ROUSSEAU
ON EDUCATION,
FREEDOM,
AND JUDGMENT

Rousseau

ON EDUCATION, FREEDOM,
AND JUDGMENT

DENISE
SCHAEFFER

The Pennsylvania State University Press
University Park, Pennsylvania

Library of Congress Cataloging-in-Publication Data

Schaeffer, Denise, 1968– , author.
Rousseau on education, freedom, and judgment /
Denise Schaeffer.
p. cm
Summary: "Explores the writings of Rousseau, including Emile,
Discourse on the Origins of Inequality, and On the Social Contract,
focusing on the problem of judgment and its role in creating the
condition for genuine self-rule"—Provided by publisher.
Includes bibliographical references and index.
ISBN 978-0-271-06209-9 (cloth : alk. paper)
1. Rousseau, Jean-Jacques, 1712–1778.
2. Judgment (Logic).
3. Rousseau, Jean-Jacques, 1712–1778. Emile.
4. Education—Philosophy.
5. Liberty—Philosophy.
I. Title.

B2137.S33   2014
194—dc23
2013032625

Copyright © 2014 The Pennsylvania State University
All rights reserved
Printed in the United States of America
Published by The Pennsylvania State University Press,
University Park, PA 16802-1003

The Pennsylvania State University Press is a member of the
Association of American University Presses.

It is the policy of The Pennsylvania State University Press to use
acid-free paper. Publications on uncoated stock satisfy the minimum
requirements of American National Standard for Information
Sciences—Permanence of Paper for
Printed Library Material, ANSI Z39.48–1992.

This book is printed on paper that contains
30% post-consumer waste.

CONTENTS

Acknowledgments / *vi*
Abbreviations of Rousseau's Works / *viii*
Introduction / *1*

1
Judgment and the Standard of Nature / *16*

2
Learning to Move:
The Body, the Senses, and the Foundations of Judgment / *36*

3
Books and Experience in the Education of Judgment / *63*

4
Judgment and Pity / *85*

5
Piety and Authority / *107*

6
Judgment, Love, and Illusion / *134*

7
Judgment and the Possibility of Partial Detachment / *158*

8
Judgment and Citizenship / *174*

Notes / *197*
Index / *217*

ACKNOWLEDGMENTS

The National Endowment for the Humanities provided support for this project in its earliest stages, which helped me to get the project off the ground. The College of the Holy Cross generously provided research leaves that gave me time to think, write, and revise. Portions of some of the chapters were originally published elsewhere. Most of chapter 3 appeared as "The Utility of Ink: Rousseau and Robinson Crusoe," *Review of Politics* 64 (Winter 2002): 121–49. A much earlier version of chapter 6 was published as "Reconsidering the Role of Sophie in Rousseau's *Emile*," *Polity* 30 (June 1998): 607–26. Chapter 8 draws material from two previously published articles, "Attending to Time and Place in Rousseau's Legislative Art," *Review of Politics* 74 (Summer 2012): 421–41, and "Realism, Rhetoric, and the Possibility of Reform in Rousseau's *Considerations on the Government of Poland*," *Polity* 42 (July 2010): 377–97. I would like to thank all of the original publishers for permission to reprint.

Over the years, I have benefited enormously from discussing Rousseau, both informally and at conferences, with many friends and colleagues, including Jonathan Badger, William Baumgarth, Ronna Burger, Michael Davis, Christopher Dustin, Herma Gjinko, Pamela Jensen, Paul Kirkland, Joseph Knippenberg, David Nichols, John Scott, and Stephen Thomas. I owe a particular debt of gratitude to Mary Nichols and David Schaefer, who read the entire manuscript with meticulous care and provided many valuable suggestions. I would also like to thank the Penn State Press reviewers for their helpful feedback; I feel fortunate to have had such attentive and insightful readers. It has also been a pleasure to work with Kendra Boileau and Laura Reed-Morrisson at Penn State Press. I would also like to thank Daniel McMurtry for his assistance with manuscript formatting, and Suzanne Wolk for her excellent copy-editing. Finally, I am grateful to my colleagues and students at the College of the Holy Cross for their collegiality and ongoing encouragement.

I have lived with this book for quite some time, and by extension so has my family. I would like to thank my amazing husband, Charles Planck, as well as my daughters, Amanda, Isabel, and Lydia, who have been patient and generous over the years in sharing their mother's attention with this mysterious person named Rousseau. I would also like to thank my parents, Ernesto and Darci Schaeffer, for their love and unwavering support. I dedicate this book to the memory of my father, a self-described philosopher of cars and mechanic of people whose distinctive perspective on the world gave me a taste for philosophical thinking before I knew what it was.

ABREVIATIONS OF ROUSSEAU'S WORKS

Parenthetical references to the following works are followed by references to volume and page number of the *Oeuvres complètes de Jean-Jacques Rousseau*, ed. Bernard Gagnebin and Marcel Raymond, 5 vols. (Paris: Gallimard, 1959–95).

CC   *Plan for a Constitution for Corsica*, in *The Collected Writings of Rousseau*, ed. Roger D. Masters and Christopher Kelly, 13 vols. (Hanover: University Press of New England, 1990–2009), 11:121–65.

E   *Emile, or On Education*, ed. and trans. Allan Bloom (New York: Basic Books, 1979).

ES   *Emile and Sophie, or The Solitaries*, trans. Christopher Kelly, in *The Collected Writings of Rousseau*, ed. Roger D. Masters and Christopher Kelly, 13 vols. (Hanover: University Press of New England, 1990–2009), 13:685–721.

GP   *The Government of Poland*, trans. Willmoore Kendall (Indianapolis: Hackett Publishing, 1985).

PE   *Discourse on Political Economy*, trans. Judith R. Bush, Roger D. Masters, Christopher Kelly, and Terrence Marshall, in *The Collected Writings of Rousseau*, ed. Roger D. Masters and Christopher Kelly, 13 vols. (Hanover: University Press of New England, 1990–2009), 3:140–70.

SC   *On the Social Contract*, trans. Judith R. Bush, Roger D. Masters, and Christopher Kelly, in *The Collected Writings of Rousseau*, ed. Roger D. Masters and Christopher Kelly, 13 vols. (Hanover: University Press of New England, 1990–2009), 4:127–224.

SD   *The First and Second Discourses*, trans. Roger D. Masters and Judith R. Masters (New York: St. Martin's Press, 1964).

INTRODUCTION

The general will is always right, but the judgment that guides it is not always enlightened.
It must be made to see objects as they are, or sometimes as they should appear to be. . . .
From this arises the necessity for a legislator. (*SC*, 154; 3:380)

The idea of democracy presupposes that human beings are capable of exercising judgment, since it requires citizens who are capable of making judgments about a shared public world. The question of how to foster this capacity in individuals is thus a fundamental question for political philosophy. Yet the process by which the ability to exercise good judgment is acquired and nurtured remains somewhat mysterious, despite a rich intellectual history of the subject.[1] This indeterminacy has to do with the very nature of judgment. As Ronald Beiner states in his landmark book *Political Judgment*, "Judgment is a form of mental activity that is not bound to rules, is not subject to explicit specification of its mode of operation (unlike methodical rationality), and comes into play beyond the confines of rule-governed intelligence."[2] Because the operation of judgment is detached from the realm of universal reason and absolute standards, yet is at the same time distinguishable from the realm of merely subjective opinion, judgment seems to rest upon "an elusive and ineffable faculty of sense," as Peter J. Steinberger puts it.[3]

In seeking to understand judgment, scholars rarely look to Rousseau,[4] at least not when the inquiry is bound together with the question of democratic politics.[5] In fact, Rousseau is often presented as suspicious of the very idea that citizens are capable of exercising good judgment,[6] and is often depicted as willing to sacrifice judgment (and therewith genuine democratic freedom) for the sake of social cohesion and republican virtue.

Rousseau certainly leaves himself open to this charge insofar as his defense of popular sovereignty in *On the Social Contract* entails the following qualification: the general will, though always legitimate, is unenlightened and tends to lack good judgment (*SC*, 154; 3:380). This deficiency in judgment is precisely what creates the need for a godlike legislator, who mythologizes the origins of the city and its laws, creates ennobling spectacles, and appeals to divine sanction—all in order to foster the underlying psychology that is necessary to facilitate the proper expression of the general will. Rousseau seems less interested in creating citizens who are capable of exercising independent judgment than in producing citizens who are conditioned to be unreflectively patriotic: "by inclination, passionately, of necessity" (*GP*, 19; 3:966). To the degree that Rousseau seeks to *guarantee* good judgment in this way, he seems to undermine democratic judgment insofar as the general will becomes an effect of external manipulations rather than an autonomous expression of popular will.[7] In short, it can appear that Rousseau is perfectly willing to substitute deep, nonrational conditioning for the genuine and independent exercise of judgment—except perhaps for the exceptional, solitary philosopher (an unlikely model for democratic politics).

On the level of the individual, similar concerns can be raised with regard to Rousseau's model of an allegedly free individual: the imaginary pupil whose education toward freedom Rousseau depicts in *Emile*. Many have raised questions about Emile's alleged autonomy in light of the veiled manipulations of his tutor.[8] Even those who evaluate the figure of Emile positively on the question of his capacity for autonomy recognize limitations when it comes to the issue of judgment specifically.[9] On this view, Rousseau's educational project, like his political project, seems to consist in the substitution of new (healthy, salutary) prejudices for existing, corrupt prejudices. To be sure, these salutary prejudices may produce better judgments than those based on corrupt ones. But a nagging question nevertheless remains: if those judgments are conditioned reflexes, and if one never learns to reflect critically on those (new) prejudices, however salutary they may be, what are the implications for human freedom? Are we left with an unbridgeable gap between the few who are wise and the rest who remain the product of their indispensable prejudices? If so, then Rousseau's idealized models of political freedom (e.g., the general will) and individual freedom (e.g., Emile) are little more than seductive but illusory chimeras that mask the deepest operations of power.

What this leads us to see is that the question of Rousseau's position on the possibility of genuine self-rule is inseparable from the question of his view of the proper orientation of individuals and communities toward the illusions or "chimeras" that operate in identity formation and political life—including those that he himself generates. If these chimeras, in performing their necessary function in promoting civic cohesion, *substitute* for the faculty of judgment, then self-rule in any meaningful sense becomes compromised, if not impossible, as charged by those who see citizenship for Rousseau as fundamentally passive and devoid of critical reflection.[10] In other words, if citizenship is to be more than a deeply conditioned, unconscious reflex, we must be able to distinguish between conditioning and education in Rousseau's political philosophy.

What, then, does "education" mean for Rousseau? At first glance, he appears to offer two mutually exclusive models. On one side, there is the civic education depicted in overtly political works such as the *Discourse on Political Economy* and *Considerations on the Government of Poland*, in which the individual is apparently subsumed by the common unity. Then there is *Emile*, which is ostensibly the education of a natural man who is a whole unto himself (albeit one who eventually inhabits a social environment). What Rousseau's civic and private models of education have in common is, at a minimum, that they are designed to overcome the contradictions that plague human beings in the modern world. The individual living in civil society, Rousseau argues, exists in a sorry state of in-betweenness. "Always in contradiction with himself, always floating between his inclinations and his duties, he will never be either man or citizen. He will be good neither for himself nor for others. . . . He will be nothing" (*E*, 40; 4:249–50). This lack of substance stems from a deeper dividedness within the bourgeois insofar as he sees himself only through the eyes of others. He lives outside himself, not within himself. He is neither whole nor part of a larger whole. He is nothing.[11]

The bourgeois may be neither man nor citizen, but one might say the same of Emile himself, who, although a "savage made to inhabit cities" (*E*, 205; 4:484), possesses neither the absolute independence of natural man living in the state of nature (since he marries and joins society) nor the fervor of the citizen who exists only in relation to the whole. He is simultaneously attached and detached. Moreover, he is taught to compare himself with his fellow men, and to see himself through his beloved's eyes. He therefore exhibits a certain degree of self-consciousness, but always in tandem (and in tension) with his unselfconscious naturalness, a tension that Rousseau suggests must somehow be reconciled. Emile's example, and the project of his education, thus raises the question of whether there can be some *positive* form of in-betweenness, in Rousseau's view. A positive in-betweenness that incorporates a healthy form of self-consciousness is necessitated by the fact that the wholeness that is the distinctive feature of Rousseau's twin poles—natural man and citizen—is utterly fragile unless maintained by some outside force. In the political realm, that external force is obviously the legislator, and in *Emile* it is the tutor, who must employ a great deal of art to maintain his pupil's alleged naturalness.

This paradox is already reflected in the *Second Discourse*, which depicts the progress of human development without any guiding hand, divorced from considerations of divine providence (or humans "left to themselves," as Rousseau puts it). In this presentation, human beings fall away from their natural independence without realizing what is happening. They lack foresight to anticipate the implications of various changes they make to their environment. They embrace new chains, thinking that they are embracing freedom. Thus the lack of foresight and self-consciousness that makes possible a perfect equilibrium between desires and faculties (and thus facilitates self-contained wholeness) is also the Achilles' heel of that wholeness.[12] Is there some way in which this potential weakness can be transformed into a strength? This transformation is, I submit, the ultimate goal of education for Rousseau.[13]

In exploring the possibility that there may be a positive form of in-betweenness for Rousseau, I join a number of scholars who understand the tensions that pervade Rousseau's work as just as (or even more) important to his project as the simple model "wholes" that he presents in a polarized fashion. For example, Mark Cladis argues that Rousseau seeks "a middle way" between individuality and social assimilation, embracing "both humanity and citizenship, morality and politics, individuality and social cooperation."[14] Rousseau's point is not to choose between the alternatives of self-possession and citizenship, but to come to see that they are mutually implicated and to combine them. Jonathan Marks also illuminates Rousseau's concern for the harmonization, rather than the utter assimilation, of disharmonious goods.[15]

One virtue of these readings is that they provide a way of explaining the paradoxes in Rousseau's thought without explaining them away. They also suggest that Rousseau is neither inconsistent nor indecisive. He is not alternately individualist and collectivist, but rather theorizes important connections between the two poles.[16] These interpretations help us to see that the common characterization of Rousseau's overriding concern in terms of the goal of achieving unselfconscious "wholeness" (whether of the naturally unified man or of the artificially unified citizenry)[17] is overdrawn, and that his writings are oriented to the problem of combining and harmonizing competing goods rather than forcing a choice between them. As Marks, for example, puts it, "Far from impatiently seeking unity at the cost of human freedom, Rousseau was willing to preserve tension in order to give the plurality of human goods their due."[18]

Scholars developing this line of thought often focus on the individual and the community as the most fundamental of the competing goods that Rousseau seeks to reconcile. The tension with which I am especially concerned is that between truth and illusion, and how these operate in Rousseau's understanding of freedom, judgment, and the relation between the two (in his theory of education as well as in his own rhetorical strategy). This does not mean that I wish to ignore the individual/collective tension in his thought, but rather that I aim to explore the underlying human psychology that makes possible the achievement of Rousseau's ideal middle state between individualism and collectivism. While I agree with Marks that "Rousseau views the human good not as a unity but as a set of disharmonious attributes or tendencies that must somehow be arranged in a life so as not to tear the human being apart,"[19] I would add that this "somehow" raises troubling questions about the role of illusions, manipulation, and conditioning in this arrangement. Does Rousseau's amelioration of this disharmony entail the sacrifice of self-rule?

To address these questions adequately, it is necessary that we rethink not only Rousseau's understanding of the relationship between the "I" and the "we," but also the stance of the "I" toward itself and toward the illusions that nourish that sense of self, whether identity is individual or collective. Whereas the bourgeois is unhappy and unfree because he sees himself only through the eyes of others, natural man and citizen do not see themselves at all, so seamlessly do they inhabit their identities, which is problematic in a different way. Is there, for Rousseau, a form of self-awareness that does not simply get in the way of freedom but actually allows one to preserve it from within? Can one achieve a measure of detachment that allows one to both be whole and *know* that one is whole, thus actively preserving that wholeness rather than having it maintained by some external force? Does this require dispensing with all illusions, which Rousseau seems to suggest is impossible, or does it require, instead, achieving some measure of detachment from those illusions while still being moved by them?

My reading of *Emile* suggests that although Rousseau sees salutary illusions as inescapably necessary to foster the conditions that make freedom possible, he nevertheless preserves a distinction between these illusions—which can and should be objects of critical reflection, and bear some essential relationship to truth—and mere prejudice. He does not simply sacrifice genuine self-rule for the sake of an illusory freedom out of a distrust of judgments that are not guided by some passionate attachment to a salutary ideal. Rather, he explores the question of whether illusions might not simply dazzle and inspire but also provoke critical reflection and judgment. Illusions might then contribute to the genuine *education* of judgment instead of simply circumventing the need for judgment, and thereby foster genuine self-rule rather than a condition that is subjectively experienced as autonomy but is actually a state of subjection. The question of whether freedom is fostered by naked truths or salutary chimeras is an undercurrent throughout *Emile*, implicated in every aspect of Emile's education, from his exposure (or lack thereof) to books, to his physical education, to his religious education, to his development of pity and his experience of falling in love—each of which I address in the chapters that follow.

I pursue these issues primarily in the context of *Emile*, and the organization of my chapters tracks the stages of Emile's education as it unfolds, but these issues resonate in Rousseau's more explicitly political writings as well, and I trace these resonances in my concluding chapter. Even in Rousseau's discussions of civic education, he indicates that the people cannot remain in a state of dependence upon the machinations of a legislator figure forever. As he states in the *Discourse on Political Economy*, citizens should one day become "the fathers of the country whose children they have been for so long" (*PE*, 156; 3:261). This is more than a matter of generational progression. The underlying question is: how will citizens subjected to a rigorous, parochial civic education from birth suddenly stop behaving like obedient children and become the "fathers"? And how then are we to understand the middle ground that Rousseau implies each time he suggests that a people must somehow be young and old at the same time?

While Rousseau does not adequately address the question in his overtly political works, he makes it a central question in his work on education. In a critical scene, as Emile approaches adulthood and marriage, the tutor explicitly reprimands him for being a mere product of his conditioning, and demands that he begin to make truly independent decisions (*E*, 326; 4:652–53). Emile is told that he must no longer simply obey his tutor but must question his advice and demand an account of his reasoning in order form an independent judgment. Whether Emile lives up to this charge remains to be seen; for now, I simply indicate that this is the professed goal of his education. *Emile* offers Rousseau's fullest exploration of the question of what it means, and what it takes, to "grow up" in the broadest and deepest sense, and this is the philosophical and political significance of its pedagogical orientation.

In other words, *Emile* takes what remains embryonic or even resolutely problematic in the overtly political works—the need to combine rational detachment with passionate attachment in order to achieve the capacity for exercising independent judgment and hence self-rule—and makes it a central concern. It is Rousseau's most sustained exploration of the possibility of a genuine self-rule in which freedom is actively maintained rather than passively enacted—a possibility on which the entire validity of Rousseau's project, from the point of view of democratic theory, rests. Whereas *On the Social Contract* considers men as they are, and laws as they might be (*SC*, 131; 3:351), *Emile* explores human beings as they *might be*, and therefore opens up new political possibilities, even if these political implications are not fully developed in *Emile* itself.[20] It is therefore a pivotal work that addresses a long-standing issue in Rousseau scholarship—the question of his support for genuine versus apparent self-rule—while also connecting Rousseau to a contemporary arena of concern: the question of judgment and how it is learned.

What does the term "judgment" mean in this context? Unlike Kant, Rousseau does not provide a formal account of judgment, although he refers to it frequently, especially in *Emile*. What he does say about judgment indicates that in his understanding judgment must be distinguished from formal reasoning, which seeks to understand particulars in light of valid universals. For Kant, the question of the relationship of judgment to purely logical reasoning results in a distinction between "determinate judgment," which involves the correct application of general rules, and "reflective judgment," which proceeds in the absence of such rules. Kantian reflective judgment operates specifically in the realm of aesthetics and taste. Hannah Arendt famously extends reflective judgment to the realm of politics. It is precisely because the particulars of political life are not fully subsumable under universal rules—which is what most fundamentally distinguishes political science from the natural sciences—that politics is both possible and necessary, and those particulars are not subsumable precisely because human beings are free.[21] The attempt to turn politics into an exact science or expertise is, from Arendt's perspective, a threat to human freedom, even if the attempt is motivated by a concern to foster freedom. In other words, the capacity for reflective judgment is both a product and a condition of our freedom. And yet this absence of determinative universal rules does not mean that we devolve to the realm of purely subjective opinion. The concept of judgment, as murky as it may be, is a marker for this necessary in-betweenness. As Linda Zerilli puts it in her influential analysis of Arendt:

> A freedom-centered practice of judgment, then, cannot be modeled on the rule-following that characterizes what Kant calls determinate judgment. To obtain critical purchase on our social arrangements and the ungrounded form of life, but without yielding to the temptation of the external standpoint, we need to develop a practice of judgment that is

not rule-governed. Judging without the mediation of a concept is a quotidian skill we do well to learn and practice. It always carries the risk that we will fall back on known concepts or rules for making sense of political reality out of our own sense of frustration or inadequacy. And yet if we want to come to terms with new objects and events, including those that have no place within our system of reference save as curious anomalies to the rule that merely preserve the rule, we need to develop the faculty of judgment.[22]

In opposite ways, both the detachment of the universal rule (and of those who seek to apply it to politics) and the partisanship of the demagogue pose a threat to judgment. Rousseau was intensely concerned with this risk (in both forms) and sought to address it rather than to circumvent it. He was also acutely aware of how difficult it is to introduce the new, or that which finds no immediate place within existing frames of reference. " 'Propose what can be done,' they never stop repeating to me; it is as if I am told, 'Propose what is done' " (E, 34; 4:242–43). He sought to change how people see, in order to disabuse them of the prejudiced conceptions of nature, freedom, and happiness that produce widespread inequality and misery. Such reform would never be achieved by rational argument alone, he believed, but required a reorientation of human sentiments, specifically by means of an appeal to the imagination. *Emile* is, in part, such an appeal. But it does not *only* appeal to the imagination; it also appeals to judgment. "In expounding freely my sentiment, I so little expect that it be taken as authoritative that I always join it to my reasons, so that they may be weighed and I be judged" (34; 4:242).

Rousseau's engagement with the question of judgment is not primarily a theoretical engagement, but rather an intervention. That Rousseau does not provide a formal account of judgment should not dissuade us from exploring his understanding of it. As Leslie Paul Thiele has observed, it is questionable whether we can "gain theoretical access to the essence of this mysterious faculty."[23] Charles Larmore similarly argues that an understanding of judgment "lies beyond the limits of theory" and requires examples "such as those we find presented by the literary imagination."[24] The effort to capture the essence of a judging stance that is simultaneously immersed in the experience of the particular to be judged, yet capable of some degree of detachment that makes critical reflection (and the very distinction between good versus poor judgment) possible, often proceeds metaphorically precisely because of this indeterminate character. Beiner, for example, drawing on Arendt, invokes the notion of spectatorship (understood as active and critical engagement, as opposed to passive watching) to capture precisely this in-between state. While one might think of spectators as governed by pathos rather than by praxis, or as mere "'patients' absorbing stimuli rather than 'agents' exercising active discrimination and intelligent reflection," the spectator in Beiner's sense *interprets* and *judges*, even as she is immersed in the experience of absorbing the spectacle.[25] I propose that this is the stance that Rousseau evokes when describing a mature individual populace or capable of exercising judgment with regard to all authoritative claims and dominant discourses and images—even as he argues that certain "chimeras" are necessary to the health and growth of that capacity for judgment.

The figure of Emile is itself such a chimera, created for Rousseau's reading audience, who are meant to be deliberately seduced by his example[26] but also invited—frequently and explicitly—to judge that example, not simply to affirm it unreflectively. The model of good judgment that is developed throughout *Emile* is thus rooted in Emile's example but also transcends that example in important respects. The education of *Emile* is not identical to the education of Emile, though at times it runs parallel to it.[27] Emile is educated to judge the world around him in increasingly complex ways, applying first a standard of utility, then of beauty, then of the good. The reader's capacity for judgment is being similarly honed, though on a higher plane. The reader, whom Rousseau addresses directly throughout *Emile*, is as much a part of Rousseau's pedagogical efforts as Emile is—perhaps even more so. Part of the reader's education involves being inspired by Emile's example, but part of it, too, is achieving some critical distance from that example; Emile's deficiencies thus serve an important function in the reader's education. That said, I would also submit that the internal education of *Emile*—Emile's education—is, at least in its *aspirations*, more oriented toward a genuinely independent faculty of judgment than is often recognized, even if those aspirations are imperfectly realized. And the unfolding of Emile's education forms but one part of the reader's education, which is also primarily an education in judgment—including the ability to judge Emile. Rousseau's ideal reader of *Emile*, initially characterized as a mother who knows how to think (*E*, 33; 4:241), is ultimately referred to in book V as a mother who is *judicious* (364; 4:701). Rousseau criticizes his readers for being too prejudiced to judge his pupil or his project soundly, yet he continually engages their judgment in different ways. By attending to how his engagement with the reader develops and changes over the course of *Emile*, we learn something about how he thinks judgment might be reformed. Rousseau, who complained that his readers did not understand him, does his part to educate them to do so.[28]

I am not the first to draw attention to the importance of this dimension of Rousseau's work. What is the character of the education he imparts to his reader? In many readings of Rousseau's rhetorical strategy, a parallel is drawn between the tutor's cultivation of necessary prejudices in Emile and Rousseau's cultivation of necessary prejudices in the reader. One such salutary prejudice would be an idealized view of the goodness of nature, which allows the reader, like Emile, to be "shielded" from "the dangers that even measured progress and a limited social life entail." While *Emile* may offer a more complex view of nature than the idealization we find in the first part of the *Second Discourse*, "downplaying or concealing this view is part of Rousseau's rhetorical strategy," employed for the political purpose of preserving a salutary prejudice in favor of the goodness of nature.[29] The primary goal of Rousseau's political/philosophical project is thus understood to be the production of certain beneficial psychological or social dynamics at the expense of revealing the truth about them. For example, we might understand Rousseau's goal as the cultivation of a salutary but unreflective love of virtue by means of identification with Emile's example.[30] On this view, Rousseau manipulates the reader (for his or her own good), just as the tutor manipulates Emile.

My analysis seeks to extend this insight by subjecting it to the persistent question with which I began: if one never learns to reflect critically on those (new) prejudices, however salutary they may be, what are the implications for self-rule? Are we left with an unbridgeable gap between the enlightened few and the rest, who remain dependent upon prejudice? Does Rousseau ultimately follow Plato in suggesting the necessity of a noble lie deployed by an enlightened elite in order to produce a certain disposition in the many, and thereby a unified whole?[31] But of course Rousseau is indisputably modern, which means that the tension between his desire for wisdom to rule and his egalitarianism (reflected in his claim that each individual has an infallible guide within, namely, conscience) is not so easily resolved. Just as there is a middle ground between the poles of radical asociality and seamless community, there is also a middle ground between mere prejudice, on the one hand, and either godlike wisdom or transparent truth, on the other. If we reconsider Rousseau's rhetorical strategy in light of *this* middle ground, a new picture emerges, for example, of the rhetoric of the *Social Contract*. While Rousseau clearly offers a great deal of ideological ammunition for the people to use in passionate defense of their sovereign rights, as Arthur Melzer has argued,[32] we must not overlook the fact that it also draws attention to the secret machinations of the legislator and thus requires that the reader *transcend* the perspective of the people for at least a few chapters. Rousseau does not of course spell out all of the legislator's techniques—he leaves that in part to the *Political Economy* (which is for Melzer the partisan education of the legislator)—but he does highlight what is probably the most important technique: the necessity of an appeal to divine sanction in order successfully to direct the general will. Rousseau thus makes explicit the instrumental and Machiavellian character of appeals to divine sanction.[33]

The *Social Contract* is not simply an education *toward* a particular illusion but is also simultaneously an education *about* illusions and the role that they play in creating and maintaining a political community. The claims of the legislator then would be checked not simply by the unreflective partisan zeal of the people but by their appreciation of the nature of his position in relation to their own.[34] I would add that while the *Social Contract* is not simply a defense of a manipulative legislator, neither is it simply an unmasking. The matter is rather more complicated, even paradoxical. The challenge for Rousseau is to encourage critical reflection while at the same time preserving a passionate attachment to the political whole. He may hope that citizens appreciate the necessity of an appeal to divine sanction, which requires some critical detachment, but at the same time he needs the appeal to *work*. Explicit demystification is therefore not the goal, nor is the goal the checking of one single-minded perspective with another, but rather a double vision that both incorporates and transcends the necessary illusion.

Thus, while I agree with commentators that Rousseau seeks not simply to explain but to produce the political effects he theorizes, I argue that *Emile* represents Rousseau's attempt to cultivate the capacity for independent judgment, and not simply to foster the salutary prejudices and illusions that might substitute for it. These prejudices and illusions play an important role, to be sure, but they are only one part of Rousseau's strategy. Focusing on the twofold character of Rousseau's project in *Emile* will enhance our understanding of the psychology that makes possible the political middle ground identified in the existing scholarship that focuses on Rousseau's concern for complex middle states over simple, unified wholes. *Emile* is certainly about combining independence and interdependence, but it is also *exemplifies* another (related) middle ground. That is, as a philosophical novel it occupies a middle ground between Rousseau's treatises and his literary works, such as *La nouvelle Heloise*. *Emile* does not simply tell the story of an idealized education; it includes commentary and critical reflection on that poetic representation throughout. Both substantively and structurally, it is a crucial text for exploring Rousseau's take on the proper perspective toward idealized images.

For a book that is often considered to be primarily about achieving wholeness and psychic unity, *Emile* is strikingly riddled with divisions that resist assimilation to a stable whole. A crucial bifurcation occurs between book III and book IV, which heralds a "second birth" for Emile. This major fault line in Emile's education separates the physical and the moral dimensions of that education, or, put another way, separates Emile's education in independence from his education in interdependence.[35]

Within this fundamental cleavage, however, others unfurl. Just as it is significant that Emile is "born" twice, it is important to note that the other characters in the book have a double or foil as well. For example, there is the awkward distinction between the tutor and Jean-Jacques (Rousseau's persona as author). The voice of Jean-Jacques interprets, reflects, and comments upon the drama of Emile's education by the tutor. This creates the illusion of a closed circuit between the tutor and Emile, with Jean-Jacques observing from above or beyond. However, Jean-Jacques also occasionally intervenes by means of a subtle narrative slippage, the implications of which are never explicitly acknowledged. The tutor seems never to make a mistake, but Jean-Jacques is an experimenter who must sometimes retrace his steps or explore alternative scenarios that involve other (often wayward) pupils who present challenges that do not arise with Emile. These challenges and mistakes are in one sense extrinsic to Emile's education, but are in another sense an important part of it, as they provide the justification for many of its features. Moreover, they form part of the educational project of *Emile* as a whole, which is not reducible to the education of Emile in particular. *Emile* depicts several educations: the education of Emile (which is itself divided into two parts), and that of Jean-Jacques himself, which is itself two discrete educations in the following sense. We see the education that he receives *about* education, as it were, as he experiments with alternative scenarios for Emile and recalls experiments with other children, but we also witness certain moments in his own (earlier) education as a young man. For example, two important lessons in *Emile*—on taste and religion—are explicitly based on an account of Jean-Jacques's own education rather than Emile's. In his dual role as both educator and (at times) the one who is educated, Jean-Jacques serves as a foil not only for the tutor but for Emile as well.

Furthermore, there is the education of Sophie—yet another of *Emile*'s multiple educations. Since Sophie is destined to marry Emile, her education is part of Emile's story, but it also stands on its own insofar as book V is not simply a chapter like other chapters but rather a "book" unto itself, with its own subtitle ("Sophie, or The Woman"). Sophie's education is partly designed to complement Emile's, but it also, I shall argue, explores alternative *human* possibilities, and therefore offers a model to *challenge*, not simply complement, Emile's.[36] (Rousseau more than once depicts men learning from women.) The book within a book on Sophie is itself further divided, consisting of a lengthy discussion of women in general followed by the story of Sophie in particular. These two accounts of "woman" (the general and the particular) are not entirely consistent. Thus the "or" in the book's subtitle might be taken as disjunctive rather than conjunctive, or at least as ambiguous. Moreover, the figure of Sophie also has a double. Rousseau offers, in the middle of her story, a digression about "a girl so similar to Sophie that her story could be Sophie's without occasioning any surprise" (*E*, 402; 4:759). This other Sophie, who ends up a victim of her own unattainable standards of virtue, is abandoned when Rousseau decides to "resuscitate this lovable girl" and "to give her a less lively imagination and a happier destiny." He returns to his original Sophie, but only after complicating his narrative of feminine education to the degree that he makes it difficult to discern which image of womanhood he wishes to present as ideal.

Finally, we must keep in mind that Emile's story does not end with *Emile* but carries over into *Emile and Sophie, or The Solitary Ones*. The existence of a sequel, even an unfinished one, raises questions about what it might mean to understand and evaluate Emile's education as a whole. Since Rousseau chose to publish *Emile* alone, with its happy ending and without any reference to Emile's subsequent experiences, *Emile* can and should be considered a whole unto itself. At the same time, it is *not* a complete whole in light of the sequel. I draw attention to these ambiguities, and to the fact that every major character in *Emile* has a double or foil, to raise the question of what it means to talk about wholeness and psychic unity in the context of so many split identities and narrative cleavages. Bifurcation is structurally important in *Emile* in another way as well.[37] There are numerous instances in which Rousseau returns to a subject he addressed earlier in order to present it in a new (and more critical) light, asking his reader to judge in both cases. In each case, the initial lesson points the reader directly to an explicitly specified conclusion, whereas the subsequent lesson introduces considerations that may call into question the initial conclusion, and then withholds any indication of the desired or correct conclusion. This pattern, which persists throughout *Emile*, brings to light (both discursively and performatively) Rousseau's considered view of what good judgment is and how it develops. By calling for increasingly sophisticated judgments on the part of the reader, as we shall see, Rousseau does much more than simply redirect readers' passions, seducing them toward virtue with necessary and noble chimeras. Rather, he cultivates a model of good judgment that calls for a more reflective stance than most commentators acknowledge—one that, to be sure, necessarily involves some degree of seduction by chimeras or illusions (of which the figures of Emile, and even of "natural man," are examples), but simultaneously entails critical awareness of their chimerical quality and the hold they have on us. *This* middle ground is my focus, for it reflects the necessary combination of attachment and detachment that makes judgment possible, inasmuch as judgment can be neither reduced to the utter subjectivity of the prejudices and opinions to which we are unreflectively attached, nor elevated to a realm of detached scientific objectivity.

My attempt to elucidate this middle ground is not without its difficulties, for Rousseau does not address it directly or provide a straightforward account of it. It emerges only indirectly, out of the collision of the various extremes in Rousseau's work and the juxtaposed episodes in Emile's education. By this I do *not* mean that Rousseau's indirectness veils a straightforward claim in order to make it obscure and accessible only to an enlightened few, which is one way of understanding philosophical esotericism. Rather, Rousseau suggests that the very nature of what he seeks to convey compels him to convey it indirectly. If, instead of providing one definitive lesson, he offers parallel episodes that revisit an issue in order to transform a simple lesson into a more complex one, it is because the moment of collision or transformation would be lost in a more direct account, which would then fail to do justice to the phenomenon in question. For it is precisely the experience of returning to a simpler "whole" with an altered perspective that produces the necessary insight; any attempt to jump directly to an explicit statement of that insight will inevitably distort the essential feature of what he seeks to convey. In other words, if (in part) the "lesson" is that the formation of ideal "wholes" is both necessary and dangerous, which suggests that a middle state between enchantment and disenchantment is necessary, then turning that middle state into yet another idealized whole would undermine the most essential part of the lesson. This middle state can be fully appreciated only in juxtaposition to the extremes that it lies between, not abstracted from them or as a separate "third way." Otherwise, the effect is not an illuminating demystification of Rousseau's lesson that increases its accessibility but rather a re-mystification, insofar as the "third way" becomes yet another oversimplified, static, and ultimately misleading ideal—an obfuscating chimera.

I admit that this difficulty necessarily haunts my reading of Rousseau as much as it haunts Rousseau's own work, but I hope to address the problem head on instead of leaping over it. In striving to do justice to what Rousseau shows rather than limit myself to what he says, I will have to do my own share of showing. But this is thoroughly consistent with a widely shared insight about the nature of judgment: that it is primarily taught by example, experience, and narrative rather than by discursive inquiry. Judgment "can in one sense be taught and in another sense not."[38] If by teaching we mean the discursive transmission of knowledge *about* judgment, then judgment itself cannot be taught. Because judgment itself occurs only in the absence of universally applicable principles (which would render judgment superfluous), education in judgment cannot be a matter of acquiring a set of universal principles or rules of judgment. It must proceed, rather, by way of example.[39] In other words, good judgment is not a discursive product to be transmitted but is, as Aristotle insisted, cultivated only by experience. "We gain such indirect experience from listening to, reading, and reflecting upon stories."[40] In other words, we must *reflect* on exemplary narratives and experiences in order to glean from them the insight they have the potential to convey.

Rousseau not only confirms this point by weaving together narrative and commentary upon that narrative, but also, in his commentary, raises important questions about the nature of such reflection. Throughout *Emile* he contends that examples are most likely to speak to (and be correctly interpreted by) those who, on some intuitive level, already understand what is being imparted, and are likely to be *mis*understood by those who most need to be instructed by the example. This suggests that the sort of reflection that moves one from a complete lack of receptivity to the force of the example toward that very receptivity is not detached reflection "on" or thinking "about" the meaning of the example. What is fundamental to the development of the capacity for judgment is a form of engagement that is neither wholly absorbed by nor utterly detached from the object of reflection. For Rousseau, this is as much the case for self-reflection as it is for reflection on the particulars of the world we inhabit. In *Emile*, he explores how this complex stance toward oneself and one's world develops over time, and the internal and external conditions that strengthen and weaken it. As such, *Emile* is an important resource for our own thinking about the nature of judgment, and how it is learned.

1

JUDGMENT AND THE STANDARD OF NATURE

It is not philosophers who know men best. They see them only through the prejudices of philosophy, and I know of no station where one has so many. A savage has a healthier judgment of us than a philosopher does. (*E*, 243; 4:535)

Whatever else good judgment means for Rousseau, it is certainly grounded in his understanding of nature, which provides a standard against which civil society is to be judged. To what degree, and in what sense (i.e., whether substantively or as a formal standard of wholeness), nature remains relevant to human beings living in society is the subject of much scholarly debate; but Rousseau is unequivocal on the point that a poor or deformed understanding of nature leads to unsound judgment of the human condition. Thus in his preface to the *Second Discourse* he claims that a correct understanding of the original state of nature (which "no longer exists, which perhaps never existed, which probably never will exist") is necessary "in order to judge our present state correctly" (*SD*, 93; 3:123). In *Emile*, Rousseau frequently holds up his pupil, the product of an education according to nature, as an example against which the misery of civil society can be judged.

It is arguable that the understanding of nature developed in *Emile* is even more relevant to civilized human beings, because while the savage state depicted in the *Second Discourse* is irretrievably lost to us, Emile is educated to live not in a savage state but in society. Rather than strictly oppose the state of nature and existence in society, Rousseau goes so far as to refer to what is "natural in the civil state" (*E*, 406; 4:764). This suggests the possibility of a second-order naturalness that might serve as an even more useful guide to our judgments of our present state than the account of the original natural state in the *Second Discourse*.

As a touchstone for guiding judgment, however, "nature" turns out to be a very slippery concept in *Emile*. Rousseau suggests that there is a natural order and direction to human development, and that a sound education follows the path that nature lays out for us. Insofar as Emile's education is to follow that path, its goal "is the very same as that of nature" (38; 4:247). Rousseau then adds, "But perhaps this word *nature* has too vague a sense," concluding that "an attempt must be made to settle on its meaning" (39; 4:247). One might understand his "attempt" to settle its meaning as consisting of the substance of the next two paragraphs, which culminate in the definition that *nature* is whatever human inclinations are before "they are more or less corrupted by our opinions." Again, this formulation is deceptively simple. What would it mean to relate everything to our "original" dispositions, if we are born in such an undeveloped state? We are *not* born independent and self-sufficient. "We are born weak, we need strength; we are born totally unprovided, we need aid; we are born stupid, we need judgment" (38; 4:247). To appeal to natural man as the ideal to which we must orient all education thus begs the question of how one develops *into* a natural man.[1] It seems odd to make such a leap in a book that devotes so much attention to the earliest stages of childhood. The human infant can hardly be the guide for us; it is thus not surprising that Rousseau follows his statement that everything must be related to these original dispositions with a description of natural man (contrasted with both the citizen and the bourgeois). This points us to the *Second Discourse*, where Rousseau takes as his starting point an image of natural man fully formed (and only subsequently addresses the question of reproduction and the status of children). Perhaps it is there that Rousseau shows us man's "original" form; but even in that work, Rousseau makes it difficult to discern when his natural man is *fully* formed, inasmuch as perfectibility is presented as part of man's original nature.[2]

In *Emile*, this doubleness is reflected not only in the contrast between the early and later (negative and positive) phases of Emile's education but in the very idea of an "original" nature as presented in the earliest stages of Rousseau's educational project. That is, even as Rousseau counsels his reader to "observe nature and follow the path it maps out for you" (47; 4:259), he suggests that it is actually rather difficult to discern an original nature to use as a formal principle on which to base an increasingly complex naturalness; it, too, is a moving target.[3] To be sure, Rousseau claims that the first part of Emile's education is a negative education, designed only to preserve what is natural while adding nothing to it. However, as early as book I, when Rousseau is most insistent upon the notion of a negative education—that is, the notion that in order to follow nature one must simply avoid opposing it—we perceive the first indications that following nature (whether we want to preserve it or to use it as a formal principle on which to base a more complex, second-order naturalness) is not quite straightforward. Book I both posits nature as a given and poses it as a question.

> But what will a man raised uniquely for himself become for others? If perchance the double object we set for ourselves could be joined in a single one by removing the contradictions of man, a great obstacle to his happiness would be removed. In order to judge of this, he would have to be seen wholly formed: his inclinations would have to have been observed, his progress seen, his development followed. In a word, the natural man would have to be known. I believe that one will have made a few steps in these researches when one has read this writing. (41; 4:251)

The "double object" of Rousseau's project refers of course to the eventual task of introducing a natural man into society in order to test his independence, but not only to that. We cannot *judge* whether this great reconciliation has been achieved unless natural man is first *known*. But, as Rousseau points out in the *Second Discourse*, the very attempt to know ourselves gets in the way (*SD*, 92; 3:122–23).[4] Later in book I of *Emile*, Rousseau observes, "We do not know what our nature permits us to be" (*E*, 62; 4:281). *Emile* thus raises anew the question of the boundary between what is natural and what is artificial in the human condition, perhaps because the *Second Discourse* problematizes that very boundary even as it purports to delineate it.[5] Although Rousseau presents an *image* of natural man that at first glance seems complete (i.e., natural man reclining under a tree, his needs satisfied), he also presents an evolutionary understanding of human nature that complicates the simplicity of that image. It is precisely by arguing for an evolutionary rather than a static conception of human nature that Rousseau disputes the Hobbesian and Lockean accounts of human nature. He not only draws the line between nature and society in a new place; he also makes it simultaneously easier and more difficult to draw the line at all. Natural man disappears by degrees, until the reader is asked to behold human beings with "all our faculties developed, memory and imagination in play, vanity aroused, reason rendered active, and the mind having almost reached the limit of the perfection of which it is susceptible." Yet, at the same time, Rousseau refers to this development as "all the *natural* qualities put into action" (*SD*, 155; 3:174, emphasis added). Insofar as perfectibility is part of human nature, it makes it difficult to delineate precisely where nature begins and ends. Unnatural faculties exist in man in potentiality (*en puissance*), although they remain latent until a chance combination of external factors actualizes them.

Scholars tend to try to work around these ambiguities by referring to the "pure" state of nature, distinguished from the successive degrees of change that occur before civil society comes into being, but the result is that we are left with no single way of designating all that comes between the pure state of nature and civil society. So we might divide the process into three parts rather than two: pure state of nature, rustic society ("the happiest and most durable epoch"), and civil society. But even then, transitional periods are unaccounted for. The essay certainly accomplishes its goal of creating a gulf between nature and civil society, but the gulf that separates them also connects them, and is not just an empty space separating/connecting two discrete entities. The space is filled with gradual transitions and alterations that cause the stages "in between" to shade into each of the extremes. Structurally, the essay is divided into two discrete parts, and the first sentence of the second part purports to identify the precise beginning of civil society: the first person who claimed private property was its founder. *The* turning point has been pinpointed, or so it seems. But this "beginning" is not where the logic of Rousseau's account of the transition to civil society actually begins; he goes on to retrace the steps that lead up to the development of private property, which is actually an effect of a series of other changes.

I emphasize these ambiguities in the *Second Discourse* (which others have discussed in more detail)[6] in order to highlight the significance of Rousseau's insistence in *Emile* that we watch natural man come into being. The account in the *Second Discourse* begins with a fully formed natural man, in the strict sense that he is not a child. The question of reproduction is addressed as a secondary issue. But human beings are not born fully formed or self-sufficient; far from it. Therefore, even if we try to work with a nonteleological conception of nature, and cast Rousseau's project in *Emile* as an attempt to preserve nature against corrupting social influences, we must acknowledge that a doubleness inheres even in the minimalist goal of preservation—since preserving nature entails letting it develop until it is *tout formé*. There is a developmental quality built into even the simplest principle of nature for Rousseau, the ideal of equilibrium, because we cannot preserve natural equilibrium until it has come into its own. At a minimum, the weak and dependent infant must develop into the strong, unspoiled child whose simple needs allow an equilibrium to exist between his desires and faculties.

In this way, *Emile* addresses a philosophically interesting lacuna in the *Second Discourse*, while raising the question of how one might be guided by the standard of "nature" even as a complete grasp of it remains elusively out of reach. The "perfection" of our form as we leave the hands of the author is itself an abstraction, an ideal—and disembodied—state of perfect freedom, altered by confinement in a human body and further altered by the unnatural confinement to which that body is subjected over the course of a human life. To understand *human* freedom, then, one must understand not only its perfect idealization (which functions as a Platonic Form) but also its embodied form. Concrete human freedom is (somehow) formed formlessness. This is the true subject of *Emile*, inasmuch as Rousseau attempts to make the abstraction of perfect freedom concrete and particular without distorting it in the process. If Emile strikes us as simultaneously ordinary and otherworldly, this is why. He is an intermediate form.

Emile thus occupies the space between what is imaginatively idealized (and thus so far removed from existing circumstances as to be irrelevant) and what is recognizably practical (thus insufficiently critical). That is, in order for Emile's example to be instructive for readers whose own experience of raising children bears little resemblance to Rousseau's imaginary scenario, his example must be at once recognizable (thus relevant) and strange (to afford critical distance). The same can be said of the figure of "natural man" in general: he must be recognizably human, yet radically other. To the degree that any imagined ideal is disconnected from existing conditions, it may offer a standpoint for critique but at the same time suffer from a deficiency: this form of critique may be either purely negative and based on fantasy (insofar as it simply retreats from the real in order to remain devoted to the purity of an unachievable ideal) or potentially dangerous (insofar as a self-appointed visionary may seek to remake the world to match the envisioned ideal, by totalitarian means). The challenge of immanent social criticism is to work from within, while harnessing the transformative powers of the creative imagination.

Judgment and the Standard of Nature   21

Appealing to the imagination, the *Second Discourse* furnishes the image of natural man, which provides a beginning point for reflection and reorientation of the reader's understanding of human nature. This is part of what it means to "clarify" (*éclaircir*) the question (of natural right), as opposed to resolving it (*SD*, 92; 3:123); the image orients the inquiry but does not simply answer the question posed. By raising the question of nature anew, *Emile* functions as Rousseau's second sailing (to use a Socratic metaphor). As such, it orients itself toward the image that motivated the inquiry in the first place, but also brings a new standard of judgment to bear on it. The image is called upon for guidance as we form our judgments about the human condition, but somehow we must also be able to look upon it with a critical eye.[7] But if we are to judge civil man in light of the standard set by Rousseau's image of natural man, in light of what standard does he expect us to judge whether the natural man has been achieved?

Beginning with the preface and throughout *Emile*, Rousseau invites his readers to judge his project for themselves. "In expounding freely my sentiment, I so little expect that it be taken as authoritative that I always join to it my reasons, so that they may be weighed and I be judged" (34; 4:242). At the same time, he thinks that his readers' standards of judgment are deeply corrupted. "All our wisdom consists in servile prejudices" (42; 4:253). Rousseau anticipates that his project will be out of step with the prevailing wisdom and may be dismissed as unrealistic. But he also challenges the value of striving to be more realistic. Proposing "what can be done," he counters, too often amounts to proposing exactly what *is* done (34; 4:242–43). While limiting one's proposals to "what can be done" may seem practical, it is less simply so than it may appear, because in order to take one's bearings from existing conditions, one must apprehend them properly, and this is precisely what his readers are ill equipped to do. "Childhood is unknown. Starting from the false idea one has of it, the farther one goes, the more one loses one's way" (33; 4:241–42). Insofar as his readers have a false idea of childhood, they are in no position to judge whether he has offered a sound education for children, or even whether his proposals are feasible.

Part of what Rousseau must do, then—perhaps the most important part of what he must do—is to elucidate the grounds on which his, or any, proposed education ought to be judged. To that end he provides an account not merely of what a natural education ought to look like but of how one ought to look at the subject of this or any education. "Begin, then, by studying your pupils better. For most assuredly you do not know them at all" (34; 4:242). By this Rousseau does not mean that empirical study of existing children will provide the requisite wisdom, any more than he thinks that man can be properly understood on the basis of civil man. Like the statue of Glaucus to which he compares civil man in the preface to the *Second Discourse* (*SD*, 91; 3:122), all the examples of children one finds in civil society are deformed. The difficulty lies in discerning the genuine form of an object of knowledge that has been deformed over time by prejudice and social influence. Thus what it means to study one's pupils "better" is not simply that one must look at them more closely or at greater length, but that one must be able to properly evaluate what one sees when one looks at them. Rousseau's turning away from actually existing pupils to focus on an imaginary pupil is, in its own way, "practical" insofar as it is designed to help his readers see their own pupils more clearly—which is to say, to judge what they properly *are*. Only then might we get to the question of how to educate them.

Rousseau's task, therefore, is not simply to add to the current discourse about a particular subject—childhood—but to challenge the prevailing construction of the subject itself. Before offering a series of recommendations about how children ought to be educated, he addresses the question of how childhood itself is to be understood, and he suggests that the true merit of his project is its elucidation of this subject. "My vision of what must be done may have been very poor, but I believe I have seen clearly the subject on which one must work" (34; 4:242). He criticizes the child-rearing experts of his day[8] on the grounds that when they look at their subject, they see not children but future men. "The wisest men concentrate on what it is important for men to know without considering what children are in a condition to learn. They are always seeking the man in the child without thinking of what he is before being a man" (33–34; 4:242).

In contrast to *les sages*, who see children simply as protomen and thus misunderstand their subject, Rousseau juxtaposes the figure of the tender mother who appreciates the child as a child and concerns herself with the child's present security and happiness. In effect, Rousseau encourages *les sages* to become more like mothers. This is perhaps not surprising given that Rousseau often counters the sophisticated "wisdom" of experts with the humble perspective of simple souls. Moreover, Rousseau is often credited with having "invented" childhood as a separate stage of life with its own requirements, inasmuch as he insists that childhood must be considered on its own terms, and we see evidence of that here. But his point here is less to celebrate childhood innocence than to use that innocence as evidence for the natural goodness of human beings. Rousseau assimilates the tender mother's desire to protect her child from harm to a more expansive imperative that she must shield the child's natural goodness from the corrupting effects of human opinions and social institutions. First nature itself, and then the child, is compared to a shrub on a busy path that must be protected from damaging external influences. Rousseau addresses himself to a tender and foresighted mother whom he asks to shield the child from the ruinous impact of human opinions. "Cultivate and water the young plant before it dies. Its fruits will one day be your delights. Form an enclosure around your child's soul at an early date. Someone else can draw its circumference, but you alone must build the fence" (38; 4:246).

Thus it seems clear that Rousseau's emphasis on the importance of maternal care reflects his larger emphasis on nature as the proper guide for our judgments and social practices. If mothers would just be mothers again, Rousseau laments, instead of turning their children over to wet nurses and dedicating themselves to the entertainments of the city, all would be well. Indeed, "from the correction of this single abuse would soon result a general reform; nature would soon have reclaimed all its rights" (46; 4:258). Here Rousseau deploys a simple formula that reduces mothering to an activity guided simply by natural instinct rather than expert knowledge. Later in book I, another representative of this simple perspective appears: the figure of the peasant, whose simple, rustic approach to child rearing Rousseau juxtaposes favorably to the corrupt practices of the upper classes (just as the tender mother is contrasted with *les sages*). With these idealized images of natural parenting, Rousseau seems to suggest that the knowledge of nature required for its preservation is itself naturally available to us. Both of these "natural" perspectives, however, are revealed as incomplete in ways that point to the necessity of good judgment, even within the context of a natural education.

The Tender Mother Reconsidered

While Rousseau effusively praises the mother-child bond as the most natural of bonds, he adds (in a footnote) that what it means to "mother" is not self-evident. "The sense I give to the name *mother* must be explained; and that is what will be done hereafter" (38; 4:246). Although he seems to want to use the mother figure to pin down the meaning of nature, which he admits is unstable, he then destabilizes the term "mother." At no point does he explicitly define the term, but we are given some guidance by the adjectives he uses in conjunction with it. From the outset, he addresses *Emile* to a mother who is both tender and foresighted. This mother is distinguished not only from the frivolous, neglectful mother whom he criticizes for abandoning her duties (and who is, arguably, no mother at all in his estimation) but also, indirectly, from the mother who exhibits "blind tenderness" toward her children, whom he (gently) criticizes in the same note. Tenderness, it seems, can be either blind or foresighted. Rousseau's project requires "a good mother who knows how to think" (33; 4:241). Rousseau will later refer to his addressee as a "judicious" mother as well (364; 4:701). If the good mother is one who thinks, has foresight, and exercises judgment, what is her relationship to nature? This question can shed light not only on what Rousseau thinks of mothers but, more broadly, on how he understands the relationship between nature and human reflection upon nature, and the bearing of each on the development of the capacity for good judgment.

Much of Rousseau's explicit practical advice with regard to early childhood suggests that nature clearly and unambiguously indicates the way, and that all we have to do is follow it. For example, children by nature seek freedom from tight clothing and other restrictions, so we should refrain from swaddling them. By nature children suffer a host of painful physical afflictions in their early years, from teething to fevers, from which they emerge stronger and healthier; we should therefore allow them to experience physical hardship in order to harden them. Nature is presented as a given, and the line between nature and nurture as easily discernible. By comparing our original nature to a shrub in the middle of a well-traveled path, Rousseau implies that if protecting the shrub is difficult, it is because social influences are many and strong and begin to operate from the moment of birth, not because the contours of the shrub are hard to see. The analogy works well, to a point, insofar as much of the advice of book I centers on how to care for an infant's body so that it might be permitted to develop naturally, without artificial restraints such as shoes and swaddling blankets. Human beings are not born physically self-sufficient. It takes about a year for them to become able to walk and feed themselves. During that year, the mother's task is to protect the "shrub"—the body—from anything that might distort its shape, as it grows into the form that is natural to it. To that end, Rousseau insists that children be bathed in cold water, fed a "natural" (vegetarian) diet, and kept away from doctors, because the natural form of the human body is to be hardy and strong.

When Rousseau focuses on the physical body, his analogy to the shrub works sufficiently well, for just as we can look to the mature plant in full flower to know the form that the young shrub ought to achieve, we can look to the adult human being to set a standard for the infant. At the same time, the fact that human infants are born so physically weak and dependent presents a difficulty for Rousseau's contention that human beings are by nature physically strong and independent. We have to "catch up" to our natural physical form, more so than other animals. On the level of the individual (if not of the species, though the two problems intersect), there is a tension between the original form and the natural form. This is problematic insofar as Rousseau seeks to draw parallels between the development of the individual and the development of the species.

In the *Second Discourse*, this difficulty is suppressed. Rousseau covers the months that it takes for the infant to learn to walk (and find its own food, and therefore leave its mother) in a mere sentence or two. Because he is imagining a time before there were swaddling blankets or shoes or wet nurses to distort the natural (physical) maturation of human babies, this brevity may seem justified. Clearly, it was not necessary for the mother to "build a fence" against unnatural influences, because nothing artificial existed to threaten the child's natural physical development.

It is therefore tempting to think that the only reason we need a book like *Emile*, and the only reason we need to build a fence, from Rousseau's point of view, is that Rousseau is trying to reproduce the condition of nature in society. What I referred to earlier as the challenge of Rousseau's "double object" would again appear to be nothing other than an effect of the already corrupted circumstances in which we cannot help but operate. However, this overlooks an important dimension of the mother's task as outlined in book I. Her job is simultaneously to allow the unfettered growth of the body and to *prevent* the growth of unnatural needs and desires. The first task would have been much easier in the savage state than in civil society; the second, however, is likely to have been just as difficult.

Why? If we look carefully at Rousseau's advice in book I of *Emile* about preventing the development of unnatural desires (specifically, the desire to dominate others), we see that the transformation of the infant's physical dependence upon the mother into a psychological need to dominate her and direct her will might easily have been triggered in the state of nature. It is for this reason that Rousseau advises his reader to allow the child to relate only to things, and never to the will of another human being. The experience of the will of another will stimulate the development of the child's. And since the child is in no position to satisfy his own desires—he is utterly dependent because he is so physically weak—the will that emerges can only be frustrated. The experience of being thwarted will give rise to anger, indignation, and the desire to dominate. It is from a faulty education in infancy, Rousseau suggests, that the corruption, inequality, unfreedom, and unhappiness of civil society all grow.

And yet such a faulty education is just as likely to come from a mother who does nurse her child as from a mother who does not, and just as likely from a mother in the state of nature (insofar as she is attentive and becomes attached) as from a mother in society. Mothers who seek to preserve their children, and to secure their happiness, may do things that, in Rousseau's view, inadvertently lead to the warping of the child's sense of self. He notes that the overly attentive mother can be just as harmful as the indifferent mother. "One leaves [nature] by the opposite route as well when, instead of neglecting a mother's care, a woman carries it to excess" (47; 4:259). For example, Rousseau directs the mother to transport the child to whatever object the child desires, rather than fetching the object and bringing it to the child. Even one deviation from this practice might suffice to cause the child to begin seeing the mother as an instrument to be directed as he wills. And yet Rousseau would be hard pressed to make the case that no mother in the state of nature *ever* brought a pine cone to her baby when he indicated his desire for it. Indeed, what little Rousseau does say about the mother-child relationship in the *Second Discourse* hints at this very possibility. He argues that because the child must express his needs, it is the child (not the mother) who must invent the words to ask his mother for a particular thing (*SD*, 121; 3:147). Rousseau goes on to insist that this private language remains private, dying out when the mother and child part company, because his larger point is to show that language in any meaningful sense was not a part of original human nature. However, his passing remarks about how a child asks its mother to fulfill his needs raises the question—a question that goes unasked in the *Second Discourse* but receives considerable attention in *Emile*—of how the mother might respond without turning her child into a little tyrant who expects other human beings to fulfill his every whim. Such an expectation can arise, Rousseau makes clear, even when the needs themselves are very simple, as they are for infants. "The first tears of children are prayers; if one is not careful, they soon become orders" (*E*, 66; 4:287).

Moreover, we must consider what triggers the development of new needs and desires, which is habit. Two critical junctures in the *Second Discourse* identify habituation as that which transforms an innocuous (and reversible) physical dependence into a pernicious (and irreversible) psychological dependence. As man discovers fire and rudimentary tools, the "repeated utilization" (*application reitérée*) of various things in relation to himself and others is what engenders the perception of relations among human beings, which is the first step on the road to the unhealthy comparisons that are a function of amour-propre. Rousseau calls this the "first stirring of pride" (*SD*, 144; 3:166). Then, when human beings leave behind their nomadic existence and settle in rustic huts, cohabitation leads to habituation, which sets in motion another major revolution: the first developments of the heart. "The habit of living together gave birth to the sweetest sentiments known to men: conjugal love and paternal love" (*SD*, 146–47; 3:168). Rousseau contends that human beings can be *exposed* to potentially transformative things such as fire and iron ore without becoming dependent upon them, and can *encounter* one another briefly (even sexually) without becoming dependent upon one another, but *repeated* exposure triggers fundamental alterations in human nature.

One must wonder, then, at the language Rousseau uses in his brief description of the prolonged encounter between mother and infant. "The mother nursed her children at first for her own need; then, habit having endeared them to her, she nourished them afterward for their need. As soon as they had the strength to seek their food, they did not delay in leaving the mother herself" (*SD*, 121; 3:147). Why wouldn't the habit of nursing endear the mother to the child just as it endears the child to the mother? Why wouldn't the habit of seeing one another lead to the desire to see one another again, leading to the first movements of the heart? Is some sort of "fence" necessary to protect against *this*? Without addressing these considerations, Rousseau maintains that the child leaves the mother easily, and that soon the two do not even recognize each other.

My point is not simply to poke holes in the argument of the *Second Discourse*. I am not the first to notice that Rousseau's account of the mother-child relationship strains credulity. But the account tends to be read as consistent with the rest of Rousseau's argument in the *Second Discourse*, whereas I am arguing that *on Rousseau's own terms*—in which the absence or presence of habituation is what maintains or destroys individual independence—the account is self-undermining. Rousseau goes to great lengths to argue that one form of physical contact that is necessary for the survival of the species (sexual intercourse) does not bring about a psychological attachment, but he says nothing about how another, equally critical form of physical contact (nursing) avoids the same potential problem—a problem to which he draws attention by mentioning in passing that one becomes "endeared" to the other.

It is perhaps for this reason that in the *Second Discourse* Rousseau moves on from the discussion of the mother-infant relationship by asking his readers to "suppose that this first difficulty [has been] conquered" (*SD*, 121; 3:147). He means the difficulty of reconciling a rudimentary language with his depiction of the state of nature as asocial; but "conquering" the problem of language by limiting language to the period of infancy only draws attention to yet another problem—the problem of infancy itself, which opens up the possibility of ruining natural independence only one generation into the story. The silence of the *Second Discourse* on this point is filled in by the extended discussion of infancy in *Emile*. *Emile* does not simply "apply" the concept of nature developed in the *Second Discourse* to a social context; it, too, explores nature as a question.

A mother in the state of nature may not have needed to build a fence to ward off corrupting social influences, because those influences did not exist; but she did have to keep her little "shrub" alive until it could survive on its own. In so doing, she had to keep the child from becoming psychologically dependent upon her—either by becoming "endeared" (attached) to her, or by wanting to dominate her will, or both. This imperative is inextricable from Rousseau's fundamental contention that the desire to dominate others is not natural to human beings. They are not born with this desire, but "as soon as they can consider the people who surround them as instruments depending on them to set them in motion, they make use of those people to follow their inclination and to supplement their own weakness. That is how they become difficult, tyrannical, imperious, wicked, unmanageable . . . for it does not require long experience to sense how pleasant it is to act with the hands of others and to need only to stir one's tongue to make the universe move" (*E*, 67–68; 4:289).

If it takes only a very small taste of the experience of wielding another person as an instrument to develop a taste for domination, then that possibility is as much a problem in nature (between mother and child) as it is in society, especially in light of Rousseau's insistence that we are born in a state of equilibrium (despite our physical weakness) precisely because the mother acts as an extension of the child's faculties. It seems that a child must wield the mother like an instrument in order to be considered a self-sufficient "whole," and yet he cannot wield her or his wholeness will be disrupted by the emergence of a spirit of domination. Reflecting on the problem of infancy in the state of nature raises interesting questions about our supposed natural independence and how it is maintained.

Although book I of *Emile* ends where the *Second Discourse* begins, so to speak (when the child can walk, talk, and feed himself), only in *Emile* does Rousseau draw attention to the fact that a very great deal can go wrong before that point. However, read alongside *Emile*, the account in the *Second Discourse* invites us to see that the problem of "building the fence" is not simply a challenge that arises within society; it is a problem generated by nature itself, and by the need to know nature in some way in order to preserve it. But the process of seeking to know nature inevitably interferes with the preservation of nature. If a mother turns her infant into a tyrant by bringing him something he wants rather than transporting him to the thing he desires, for example, it is not due to the corruption of society; corruption would account for her lack of attentiveness, but not to her misplaced attentiveness. Her misplaced attentiveness is an expression of the very attachment that Rousseau sees as necessary to preserving a child's potential for natural freedom and happiness until his weak infant body develops enough strength for the idea of freedom to have any meaning.

While "there is no substitute for maternal solicitude" (*E*, 45; 4:257), it is precisely the mother's attachment to *this particular child* that works against her ability to raise the child to become, like natural man, an "abstract man" (42; 4:252) who is prepared to suffer the blows of fate and accidents of fortune throughout life. To raise such a man, "we must generalize our views" (42; 4:252). It is exactly this broader, more generalized view that is not natural to us. Solicitous mothers are in one sense like Thetis, seeking to dip their children in the water of the Styx; their good but misguided intentions lead them to plunge their children into "softness," which "open[s] their pores to ills of every sort to which they will not fail to be prey when grown" (47; 4:259). Thus, while Rousseau's advice to protect the child requires a tender and attentive mother, he suggests at the same time that the instinctive desire to protect one's child is insufficient. Rousseau's most explicit correction of the perspective of the tender mother comes in a note: "The mother wants her child to be happy, happy now. In that she is right. When she is mistaken about the means, she must be enlightened" (38; 4:246). While Rousseau may appeal to natural motherhood as an antidote to social corruption, the model of motherhood he ultimately portrays is an instructed, rather than simply natural, model.

Thus, although Rousseau initially presents the tender mother's solicitude as a corrective to the tendency of *les sages* to "seek the man in the child" without focusing on the child per se, he offers several indications that this maternal perspective, too, requires correction insofar as maternal tenderness can, as mentioned earlier, be "blind." Rousseau reprimands mothers whose protective focus on keeping a child safe (which is, of course, a sort of fence building) works against the child's development of the capacity to *live* in the fullest sense, and in the fullness of time. "One thinks only of preserving one's child. That is not enough. One ought to teach him to preserve himself as a man" (42; 4:253). In other words, the protective mother needs to see the man in the child. It is precisely for this reason that Rousseau requires a good mother who knows how to *think*; one who is not only tender but also foresighted. Feminine care and philosophical reflection are conjoined in Rousseau's ideal reader (and will eventually come to resemble Sophie, whose name means wisdom). Only by tapping into the mother in the thinker, and the thinker in the mother, might one develop the perspective that enables one to discern the child in the man and the man in the child.

Because human beings are inevitably shaped by environmental influences, the art of education—that is, conscious influence—is necessary. Rousseau's gardening metaphor captures these two sides of education, negative and positive. Education is like the cultivation of a nascent plant. This cultivation is a matter of both preserving the plant's original form and allowing it to grow into its fully developed form. On the one hand, education means building a fence in order to protect the original form. On the other hand, education "gives us" everything we need as grownups, which we lack as children. The problem is that in civil society we reverse these functions; we "teach children what they would learn much better by themselves" and "forget what only we could teach them" (78; 4:300). That is, we pervert nature where we ought to preserve it through a negative education, and fail to provide the positive education essential to human flourishing. Because we have utterly confused the two, Rousseau separates them in order to clarify each. Thus Emile's education appears to be divisible into two stages: negative (preserving) in books I–III, and positive in books IV–V. But these two dimensions of education are two sides of one coin—essentially, not sequentially, related. Again, this reflects Rousseau's attempt to correct the perspectives of both the mother and the sage insofar as the task of discerning the child in the man is inseparable from the task of discerning the man (that is, the well-formed man) in the child.

Preserving nature requires more than a natural bond between mother and child, because it requires more than instinct. It requires an unnatural knowledge of nature. Foresight, which is characterized as inimical to natural human independence and happiness in the earliest stages (of infancy, or of the history of the human species), is at the same time necessary to the achievement of that independence and happiness, even in the context of the "natural" family unit. Rousseau needs to replace the nuclear family with an "expert," not because he can't find a mother willing to nurse her baby but because however "good" such a mother might be, there is no guarantee that she knows how to think. Rousseau needs something beyond the natural attachment of parents for children, even as he insists that *only* the natural attachment of parents for children will generate the level of commitment necessary to the intensive task of "building the fence." But knowledge of where to build the fence—the "circumference" or parameters of nature—is not natural. It is no wonder, then, that Rousseau presents these two steps as separable, allowing that someone other than the mother may draw the circumference of the fence that she must build. But these two apparently separable steps are *not* in fact sequential or separable, because each presupposes the other. The preservation of nature presupposes knowledge of its boundaries, or "the circumference," just as one must see natural man "fully formed" in order to preserve his original form. And yet he must be preserved in order to achieve that form.

What Rousseau initially presents as separate—unselfconscious affection on the one hand, and cultivated expertise on the other—he spends the rest of *Emile* trying to put together. That this is his goal is already reflected in his identification of "a mother who knows how to think" as his ideal reader, a figure who is not presupposed but rather (ideally, by design) brought about by reading *Emile*. Her judiciousness, in other words, only emerges over the course of the five books of *Emile*.

The Ambiguous Origins of a Good Education

It turns out, then, that a mother is both necessary and insufficient in order to carry out Rousseau's project. Rousseau first hints at this insufficiency when he insists that fathers as well as mothers must be wholly invested in raising their children. (The father is the first candidate for the "someone else" who is to determine the circumference—soon to be replaced by the tutor.) With this move, Rousseau rather quickly begins introducing consideration upon consideration that complicate his own simple formulas and prescriptions. To be sure, these complications arise initially from the fact of the already corrupt state of civil society. Fathers claim that they are too busy to raise their own children, and hire governors. The "natural" answer to the needs of nature is no longer available. It is in response to this situation, it seems, that Rousseau launches into a discussion of the difficulties of finding a good governor. But the difficulties he identifies do not simply stem from the fact that the governor is someone other than the father; they would apply equally to any father. The major difficulty is that in order to know how to provide a good education, one must oneself be the product of a good education. Therefore, identifying the original source of a good education is nearly impossible.

> The more one thinks about it, the more one perceives new difficulties. It would be necessary that the governor had been raised for his pupil, that the pupil's domestics had been raised for their master, that all those who have contact with him had received the impressions that they ought to communicate to him. It would be necessary to go from education to education back to I know not where. How is it possible for a child to be well raised by one who was not well raised himself? (50; 4:263)

Each good educator presupposes a previous good educator, going back to "I know not where." This difficulty is the difficulty of all origins. It cannot be avoided by preserving the family structure. A simply "natural" education was never available, because the problem is built into nature itself, as a careful analysis of Rousseau's requirements of natural mothers (and now fathers) has shown.

The requisite knowledge that grounds a legitimate education, Rousseau suggests, can be acquired only in practice, by blocking out all social influences and watching the form that an individual takes over a lifetime. Although it would be preferable if the governor had already educated someone, Rousseau adds that this would be "too much to wish for," because "the same man can give only one education." This raises a question of legitimacy: "If two were required in order to succeed, by what right would one undertake the first?" (51; 4:265). If one is required to have educated in order to be entitled to educate, and to be educated in order to be receptive to education, then how can one ever begin? This crisis reverberates throughout Rousseau's major works. In the *Social Contract*, the formation of a people is a task that seems to require a people already formed. "Just as the architect, before putting up a big building, observes and tests the ground to see whether it can bear the weight, so the wise founder does not start by drafting laws that are good in themselves, but first examines whether the people for whom he destines them is suited to bear them" (*SC*, 157; 3:384–85). Rousseau goes on to explain that nations, like men, must reach maturity before they are ready to be made subject to law (158; 3:386). This puts the lawgiver in a difficult position, since this necessary "maturity" is achieved primarily by living under good laws and institutions. "For a newly formed people to understand wise principles of politics and to follow the basic rules of statecraft, the effect would have to become the cause; the social spirit which must be the product of social institutions would have to preside over the setting up of those institutions; men would have to have already become before the advent of the law that which they become as a result of law" (156; 3:383).

It is not surprising, then, that when Rousseau fantasizes about where he would like to have been born, had he not had the good fortune of being born in Geneva, he chooses a "long-standing republic" whose origins are "lost in the darkness of time" (*SD*, 81; 3:113). Such a wish simply defers the problem of origins.

A parallel conundrum surfaces in the opening dialogue of *Rousseau, Judge of Jean-Jacques*, as "Rousseau" first begins to converse with "a Frenchman." In response to the Frenchman's demand that he "explain" himself, "Rousseau" laments, "I'll explain what I mean, but it will be either the most useless or most superfluous of efforts, since everything I will say to you can be understood only by those to whom there is no need to say it."[9] Rousseau suggests that although he wishes to instruct his readers, the only readers who will learn from him are the ones who already know, at least on some level, what he is trying to teach them.

How does a good lawmaker or educator come to be? How does a well-governed populace or individual come to be? How does a good reader come to be? These are all different versions of the same problem for Rousseau, who seems tempted by the resolution of divine intervention. The legislator *must* have divine qualities in order to effect the necessary coincidence of good laws and a good people, as each presupposes the other (echoing the *Republic*'s miraculous coincidence of philosophy and political power in the philosopher-king). The education of Emile—the education of nature—is the "first," or original, education that makes others possible, grounding them not only in the experience of the author in writing the book but also in that of the reader in reading the book. Emile's education is analogous to the *Republic*'s city-in-speech in allowing the pursuit of a philosophical question that has concrete political consequences without actually setting into motion any of those political consequences. As an education "in speech," or a first education, *Emile* is designed to make a certain experience available to the reader while avoiding the degeneration that Rousseau believes tends to result from the expansion of human experience.

It is for this reason that Rousseau contrives to proceed independently of any preexisting context for his thought experiment. He declares Emile an orphan. Moreover, without reflecting on the kind of education that a suitable tutor would need to have had in order to carry out a "natural" education, he takes for granted that he possesses the necessary qualities. In other words, the origins of the tutor's own wisdom are erased, or at least "lost in the darkness of time," to borrow the language of the *Second Discourse*. This creates an illusion of a radically new beginning, which is possible only in theory or in fiction. Political and educational programs—even the most revolutionary—always begin *in medias res*. It is only as author that Rousseau can put an end to the infinite regress, functioning (like "the author of things") as an unmoved mover. The question becomes whether it is possible to be a nonauthoritarian author. Rousseau certainly distances himself from his own authority by repeatedly inviting the reader to judge his efforts. And yet this could be dismissed as yet another ruse of a master manipulator. We seem to be left with the unsatisfying choice between requiring a radically new beginning and allowing the problem of legitimacy to be covered over by poetic illusion.

In book I of *Emile*, however, Rousseau does not cover over the problem of origins but rather draws attention to the difficulties that inhere in his attempt to resolve it. For example, he draws attention to the problem of time. By raising the question of the proper age for a governor, Rousseau acknowledges that the wisdom that confers legitimacy can be developed only over time, but meanwhile time passes, conditions change, and it may be too late to begin anew. Wisdom lends legitimacy to rule but exacerbates inequality, while youthfulness creates the appearance of equality but limits the degree of wisdom that can be expected, and therefore undermines the legitimacy of any authority that is exercised. The younger the governor is, the less likely he is to have had any previous teaching experience. Rousseau tries to narrow the inevitable gap between the governor and the student by insisting that they be as close in age as possible. He acknowledges the paradoxical nature of this requirement, however, when he states that the governor should be "as young as a wise man can be" (*E*, 51; 4:265). With this comment, along with his remark that it would be "too much to wish for" an educator to have already educated someone (ad infinitum), Rousseau points to the impossibility of the very conditions of legitimacy he has invoked.[10] It is by simultaneously appealing to them and questioning the appeal that he models an intermediate standard of "authorial" authority that avoids the twin extremes discussed above. Book I of *Emile* both makes a beginning and draws attention to the problem of making a beginning. In light of this, we must pay careful attention not only to how the precepts laid out in book I provide a foundation for the project as a whole, allowing these to condition our reading of the subsequent chapters, but also to how these precepts are revisited, qualified, and refined as Rousseau's project in *Emile* unfolds.

A pattern has emerged: the tender and foresighted mother requires that someone else draw the circumference for her as she builds a fence around her child's soul; the existence of a suitable governor requires that a suitable governor already exist in order to raise the child; moreover, that governor needs to have already educated a pupil before he is fit to educate another one. And yet all of these double requirements must be met somehow simultaneously; the ideal mother both is natural *and* knows how to think. Finally, and most important, we must know nature in order to preserve it, but we must preserve it if it is to be available to us as an object of knowledge. Even as Rousseau claims to begin with nature, he suggests that the question of what nature *is* cannot be answered before the project (which nature supposedly guides) is completed, and hence cannot function as a direct or unmediated source of universal rules or standards that can be applied to all particulars. This, again, is what calls for judgment and also makes judgment possible. Rousseau's opening claim that everything is good in the hands of the "author" of things and degenerates in the hands of man (37; 4:245) points indirectly to the need for a realm between natural perfection (which denies freedom and makes judgment superfluous) and utter deformity (in which our judgments are indistinguishable from corrupt prejudices and in which we are thus also left fundamentally unfree in a different way). Rousseau's exploration of the question of a "natural education" aspires to locate the genuinely human somewhere between these two poles in order to preserve both human freedom and the possibility of judgment.

2

LEARNING TO MOVE

The Body, the Senses, and the Foundations of Judgment

[Emile] gets his lessons from nature and not from men. . . . His body and his mind are exercised together. Acting always according to his own thought and not someone else's, he continually unites two operations: the more he makes himself strong and robust, the more he becomes sensible and judicious. (*E*, 119; 4:361)

The first three books of *Emile* are generally understood to constitute Emile's "negative" (93; 4:323) education, that is, an education designed to preserve his natural wholeness while forestalling the development of prejudices and passions (especially amour-propre) by warding off all social influences. Rousseau states that this first, negative education "consists not at all in teaching virtue or truth but in securing the heart from vice and the mind from error." One must "let childhood ripen in children" (94; 4:324) rather than hurry to fill their minds and souls with lessons and virtues that they are unprepared to acquire, and that are unnecessary in any case. He insists that children are not naturally inclined toward the vices we attribute to them. Those vices are the product of a faulty education. By nature, children are "little innocents" whose simplicity should be preserved for as long as possible. Rousseau prefers that children remain "ignorant and true" rather than "learn their lessons and lie" (102; 4:336). The task of the educator is therefore "to do nothing and let nothing be done" (93; 4:323).

But Rousseau follows this general rule by raising "another consideration," one that suggests an altogether different reason for "doing nothing" and invites us to reconsider the idea of a purely negative education. Rousseau advises the educator to observe the child closely and over a long period of time before beginning to educate—indeed, before saying "the first word to him." His rationale is that "one must know well the particular genius of the child in order to know what moral diet suits him. Each mind has its own form." The educator must let the germ of the child's unique individual character "reveal itself freely" (94; 4:324). If childhood must be allowed to ripen, it is not simply to preserve a universal, original state as long as possible but to allow the development (unfettered, without distortion) of the child's unique self, which is revealed over time. Thus, although Rousseau argues vehemently against turning children into miniature adults with a precocious pseudomaturity, he also conceives of growth and maturation within childhood. "Each age, each condition of life, has its suitable perfection, a sort of maturity proper to it" (158; 4:418). Is "doing nothing" sufficient to bring about this maturation?

What exactly Rousseau means by the distinctive maturity of childhood, and how it is cultivated, complicates the notion of a purely negative education while bearing on several fundamental issues with regard to his views on the education of judgment. The mark of a child's having reached "the perfection of his age" (161; 4:423) is precisely the development of a certain species of judgment, not simply physical maturation. While initially in book II Rousseau insists that children are incapable of judging, he later refers to their capacity to exercise good judgment, at least with regard to the physical world. And he concludes book II with an anecdote about a child whose judgment he praises as "incisive" (163; 4:425). This refers to a rudimentary form of judgment that is distinctly appropriate to children as children, but at the same time sets the stage for—and in some ways serves as a model for—good judgment at any age. "One must have a great deal of judgment oneself to appreciate a child's" (162; 4:424). Rousseau's admiration of the incisive child is matched by his admiration for the child's father, who is able to perceive this trait in his child. This ability marks the father not only as a good father but as a wise man. Such wisdom is rare. "None of us is philosophic enough to know how to put himself in a child's place" (115; 4:355). Time after time, in the course of explaining the limitations and characteristics of a child's perspective, Rousseau offers parallel reflections on various adult figures and their good or poor judgment. Specifically, in order to achieve the distinctive maturity of childhood, children must be taught both to run well and to see well. Rousseau's treatment of each of these lessons unfolds in two registers. Learning to run entails learning to exist as a being whose nature cannot remain static but rather *moves* (since we are, after all, perfectible beings). Learning to see means developing not only visual acuity with regard to physical distances but also the ability to discern the nature of reality. By attending to *both* registers of Rousseau's lessons on these points, we can better understand the broader significance of this educational stage of *Emile*.

On one level, then, Rousseau's concerns center on physical education of the body and the senses in order to prevent the stimulation of imagination or any passions before their time. On another, he explores the nature of judgment, which is rooted in the "natural" perspective of a purely physical being but not reducible to it. The point of this second stage of Emile's education is not simply to preserve the simplicity of his existence (and to establish the importance of such simplicity for human beings in general), but rather to establish the complexity of what it truly means for a being whose origins lie in a purely physical existence (in which Emile represents human beings as such) to learn to judge.[1] In this chapter, I explore this complexity with regard to the relationship between the physical and the intellectual in Emile's education and, more broadly, in Rousseau's understanding of good judgment.

The Child as a Physical Being

Inasmuch as Rousseau continues to emphasize the importance of a negative education, book II in some ways simply extends the principles developed in book I to the growing child. The prepubescent Emile is primarily a physical being, and his lessons reflect this. On this issue Rousseau is critical of Locke, who maintains that one must reason with children. "The masterpiece of a good education is to make a reasonable man, and they claim they raise a child by reason! This is to begin with the end, to want to make the product the instrument. If children understood reason, they would not need to be raised" (89; 4:317). Attempting to use reason with children does not simply miss the mark; its impact turns out to be harmful rather than neutral. Reasoning with children involves the use of language that they are not equipped to comprehend. They may in fact learn to speak as they are spoken to, but this is only a façade, Rousseau insists. Their apparently sophisticated bons mots are at best empty chatter, and at worst pernicious indicators that they are well on their way to becoming miserable adults (civil men) who speak and live inauthentically.[2]

Learning to Move   ✳   *39*

What language, then, is appropriate for the child learning to speak? The language of the body. At this stage the tutor couches all lessons in the language of the body and encourages Emile to interpret the world around him based on two bodily experiences that children have on a regular basis: hunger and illness. For example, Emile learns the utility of astronomy when he is lost in the middle of the forest at lunchtime, and he is inspired to run faster for the sake of a very specific prize: a cake. The tutor also mentions another child who was taught geometry "by being given the choice every day of waffles with equal perimeters done in all the geometric figures. The little glutton had exhausted the art of Archimedes in finding out in which there was the most to eat" (146; 4:401). If Locke's motto can be said to be "lead them with reason," Rousseau's is surely "lead them with cakes," for "a child would rather give [away] a hundred louis than a cake" (103; 4:338). Even complex human emotions can be explained to children in purely physical terms. What does a child see when looking at an angry person, for example? "He sees an inflamed face, glittering eyes, threatening gestures; he hears shouts—all signs that the body is out of kilter." Thus one should tell the child calmly, "This poor man is sick; he is in a fit of fever" (96; 4:328).

Thus moral lessons must be postponed, Rousseau contends, because attempts to inculcate them at this age will inevitably result in unintended consequences due to the bodily character of the child's perspective. At the same time, Rousseau suggests that the child must begin to move beyond this limited perspective. Book II opens with the announcement that we have entered into "the second period of life," which refers to the period just beyond infancy through age twelve. However, this second stage is actually a first insofar as it is only now that, "strictly speaking [*proprement*], the life of the individual begins" (78; 4:301). This birth of individuality functions as a second beginning and prefigures the "second birth" at the beginning of book IV (that is, the beginning of the significance of the individual's sex/gender). It is the first of these two rebirths.[3]

Just as it is only after infancy that, strictly speaking, the life of the individual begins, so too is it only at this point that the story of Emile truly begins. In other words, Emile is "reborn" for the reader as a concrete example rather than an abstraction; he is particularized. To be sure, the *idea* of Emile figures briefly in book I, when Rousseau first sets up his thought experiment, but the child does not yet come alive on the page. We are told that Emile is an orphan, and then in effect he disappears into a field of generalities. Rousseau's subsequent remarks refer to "one's child" or "all children." Occasionally, he mentions his imaginary pupil in passing (with a pronoun), but Emile does not actually *appear* as a character. We are not invited to picture little Emile crawling about. Rather, "the child" functions as an abstraction in book I. Only in book II do the details of Emile's particular experiences become significant. From this point forward, Rousseau illustrates his arguments with anecdotes depicting the tutor's interaction with Emile. Emile appears by degrees, just as natural man in the *Second Discourse* vanishes by degrees. As Emile must learn gradually to see and judge the world around him, the reader must learn to see and judge Emile.

Once individuality becomes an issue, so does happiness—and not before. Rousseau waits until book II to explain the understanding of happiness that guides his entire endeavor, or at least serves as a point of departure. "A being endowed with senses whose faculties equaled his desires would be an *absolutely* happy being" (80; 4:304, emphasis added). This would seem to suggest that for Rousseau the natural man, in his simplicity and physical robustness, is the best judge, or sets the standard against which the human condition must be judged. "The closer to his natural condition man has stayed, the smaller is the difference between his faculty and his desires, and consequently the less removed he is from being happy" (81; 4:304). But it is precisely the perfect equilibrium of absolute happiness that makes it impossible to stay close to this natural condition, for natural man lacks the foresight and experience to understand and maintain his condition.[4] Our perfectibility may be what moves us away, but our unselfconsciousness and ignorance are what make us susceptible to moving in directions that diminish our happiness and freedom.

This helps us to make sense of why Rousseau introduces his definition of the absolutely happy being with the remark that we cannot know what absolute happiness or unhappiness is (80; 4:303). Even as he states this unequivocally, Rousseau at the same time implies that it might be possible to *experience* absolute happiness. The absolutely happy being thus resembles the natural man of the *Second Discourse* insofar as he experiences perfect contentment but does not know enough to appreciate its fragility. Such a being *is* an absolutely happy being but does not *know* it. The underlying question is whether knowing that one is happy is an essential component of being happy.

To the degree that Emile exemplifies the happy equilibrium of desires and faculties, his equilibrium is maintained artificially by the tutor's absolute control over him. He resembles natural man but has the added benefit of the tutor's guiding hand to protect his innocence (whereas Rousseau introduces his portrait of natural man in the *Second Discourse* with the remark that he will consider what human beings would become if left to themselves). Emile does not know what happiness is, or even that he is happy (awareness of which requires comparison to other states, a lesson Rousseau saves for a later time). One should not mistake Emile's lack of self-awareness for evidence that Rousseau's model of human happiness (and, by extension, human freedom) excludes self-reflection. Rousseau gives us several indications, even at this early stage in Emile's upbringing, that a perfect equilibrium maintained by external force(s) rather than by self-consciousness is *not* in fact his ultimate model.

Rousseau begins by distinguishing the happy child from the spoiled (*gaté*) child, clarifying that his point is not to fulfill every desire (which is a recipe not for equilibrium but for disequilibrium, since desires can be limitless) but precisely to limit desire in the first place. Making a child happy does not mean making him spoiled, and making a child good does not mean making him unhappy. So far, we are in familiar territory, for this is all quite consistent with Rousseau's conception of man's natural goodness. However, once Rousseau has articulated this formulaic conception of happiness (happiness equals equilibrium), he raises the following question: "In what, then, consists human wisdom or the road of true happiness?" (80; 4:304). Rousseau's initial answer to this question reinforces the importance of equilibrium between desires and faculties. Of all the animals, human beings alone have superfluous faculties, and these become the instruments of our unhappiness. Specifically, foresight and imagination awaken new hopes and desires and extend the "measure of the possible" (91; 4:304), causing us to project goals and destinations at which we never arrive. Therefore, Rousseau advises that we restrict ourselves to a very narrow, simple sphere of existence, within which equilibrium is possible. "Let us measure the radius of our sphere and stay in the center like the insect in the middle of his web; we shall always be sufficient unto ourselves; and we shall not have to complain of our weakness, for we shall never feel it" (81; 4:305).

However, as Rousseau continues his discussion of human wisdom and its relation to happiness, he leaves behind the image of an insect caught it its own web and begins to emphasize the reflective dimension of human happiness. While he advises man to "remain in the place which nature assigns to you in the chain of being" (83; 4:308), he also notes that the wise man "knows *how* to stay in his place" (84; 4:310, emphasis added). Unlike the insect, who remains in place by instinct or impotence, or natural man, who lacks the foresight and experience to understand the consequences of leaving it, the wise man understands his distinctive place in the chain of being and knows how to maintain it. Rousseau contrasts this wisdom not only with the simplicity of other animals but with that of the human child, who "does not know his place [and] would not be able to keep to it" (84; 4:310). Unlike the child, whose equilibrium and thus happiness must be maintained by an external force (in this case, the tutor), the wise man must possess, in addition to an equilibrium of desires and faculties, some faculty that allows him to reflect on and maintain that very equilibrium. This is likely to involve the "superfluous" faculties that, Rousseau laments, tend to serve as instruments of unhappiness rather than happiness (81; 4:305). Rousseau's implicit question seems to be not simply whether this superfluity can be severely curtailed or even avoided altogether but whether it can be harnessed to serve the cause of happiness rather than unhappiness.

Rousseau's distinction between childish happiness and adult happiness implies that only children (specifically, children whose equilibrium has been maintained for them) can be perfectly happy. But this happiness is fleeting. Rousseau insists that childhood gaiety and innocence be preserved and cherished rather than sacrificed to an uncertain future, but at the same time he has long-term aspirations for his pupil's happiness. "I shall not seek a distant happiness for him at the expense of the present. I want him to be happy not once but always, if it is possible" (326–27; 4:653). Insofar as growing up means learning to maintain your own equilibrium—learning how to stay in your place—it means relinquishing a perfect (but externally maintained) equilibrium for a less perfect but more independently maintained equilibrium. This raises the question of how a child held to one standard becomes an adult held to a very different standard. How does one *learn* to stay in one's place if one has always been *made* to stay in one's place? Rousseau underscores the importance of this transition at the beginning of book III, when he begins to characterize his subject not simply as "the child" but as "the child whom one wants to make wise" (166; 4:428).

The implied distinction between being happy and knowing what happiness is runs parallel to the distinction between staying in place and knowing how to stay in place. Both are related to the central issue of book II: how to combine integrity and motion, or movement and staying in place. Rousseau's prescribed education for the preadolescent is designed at once to preserve childhood innocence and to bring the child to "the maturity of childhood" (162; 4:423). One *must* therefore grow and learn—both in order to achieve the maturity of childhood and, more fundamentally, because perfectibility is part of human nature. The challenge is to do so while remaining unified and whole. Perfect equilibrium is a static condition, but it is in the nature of human beings to *move*. In light of this fundamental tension, Rousseau's choice of illustration for book II—Chiron training the young Achilles to run—takes on added significance. At stake is not only the matter of teaching a child to move with swiftness and agility but also the underlying issue of how one might encourage a child to run or, more broadly, to *move*—that is to grow, learn, and change—while keeping him in his place by forestalling the development of all his superfluous faculties. The two objectives are intimately related inasmuch as Rousseau claims that the key to forestalling the development of superfluous faculties involves preserving the child as a purely physical being. Thus running is an appropriate activity for the child, whereas reading, which stimulates the imagination, is not. But there is more to Rousseau's discussion of learning to run; he raises the broader question of how, in light of his insistence on a negative education, one might properly learn anything at all.

Learning to Run

It is far from immediately clear why Rousseau focuses any attention at all on the issue of teaching a child to run, as opposed to simply letting the child run free, since he ridicules the common practice of teaching children to walk. "Is there anything more foolish than the effort made to teach them to walk, as if anyone were ever seen who, due to his nurse's negligence, did not when grown know how to walk?" We tend to teach children what they would better learn by themselves, he complains, and forget to teach them "what we alone can teach them" (78; 4:300). Rousseau argues that the child ought to be allowed complete freedom of movement and learn to accept the consequences of that freedom. A child should be taken daily to an open field. "There let him run and risk about; let him fall a hundred times a day. So much the better. That way he will learn how to get up sooner" (78; 4:301). Ideally, children teach themselves to run, it would seem, just as they teach themselves to walk. Yet the illustration that introduces book II is not of a child spontaneously running free but of Achilles being trained by Chiron. What is the true lesson of this stage of Rousseau's educational project?

Rousseau's discussion of children learning to run involves more than honing physical skills; it also introduces questions of motivation and direction. His main anecdote about teaching a young man to run (which includes the only reference to Chiron in the text) concerns an indolent boy who lacks not only the strength and skill to run but also the motivation. For the educator facing the task of motivating the boy, Rousseau remarks, "the skill of Chiron himself would have hardly sufficed." He adds, "The difficulty was all the greater since I wanted to prescribe to him absolutely nothing. I had banished from among my rights exhortations, promises, threats, emulation, the desire to be conspicuous. How could I give him the desire to run without saying anything to him?" (141; 4:393).

This passage distills a well-recognized difficulty that pervades Rousseau's entire corpus: the tension between will formation, on the one hand, and agency and authenticity, on the other. Rousseau's various legislator figures condition the will of their subjects to love the objects that will best support their freedom—yet this conditioning calls into question the value or character of that freedom. Of course, Emile is a child at this point in Rousseau's narrative, and careful control of his environment and experiences is arguably justified by his young age. The question of whether his freedom is ultimately genuine must be reserved for later. But the passage raises a related question, having to do with integrity as well as freedom. Before we come to the question of whether Emile is free, we must address the question of whether he is himself—or a *self* at all. "Doubtless he ought to do only what he wants; but he ought to want only what you want him to do. He ought not to make a step without your having foreseen it" (120; 4:363). How are we to reconcile Rousseau's emphasis on active formation of the will with his admonition to allow the child's character to reveal itself, unfettered? Rousseau's confidence that the child who experiences no direct opposition to his desires will show himself "fearlessly" and "precisely as he is" (120; 4:363) belies the catch-22 that he has introduced. Indeed, he claims that precisely because the child will reveal himself entirely unselfconsciously, the educator will be in a position to study him at leisure—with the same careful study that must be conducted as preparation for shaping his every desire. In other words, the anecdote in book II that relates most directly to the book's thematic illustration raises an issue that has to do not simply with physical strength but also with integrity of character— that is, with remaining oneself.

New skills cannot be acquired authentically, according to Rousseau, unless the acquisition is driven by the pupil's own desire for them. But the desire to acquire a new skill, once stimulated, is almost always linked to some form of desire for recognition. The lazy boy whom Rousseau teaches to run is motivated by the desire for the cakes that are the prize in a race. For Rousseau, the desire for cakes is natural, but the desire for recognition as the winner is born of unnatural amour-propre. In this particular anecdote, Rousseau downplays this potential hazard. He notes that the first few times he and his charge passed by the young boys racing one another to win a cake, "it did not register and produced nothing." So Rousseau expands the event (which was, of course, prearranged) to include more contestants and draw more attention to the winner. "The one who won [the prize] was praised and given a celebration; it was all done with ceremony." Predictably, his young charge gets caught up in the excitement, as passersby clap and cheer for the runners. "These were for him the Olympic games." Finally, it enters the boy's head that "running well could be good for something" (141–42; 4:394).

While it is clear that the child's interest has been stimulated by the spectacle and ceremony and not simply by the cakes, Rousseau moves on as though the potential for triggering amour-propre had never arisen. Indeed, he suggests that winning makes the boy generous, and he happily shares his cake with the others. In later episodes (beginning in book III), however, Rousseau further develops his reflections on a difficulty that is raised here only indirectly. These arise when the newly developed desire is the desire to learn new things—a desire that an educator must stoke if the child is to grow and mature but that threatens to disturb the fragile equilibrium between desires and faculties that is the hallmark of self-sufficiency, according to Rousseau. Whereas teaching a child to run will augment his strength, thus enhancing his independence, stimulating his desire for knowledge will expand his needs insofar as it makes him want something he lacks. The desire to learn takes one outside oneself, and therein lies the danger, for it is because he lives outside himself that civil man is so miserable.

In addition to creating a potential disequilibrium between desires and faculties, the desire to learn can easily turn into the desire to be learned. This desire not only stimulates vanity but leads to the desire to *appear* learned rather than to be learned. One therefore risks inflaming amour-propre in an effort to stimulate intellectual curiosity. For Emile, this problem is addressed through a contrived encounter with a magician who publicly humiliates Emile when he tries to show off some newly acquired knowledge. After watching the magician make a toy duck move at will, Emile is inspired to figure out the trick, and thus to discover the underlying scientific principles (that is, to learn the cause of the magician's effects). Once he learns how magnets make the duck move, he cannot wait to reveal his knowledge to the magician, and to the audience; "he would want the whole of humankind to be witness to his glory" (173; 4:438). Emile declares in front of the crowd that the trick is easy, and shows off his ability to manipulate the duck with a magnet hidden in a piece of bread. The magician responds graciously and invites Emile and his tutor back the next day to perform in front of an even larger crowd. This time, however, the duck flees. The crowd jeers; Emile complains and challenges the magician to attract the duck. The magician pulls the iron out of the bread, revealing Emile's attempted deceit, and goes on to manipulate the duck with another piece of bread, his gloved finger, even his voice. Emile and the tutor sneak away, humiliated.

The next day, the magician comes to their door to confront them about their conduct. He chastises them for seeking honor "at the expense of an honest man's subsistence" (174; 4:439). He explains that he did not show them his master strokes straightaway, for he keeps them in reserve rather than showing off giddily all that he knows. He then reveals his secret device for manipulating the duck: a lodestone. He begs them not to abuse this knowledge and to exercise restraint in the future. Specifically, he reprimands the tutor for failing to guide Emile and protect him from his humiliating mistake. The following day they return to the fair and do not breathe a word of what they know.[5] Emile's incipient amour-propre has been squelched, but his perspective has also been broadened.

A child does not simply grow into his body at this age; he grows into his individual identity. Inasmuch as this is when "the life of the individual begins," it is also at this stage that the child "gains consciousness of himself. . . . He becomes *truly one, the same*, and consequently already capable of happiness or unhappiness. It is important, therefore, to begin to consider him as a moral being" (78; 4:301, emphasis added). Gaining consciousness of oneself is the first step toward becoming self-conscious in the sense of living in the opinion of others; the *Second Discourse* presents this as a very slippery slope. In *Emile* Rousseau considers whether we can grow and learn while staying "truly one, the same." To put it another way, one must learn to move while staying in place. Rousseau's exploration of the matter of learning to run, which seems philosophically inconsequential, introduces the larger issue of learning, growing, and changing while remaining within various boundaries: the boundary of childhood simplicity, the boundary of the self, and, most broadly, the boundaries that nature imposes on human beings.

Rousseau argues explicitly in book II that the education from postinfancy to preadolescence must concern itself primarily with the child's physical development, so that a child's strength can "catch up" to his desires before his desires extend beyond what a self-sufficient individual can satisfy. The child is born too weak to satisfy even his limited needs for food and physical comfort. Limiting his needs and desires to these things while he grows and matures physically allows the child to achieve the perfect equilibrium between faculties and desires that makes human beings happy and free in the original state of nature. Beyond this, however, there is a second objective built into Rousseau's concern with training the muscles and physical senses. To "learn to think," it is necessary to hone "the instruments of our intelligence," which are "our limbs, our senses, our organs" (125; 4:370). Thus the child concentrates on physical education—not to avoid thinking but precisely in order to learn to think. "Let him be a man in his vigor, and soon he will be one in his reason" (118; 4:359). How are these goals connected for Rousseau? The link between physical strength and reason is that both are essential to an individual's independence and self-sufficiency. Precisely by learning to fend for oneself physically, one learns to think independently. "Since [Emile] is constantly in motion, he is forced to observe many things, to know many effects. . . . Thus his body and his mind are exercised together. Acting always in accordance with his own thought and not someone else's, he continually unites two operations: the more he makes himself strong and robust, the more he becomes sensible and judicious" (119; 4:361). The scope of a child's exercise of judgment is strictly delimited, pertaining only to everything immediately (that is, physically) related to him. Rousseau depicts children learning to judge heights, lengths, depths, and distances with a view to acquiring cherries, cakes, and other edible treats.[6] In other words, they learn to judge the physical world around them as a means to fulfilling a physical desire. Even the single positive lesson Rousseau allows during this stage—a lesson about respecting private property—is organized around the child's desire to eat some delicious melons. Education at this stage involves manipulating the child's desire for sweets in order to stimulate him to learn how to fulfill that need himself—by judging the shortest path to winning the cake, for example, or judging a tree's height accurately in order to pick the cherries. Within a small radius, equilibrium between desires and faculties is thus achieved.

Many of these judgments involve correctly calculating distances with the naked eye. With practice, the child learns to rely on himself rather than on others or even on instruments, and develops "a glance almost as sure as a surveyor's chain" (143; 4:396). In characterizing the five senses as the instruments of human intelligence, Rousseau emphasizes sight in particular as the key to demonstrating how the senses can serve as the foundation of judgment. "Sight is, of all the respects, the one from which the mind's judgments can least be separated" (143; 4:396). Rousseau introduces this issue in the anecdote about the lazy boy who learned to run, in which the boy's ability to see was educated in two senses: in order to win, he had to learn to measure distances accurately by sight, but in order to develop the desire to run at all, he had to learn to see it as good for something. Rousseau yokes together the issues of learning to run and learning to see because his concern is how one *moves* from a rudimentary to a more complex form of judgment.

Learning to See

Rousseau presents seeing as both utterly simple and highly complex. It is simple insofar as it is natural and physical; it is complex insofar as appearances can be deceiving. Every child has the capacity to see well as long as misguided parents and educators do not hamper this ability by taking away opportunities to hone and exercise it. In this sense, seeing is spontaneous, and a negative education is all that is necessary to preserve it. At the same time, however, "much time is needed to learn how to see" (143; 4:396). As in the case of running, the training Rousseau prescribes for learning to see links seeing to both the skill of estimating distances at a glance and the capacity for philosophy and independent reasoning. "Our first masters of philosophy are our feet, our hands, our eyes." To seek knowledge without using the senses is "to teach us to use the reason of others. It is to teach us to believe much and never to know anything" (125; 4:370). At the same time, the simple acquisition of sense data is by itself insufficient. "To exercise the senses is not only to make use of them, it is to learn to judge well with them" (132; 4:380). The issue thus becomes how to understand the faculty of judgment as grounded in accurate and autonomous sense perception but not reducible to it.[7] In insisting on this irreducibility, Rousseau challenges Helvétius, whose influential *De l'esprit* promoted a sensationalist view of judgment that grounded judgment in nothing other than sensation: "Juger n'est jamais que sentir." Helvétius argued that the mind passively receives impressions from external objects and experiences a sensation in response. The mind is able to remember the sensation and the object(s) to which it is attached, and as a result can piece together judgments about the world. There is no judging faculty, according to Helvétius, apart from sensation and memory. Rousseau, in contrast, held this view to be too passive. Even as he insisted on the importance of sensation in human cognition and judgment, he nevertheless argued for an understanding of judgment as active rather than passive.[8] "Our sensations are purely passive," he says in *Emile*, "while all our perceptions or ideas are born out of an active principle which judges" (107; 4:344).

While Rousseau's more direct response to Helvétius is found in the context of the Savoyard Vicar's profession of faith in book IV, in book II his discussion of the senses—especially that of sight—addresses not only the distinction between the passive and active senses of judging but also their interdependence. Thus the relationship between Rousseau's two senses of learning to see bears on the question of his understanding of good judgment and how it is formed. Since he also links seeing with philosophizing (just as Aristotle identifies sight as the sense most closely linked with the desire to know), an analysis of the way in which Rousseau teaches his pupil(s) to see also sheds light on what he thinks it means to make a human being wise. "Man learns to see with the eyes of the mind as well as with the eyes of the body."[9]

The explicit pedagogical advice of book II elaborates the connection between both senses of seeing well. Rousseau focuses on the first, physical sense when recommending exercises (such as night games) to sharpen the child's sight (and other senses). At first, Rousseau suggests that learning to see well is simply a matter of training the naked eye to see independently. The goal is to prevent the child from adding any extraneous interpretation to what his senses reveal to him. To that end, parents should avoid *any* reaction to the child's experiences, so as not to influence his perception of them, and prohibit the use of external aids such as binoculars. Clarity in sense perception, unadulterated by anything that the mind might add, is the goal. Similarly, when teaching a child to draw, one must ensure that the child has "no other master than nature and no other model than objects. I want him to have before his eyes the original itself and not the paper representing it, to sketch a house from a house, a tree from a tree, a man from a man, so that he gets accustomed to observing bodies and their appearances well and not to taking false and conventional imitations for true imitations" (144; 4:397).

However, Rousseau's insistence on the purely negative quality of such seeing—in the sense of seeing without interference—soon falters, when he acknowledges the inaccuracy of the senses, which may lead even the most rudimentary judgments astray. He takes a two-pronged approach to this problem. First, one must aim to be as accurate as possible; each sense must be fine-tuned to its peak performance. Even so, it is not possible to rely on the accuracy of each sense by itself. The only recourse, if one wants to remain on the level of the senses, is to draw on the assistance of another sense—a system of checks and balances among the five senses. "Instead of simplifying the sensation, double it, always verify it by another. Subject the visual organ to the tactile organ" (140; 4:92). This solution falters as well, however, and Rousseau ultimately moves from the purely physical to the intellectual:

It remains for me to speak in the following books of the cultivation of a sort of sixth sense called *common sense*, less because it is common to all men than because it results from the well-regulated use of the other senses, and because it instructs us about the nature of things by the conjunction of all their appearances. This sixth sense has consequently no special organ. It resides only in the brain, and its sensations, purely internal, are called *perceptions* or *ideas*. It is by the number of these ideas that the extent of our knowledge is measured. It is their distinctness, their clarity which constitutes the accuracy of the mind. It is the art of comparing them among themselves that is called *human reason*. (157–58; 4:417)

The "sixth sense" links a conception of human reason as independent of the senses with the senses themselves, functioning as a middle ground. Reason emerges as neither reducible to the senses (as it is for Helvétius) nor independent of them. If "the child whom one wants to make wise" *must* first learn how to see, this is why. Rousseau may insist that the child be preserved as a primarily physical being who interacts with the world around him on physical (not moral) terms, but this goal is not opposed to the goal of teaching the child to reason. It in fact lays the groundwork for the independent exercise of reason. A child whose senses have been properly developed can become an accurate judge within the context of the physical world around him. "Now we are well informed about the character of foreign bodies in relation to our own, about their weight, shape, color, solidity, size, distance, temperature, rest, and motion" (150; 4:407). In other words, the child, understood as a strictly physical being, has become a good judge of physical reality insofar as it relates to his immediate surroundings; "he judges, he foresees, in everything immediately related to him" (119; 4:361). Having learned to run well and to see well, he has thereby learned to judge well within the limits appropriate to childhood.

Learning to Learn

Of course, the human child is not meant to remain forever a purely physical being, and arguably the goal of childhood education is preparation for adulthood. While, as I noted in chapter 1, Rousseau is critical of those who see children only as future men, he is also critical of the tender mother who thinks only of her child's present happiness. "That is not enough," Rousseau counters. "One ought to teach him to preserve himself as a man" (42; 4:253). Thus, by Rousseau's own admission, childhood education must prepare a child for adulthood, even as it aims toward the "maturity of childhood" rather than full maturity. To what degree does Rousseau succeed in meeting this challenge? The education he lays out in the first half of book II may suffice to teach a child how to move in a physical sense, but does it teach a child to move in the sense of learning, growing, changing?

To address this question, we might consider Rousseau's argument that adults must refrain from encouraging children to consider what lies beyond their immediate physical existence, putting off moral lessons until much later. The goal at this point, he insists, is to prevent vice from developing, rather than to encourage the development of virtue. Rousseau's claim, however, is not simply that children are not far enough along the path of development to be genuinely virtuous, for such a claim could easily be countered with the argument that they should therefore be encouraged to "practice" virtuous behavior as they grow. Rousseau rejects the assumption that going through the motions of virtue produces virtue; such attempts at habituation, he maintains, encourage a discrepancy between the internal state of mind and external behavior—inadvertently cultivating an insincerity that begets vice, not virtue. Thus, for the same reason that it is wrong to try to reason with children, it is futile at best to coax children to do virtuous deeds in an effort to habituate them. A child who is trained to go through the motions of being charitable, for example, does not become charitable; he becomes an imposter. Coaxing such behavior from children cultivates "virtues by imitation," which is to say, "the virtues of apes" (104; 4:339). In Rousseau's view, the child who imitates adults only *appears* to learn and mature; the maturation is a superficial veneer. The child learns not how to become virtuous but how to hide his lack of virtue. This is one origin of the false front that civil man wears. At stake here is the ability to distinguish between true learning and false (merely apparent) learning, such as that exhibited by the child who chatters precociously. But Rousseau makes it easier for us to discern the mark of false learning. He insists that children at this age should be made to "taste" their lessons, rather than be taught the names for things. But this "tasting" is characterized as unconscious conditioning. We are left with two inadequate models: tasting without knowing, on the one hand, and superficial knowledge (knowing names without tasting), on the other. The question remains, how does one achieve real knowledge? How does one actually and truly *learn*?

Teaching inappropriate lessons produces false learning (or worse). Fables are out, and so is coaxing certain behavior. What, then, are appropriate lessons? Rousseau offers two pieces of advice on this point, both of which raise more problems than they answer. First, he counsels his readers to "know well the particular genius of the child in order to know what moral diet suits him" (94; 4:324). This suggests that the child's unique character must be known before we can know what education suits him; but by the time his character is fully formed, it may be too late to educate him. Still, Rousseau recommends taking the time to allow the child's nature to reveal itself before one begins, which strikingly recalls the paradox we saw in book I: that nature (in this case the child's innate temperament) must guide the process of discovery even as it is what is discovered in the process. Here, Rousseau generates a similar paradox by advising educators to "spy out nature for a long time; observe your pupil well before saying the first word to him. To start with, let the germ of his character reveal itself freely; constrain it in no way whatsoever in order better to see the whole of it" (94; 4:324). We are back to the difficulty of knowing when the whole is a completed whole, to say nothing of the more immediate difficulty of how one might manage to say nothing to a child until his character is fully revealed.

Rousseau acknowledges that this requirement may present an insurmountable hurdle. "I sense these difficulties; I agree they are difficulties. Perhaps they are insurmountable. But it is still certain that in applying oneself to overcoming them, one does overcome them up to a certain point. I show the goal that must be set; I do not say that it can be reached" (94–95; 4:325). At this point, perhaps in order to resolve this impasse, he introduces the idea that there is in fact a place for imitation in this otherwise "negative" education. "Remember that before daring to undertake the formation of a man, one must have made oneself a man. One must find within oneself the example the pupil ought to take for his own" (95; 4:325). A governor should lead by example rather than try to coax virtuous deeds from the child. "Be virtuous and good. Let your examples be graven in your pupils' memories until they can enter their hearts. Instead of hastening to exact acts of charity from my pupil, I prefer to do them in his presence and to deprive him of even the means of imitating me in this, as an honor which is not for his age" (104; 4:339).

The proposition that one must lead by example is perplexing, however, in light of Rousseau's scathing critique of "the virtues of apes." Is he for or against imitation? On the one hand, he contends that if Emile begins to imitate the tutor's acts of charity (behaving like the rich man that he is not), he must be forbidden to do so. However, Rousseau goes on to add that he would not mind if Emile should steal some money from him in order to give it away covertly. "This is a fraud appropriate to his age, and the only one I would pardon him" (104; 4:339). Rousseau would pardon this fraud because it is committed with a view to *being* good, not with a view to appearing good. Only if the act is covert—if it does not *appear*—is it truly virtuous rather than an empty gesture.[10]

Learning to Move ✳ 53

A good deed done in secret avoids the superficiality of imitation and becomes in some sense genuine. Still, imitation seems to play an important role in *motivating* the behavior.

Imitation is both problematic and necessary, it seems. While Rousseau at first allows that "at an age when the heart feels nothing yet, children just have to be made to imitate the acts whose habit one wants to give them," he nevertheless resolves that we must "give up the apparent good which imitation can produce" (104; 4:338–39). He uses imitation to solve a problem—that there is no other way to begin to teach children to be virtuous—but then rejects the solution. However, he continues to proceed as though the problem were solved. His rejection is therefore somewhat disingenuous. But it points to a larger, recurring issue. To overcome the difficulty generated by the requirement that the child be a completed whole before education can begin, Rousseau shifts the burden onto the tutor, demanding that he be a completed whole before he can begin the education of another. In other words, wholeness must somehow precede the very educational process that is supposed to produce wholeness. Moreover, the idea that the child would at some level emulate the wholeness of the tutor in order to achieve wholeness himself leaps over the need to educate someone to be an independent self who does not imitate others—in other words, it leaps over the possibility of what Rousseau would consider a genuine education and resorts instead to something that could just as easily produce the "virtues of apes." Either the child imitates the adult who gives alms, for example (and therefore does not develop virtue but only the appearance of it), or he does not merely imitate because he is already virtuous—and therefore does not need to develop virtue. Education is either absent or superfluous. The fundamental question that remains is how virtue might come into being if it is not already there. Once again, as we saw in chapter 1, Rousseau's argument founders on the question of origins.

The ambiguity in Rousseau's treatment of imitation suggests why even the early part of Emile's education cannot, despite Rousseau's rhetoric, be a purely "negative" education. It is noteworthy that one of his strongest statements about the need to "put off, if possible, a good lesson for fear of giving a bad one" (96; 4:327) is followed by an admission that one cannot avoid lessons altogether and must therefore choose carefully. A pattern is beginning to emerge, in which Rousseau adds a caveat to what he initially presents as an absolute rule. Rousseau "breaks" his own rules against imitation and positive lessons. This pattern continues well into book III, in which he lifts his supposedly absolute ban on books and allows Emile to read *Robinson Crusoe*, "since we absolutely must have books" (184; 4:454). In the chapters that follow, we shall explore the ways in which this tendency to qualify absolutes extends also to the poetic images (such as natural man and citizen) that function as absolute standards in Rousseau's thought as a whole.

The first positive lesson that Emile receives concerns property. He and the tutor mix their labor with the earth, cultivating some beans. Emile is told that the beans "belong" to him. One day, they arrive at the garden and find to their dismay that their bean plants have been torn up. They are indignant. The gardener is summoned. He, too, is indignant, because he had already sowed Maltese melons, which were destroyed when the beans were planted. The gardener complains that he has been done "an irreparable wrong" and also points out that Emile and the tutor have deprived themselves of the pleasure of eating the exquisite melons (99; 4:331). Rousseau makes two points here. The first is that the child can understand property to the degree that he can understand physical labor. But this requires only a static notion of property and does not address the potential for conflict between two individuals who have both invested their labor. The child's capacity for comprehending this conflict, and its resolution, is grounded once again in the body. Emile learns to respect the property of others (which is a step beyond understanding what is his own property, or what counts as property in general) because he loves melons. The story illustrates Rousseau's contention that human beings can be both self-interested and good, as long as their interests or desires are moderate.

At this point Rousseau does identify one principle that transcends self-interest. "The only lesson of morality appropriate to childhood, and the most important for every age, is never to harm anyone" (104; 4:340). Rousseau's formulation of this principle is surprisingly less self-referential than his formulation of the "golden rule" in the *Second Discourse:* "Do what is good for you with the least possible harm to others" (*SD*, 133; 3:156). That rule seems more appropriate to Emile than the admonition never to harm anyone, if only because he is supposedly devoid of any desire to harm anyone. Moreover, Rousseau has just stated that "a child does not attack persons but things" (*E*, 97; 4:329). In light of this comment, the injunction never to harm anyone hardly makes sense, or is hardly necessary. The lesson of the garden—do not harm another's *property*, for they might then harm yours, or you might be deprived of something good—would seem to suffice.

How are we to understand the instruction never to harm anyone in the context of *Emile*, especially at this stage, since Emile is still such a physical being and Rousseau continues to insist on a (supposedly) negative education? The capacity to honor this principle requires the capacity for pity, the repugnance at seeing one's fellow man suffer, which Rousseau argues in the *Second Discourse* is part of natural man's constitution. But Emile's sense of pity is not discussed, and seems not to emerge, until book IV. Therefore, Emile cannot fully appreciate the principle "never harm anyone" at this stage. Indeed, we are given no indication that the tutor articulates the principle for Emile. It is articulated only on the level of the commentary that accompanies the action of book II.

If Rousseau introduces the principle in some sense prematurely, we have to wonder why. I submit that he does so for the benefit of the reader, rather than for Emile's benefit. As Rousseau points out, it is the most important lesson not only for a child but *for every age*. It is likely to be an especially important lesson for adults who *do* attack persons rather than things. Emile has no such desire, and he does not need to be told not to harm others. He has no such desire because the tutor has controlled his environment and interactions so that Emile never perceives it to be in his interest to harm another. Even if the child's only duty is not to harm anyone, he will be able to honor this maxim only if it does not go against his inclination. This is a fundamental principle in Rousseau's moral philosophy: duty and inclination must be reconciled. This reconciliation hardly seems necessary in Emile's case, but at the same time it seems impossible in the case of civil man, who has already developed such an inclination to harm another. Emile doesn't need to be told (since he already "tastes" it), and it is certainly not enough for the reader simply to be told (or she will *never* taste it). Even before we get to the problem of reconciling duty and inclination, a more fundamental reconciliation between these two aspects of learning must be achieved.

In book II of his *Confessions* Rousseau offers a more complex formulation of the principle that one must never harm anyone. He refers to his growing appreciation for the "profound solidity" of a "great maxim of morality," which is "to avoid situations which place our duties in opposition to our interests and which show us our good in another's harm." It takes a great deal of foresight as well as insight to avoid situations where one might be in a position to benefit from harming someone, foresight that Emile lacks. Whereas the tutor avoids putting Emile in such a position, a grown man must know how to avoid such situations by his own efforts. It is not enough simply to avoid doing harm, because in following this simpler maxim one risks being put in a situation where one desires to do harm to another but must choose not to. Rousseau seeks to avoid this internal conflict for two reasons. The first is sheer pessimism about the feasibility of expecting anyone to make the right choice, once they see their own good in another's harm, for human beings naturally pursue their own good. Second, even if duty should be the victor in an internal moral struggle, the struggle itself is unpleasant and therefore detracts from one's happiness. Thus, for the sake of virtue as well as happiness, Rousseau's maxim requires that one avoid *seeing* one's good in another's harm. This is not simply a matter of restricting one's line of vision but of honing one's interpretative skills. It is not simply a matter of what one sees (or does not), but of *how* one sees. This cannot be achieved by means of a purely negative education.

A well-ordered society helps a great deal in this respect, while a badly ordered society is organized along lines that encourage each citizen to conceive his own good in opposition to the good of others. However, Rousseau does not place all of the responsibility on institutions, which in his view are only as good as the souls of the individuals who participate in them. It is up to the individual, regardless of where he or she lives, to avoid seeing good in harming others. This would seem to require a certain innocence, but at the same time a great deal of insight and self-consciousness in order to understand and maintain that highly restricted perspective. Rousseau's maxim thus demands, we might say, knowledge of ignorance.

At this point in *Emile*, the reader has been presented with what are in effect two ideal or pure types: perfect knowledge (the tutor, who sees everything) and perfect ignorance (Emile, who is blind to the forces that control his life). Initially, these two models are radically separate. Emile serves as a model of innocence rather than a model of knowledge of ignorance. The tutor supplements Emile by exemplifying the necessary foresight and knowledge required to cultivate that innocence, but he does so for another rather than for himself. His own goodness is assumed rather than demonstrated. The tutor deliberately cultivates Emile's blindness to the possible good in harming others by limiting Emile's interaction with others to instances in which he will not see any good in harming others. In fact, as Emile's lesson in property rights demonstrates, he will be put in situations where he will see that harming the property of others goes *against* his own good. By controlling Emile's experiences, the tutor controls how he sees the world and his own interests in that world. The tutor must thus be able to foresee various possibilities, both ideal and corrupt, in order to anticipate every move the pupil makes, and every consequence. To become a good judge, the reader must see these as well, and yet at the same time must see that Emile's example is superior. This is unlikely given the reader's corrupt standards (from Rousseau's point of view), so Emile's example must be compelling enough to reorient those standards.

Emile is effectively blinded to seeing things in any other way than the way in which he sees them—or more precisely, the way in which the tutor allows him to see them. Because of this blindness, Emile is incapable of conscious avoidance. The reader, however, is made privy to the tutor's foresight and knowledge as well as to Emile's blindness. Rousseau weaves together the two dimensions of his narrative because both contribute to the reader's education in judgment. The reader's goal is not to emulate either of these pure types unreflectively (that is, not merely to imitate) but rather to become like the wise man who *knows* how to stay in his place, or the mature Rousseau, who knows how to avoid situations in which his duty might run contrary to his inclinations. But the pure types operate to move the reader to be able to do this, just as imitation is a necessary step in a child's education even though it must be transcended. Conscious avoidance, as opposed to spontaneous (though conditioned) inclination, requires the exercise of judgment.

The Reader as Judge

For much of book II, the reader is admonished to avoid judging Emile—indeed, to avoid judging childhood. Just as one must keep the child from entering into judgments that he is ill prepared to make (and will err in making), the reader is prevented from judging prematurely. "Respect childhood, and do not be in a hurry to judge it, either for good or for ill" (107; 4:343). Just as the educator must delay certain experiences and lessons until his pupil is ready, Rousseau creates delays for the reader. This is not because he is waiting for Emile to be ready to be judged but rather because he waits for the reader to be ready to judge well. Emile's perfection is "visible only to clear-sighted men" (162; 4:424). Here we run up against the central problem of book II: the example of Emile is intended to educate the reader to see what a well-raised child looks like, but only a reader who already knows what to look for will see that he is well raised. And yet the example of Emile is central to the development of that perspective. When at first Rousseau argues against judging Emile, he emphasizes in particular the need to avoid judging him in comparison to other children (92; 4:321). By the end of book II, however—the book in which Emile's example first comes to light—Rousseau indulges the reader's tendency to judge by comparisons. "Do you now want to judge him by comparisons? Let him mix with other children and do as he pleases. You will soon see which is the most truly formed, which best approaches the perfection of his age" (161; 4:423).

Rousseau's earlier lack of confidence in the reader's ability to judge well is superseded by his conviction that Emile's superiority will be clearly evident. Emile's example redirects the reader's judgment, but that judgment must now be turned on Emile himself. We might say that the example of Emile is designed to give the reader a "taste" for what is good, just as children must be given a taste for virtue without understanding it. And yet one must surpass Emile in order to develop the understanding that a child lacks.

Rousseau not only calls upon the reader to judge Emile; he also raises the question of *how* we should judge Emile. He provides a model of a well-raised child and also a model of how to judge whether a child is well raised. This model of good judgment on the part of an adult is derived from a story Rousseau heard about a man who returned after a three-year absence and wanted to examine his young son's progress. The father

> went for a walk one evening with the boy and his governor in a field where schoolboys were playing at flying kites. The father asked his son, in passing, "Where is the kite whose shadow is here?" Without hesitation, without lifting his head, the child said, "Over the highway." "And, indeed," added Lord Hyde, "the highway was between us and the sun." The father at this response kissed his son and, leaving his examination at that, went away without saying anything. The next day he sent the governor the title to a lifetime pension in addition to his salary. (162–63; 4:424)

Like the father, Rousseau finds the answer appropriate to a child because the highway was indeed between the boy and the sun, and thus the boy had indicated his understanding that the sun had to be behind the kite in order to create the shadow. The son relies only on what he himself can see. The answer indicates that the child is satisfied knowing only that much; he does not require a greater level of precision in his answer, and neither does his father, because he understands the perspective that is appropriate to a child. The episode makes clear to the father that the child has stayed in his place; he has received an appropriately "negative" education from the governor to keep him there. The father infers the excellence of the child's education from one question and one answer. Yet Rousseau precedes this anecdote with the observation that "a child, no more than a man, is not to be seen in a moment" (162; 4:424). He notes that very few observers know how to grasp in a glance the traits that characterize a particular child. This is precisely what the father does, and presumably what anyone must do in order to judge. The whole cannot be seen in a moment, and yet the whole *must* be seen in a moment, that is, must be captured all at once. This wholeness can only be inferred; it is not immediately or directly present. Rousseau stresses both its availability and its elusiveness at once. Good judgment consists in appreciation of that combination; it is a matter of seeing both what is there and what is only implicitly there.

Rousseau's final gloss on the anecdote demands just this sort of double vision from the reader. He praises both father and son for exhibiting excellent judgment; the judgment of each is appropriate to his age. Rousseau then concludes, "It is thus [*C'est ainsi*] that Aristotle's pupil tamed that famous steed which no horseman had been able to break" (163; 4:425). With this pronouncement he seems to spell out the moral of the story, but the pronouncement is so ambiguous that on a deeper level the moral is withheld. The reference to Alexander may, at first glance, seem perfectly straightforward. As Plutarch tells the story, Alexander was able to tame the horse by noticing that the horse was frightened by his shadow. Alexander turned the horse toward the sun so that his shadow would be behind him. This calmed the horse enough that Alexander could tame and ride him. As in the story about the boy and the kite, a simple appreciation of the relationship between sun and shadow plays a central role. But it is more difficult to draw further parallels between the two tales, because Rousseau's "thus" (*ainsi*) is ambiguous. What is the nature of the parallel? Is the father who is able to appreciate his son's point of view being compared to Alexander, who can appreciate the horse's point of view? Or is Alexander like the child who takes a very simple view of shadows? Alexander is, after all, called the pupil. The educator is Aristotle. But Alexander is an educator as well, the educator of his horse, and he is praised for his ability to see the horse's perspective.

Rousseau's ambiguity may be expected from one who repeatedly insists that he wishes to avoid saying everything. Rousseau's "thus" may refer to either character in the story; the reader is left to make his or her own identification. He even omits Alexander's name, referring to him only as Aristotle's pupil. After all, as we have seen, good judgment is not simply a matter of knowing the name, but neither is it simply tasting without understanding. A pattern has emerged: judgment both is and is not rooted in sense perception; character is and is not revealed in a moment; and lessons must and must not be expressed directly.

Developing good judgment therefore requires that one learn to see as a child sees, but it is not reducible to a child's simplistic perspective. The wise man who knows *how* to stay in his place differs from the child who occupies his place innocently, dependent upon external assistance. Book II deals with the question of in what sense and to what extent the wise man's wisdom consists of appreciating the child's perspective. "None of us is philosophic enough to know how to put himself in a child's place" (115; 4:355). Learning to see as a child sees is the first step—but *only* the first step—in learning *why* one ought to see as a child sees, in learning the value of the child's perspective, which can be appreciated only from a perspective that transcends it. Rousseau's elaboration of a perspective that both incorporates a child's judgment and transcends it to form a more active, mature judgment is the pedagogical counterpart to his insistence that judgment is grounded in sensation but is at the same time more active and reflective than passive sensation.

Wholeness, Transparency, Judgment

Although, as we have seen, Rousseau's claim that a teacher should wait for a child's character to reveal itself before beginning his education suggests that this character will make itself manifest, he also acknowledges that character is not so easy to discern. This is precisely why the child should not be judged hastily but rather observed over time. What remains unclear in Rousseau's account is how and when one is to recognize the moment of revelation. Rousseau mentions having a friend (Condillac, as it turns out) who "at a rather advanced age" was assumed to possess "a limited mind by his family and his friends." But they were wrong; "this excellent head had ripened in silence. Suddenly he proved to be a philosopher" (107; 4:343). Here Rousseau tacitly echoes the question Aristotle poses in the *Nicomachean Ethics*: at what point can a man be judged to have led a happy life? One must look at the whole life, it seems. This causes Aristotle to wonder whether a man can be judged happy only after death. For Rousseau, as for Aristotle, the issue is not only how one might be happy but how one might know that one is happy. The latter judgment is susceptible to being misled by false appearances. At stake is the possibility not only of happiness but also of knowledge. Knowledge, it seems, requires wholeness, but our experience of reality is never the experience of wholeness, except through the idealization of memory.

The child has been led "up to the boundaries of childish reason" and must soon move "beyond these boundaries" to take "a man's step." Rousseau thus pauses to invite the reader to judge the "spectacle" he has produced in the form of his imagined pupil. His educational project is about to enter into a new stage. "Before entering upon this new career, let us for a moment cast our eyes back over the one we have just completed" (158; 4:417–18). In other words, Rousseau makes a whole of the stage just completed so that it might be judged. This both creates an illusory wholeness and reveals its illusory quality. Referring to the object under consideration as a "spectacle," which is apt, he reflects not only on his handiwork thus far but on the broader question of why it is that we must make an illusory whole in order to judge at all.

When we look at a man, our awareness of his impending death detracts from the pleasure of contemplating him. It is more pleasant to contemplate the spectacle of springtime than that of autumn, and the spectacle of a child more than that of a man, because the specter of death "makes everything ugly" (158; 4:419). The only way that unadulterated pleasure can be found in contemplating a human being is to remove the possibility of death by contemplating him after death has already occurred. "When is it that we taste a true pleasure in seeing a man? It is when the memory of his actions causes us to go back over his life and rejuvenates him, so to speak, in our eyes" (158; 4:418–19). In memory, a human being becomes whole. The threat of death is what makes the limits of a life uncertain. One can be seen as a whole (and experience oneself as a whole) only in retrospect, or before consciousness of the passage of time becomes a pressing issue—that is, as a child. Both possibilities are chimeras that Rousseau simultaneously creates and dispels. He goes on to explain that when he looks at a child of ten or twelve, he sees someone "without long and painful foresight, whole in his present being." The pleasure Rousseau takes in such contemplation leads him to identify with the child. "I believe I am living his life" (159; 4:419).

Here we see Rousseau's defense of childhood linked with his defense of wholeness. And yet, even as he extols the beauty of this stage of life, he draws attention to the fact that this beauty is fundamentally illusory. Rousseau is obviously *not* living the child's life, although the belief that he is "rejuvenates" him. Wholeness is pleasurable, but it is always illusory. The child will grow (and autumn follows spring, even if summer provides a lovely buffer). Nature is a moving target. Again, "a child, no more than a man, is not to be seen in a moment" (162; 4:424). And yet it is only in a moment that we can see anything at all. Rousseau "freezes" various moments—over the course of a human life and over the history of the species—in order to make them intelligible. Even as he does so, however, he reminds his readers that this move both reveals and conceals. This pattern is repeated several times throughout book II and throughout *Emile* as a whole. Rousseau would have us leap over the problem of death for the sake of an illusory wholeness. Yet he follows this rhetorical move with another move that reintroduces consciousness of death. In this sense he teaches his reader to learn to die. To know death one must first know what it means to live, and to that end illusory wholes are necessary. We have to forget about death in order to create a sense of wholeness, but this wholeness is necessary to develop the proper consciousness of death, which is not living in fear and avoiding risk to preserve mere life, but rather living philosophically. Natural man's lack of self-consciousness allows him to avoid the question of death as well as the meaning of life; civil man's distorted self-consciousness distracts him from genuine engagement with the significance of death; the philosopher's consciousness of death, in contrast—a sort of conscious lack of self-consciousness—avoids both defects.

Illusions and truth are not simply opposed for Rousseau; rather, one serves the pursuit of the other. For the sake of the *love* of truth, Rousseau suggests, the illusion of wholeness is necessary and salutary—but at the same time he reminds us (again for the sake of truth) that this wholeness is only an illusion. "The existence of finite beings is so poor and so limited that when we see only what is, we are never moved. Chimeras adorn real objects; and if imagination does not add charm to what strikes us, the sterile pleasure one takes in it is limited to the perceiving organ and always leaves the heart cold" (158; 4:418). Following this observation, Rousseau paints a picture, so to speak, of a perfectly unselfconscious, happy child whose outward demeanor makes the virtues of his education crystal clear. "Just look at him!" Rousseau seems to say. The outer is assumed to reveal the inner perfectly. This is the side of Rousseau associated with the (failed) pursuit of "transparency."[11] And yet he follows this spectacle with a reminder about just how difficult it is to see the merits of this education—in other words, with a reminder that *the ideal of transparency is itself a chimera*. "The great difficulty with this first education is that it is perceptible only to clear-sighted men and that in a child raised with so much care, vulgar eyes see only a little rascal" (162; 4:424). By exaggerating the charms of such a child, Rousseau makes it almost impossible to see a rascal. A charming spectacle is necessary in order to move the reader to see well, to lead the observer to the truth. Without it, one might never see what is good in childhood; one might not be able to judge it well. Judging well is presented as a matter of being moved by a necessarily illusory ideal, combined with awareness that it is an illusion. The trick is to hold these two moments together, to achieve a sort of double vision.

3

BOOKS AND EXPERIENCE IN THE EDUCATION OF JUDGMENT

To substitute books for [experience] is not to teach us to reason. It is to teach us to use the reason of others. It is to teach us to believe much and never to know anything. (*E*, 125; 4:370)

I have argued that the issue of learning (growing, changing) while staying in place, or combining integrity and change, is a fundamental challenge of Emile's education—and, more broadly for Rousseau, the fundamental challenge of what it means to be truly human, insofar as human beings are understood to possess both an original nature and the quality of perfectibility. This issue is present in *Emile* from the outset, but from the moment that Rousseau shifts focus from the child to "the child whom one wants to make wise" (166; 4:428), the task of combining integrity and change dominates his educational project. In this chapter I explore this issue in a new register, focusing directly on Rousseau's opposition to the practice of using books to teach children to think. Specifically, he denounces the tendency to substitute books for direct experience in the education of children; children should learn from the world around them. "Reading is the plague of childhood and almost the only occupation we know how to give it" (116; 4:357). Emile is shielded even from La Fontaine's fables, which, as Susan Shell notes, was in Rousseau's time "the most popular French literary work for children (outside of the Bible)."[1]

"I hate books," Rousseau insists, because books "only teach one to talk about what one does not know" (184; 4:454). In other words, they do not really teach one to know, but only to pretend to know. Moreover, they invite one to substitute the judgments of the author for one's own. Such arguments are familiar to readers of the *First Discourse*. There is ample evidence to suggest that Rousseau sees books as detrimental to the development of good judgment, especially in children. As Emile matures, however, Rousseau draws on some of the very same reading material that he rules out in Emile's earlier years, in order to teach Emile about his fellow human beings. We might explain this shift simply in terms of timing: what was inappropriate for Emile at one age is appropriate at another. But the sharp contrast between Rousseau's general remarks about fables and history in the early and later stages of Emile's education is not adequately accounted for by the age of his pupil. Rather, what emerges from this contrast is insight into Rousseau's considered view of what it means to read, and to write, well—that is, in a manner that contributes to the development of good judgment.

In light of Rousseau's scathing critique of books in early childhood, it is somewhat puzzling that in the next breath he makes an exception to his own rule and permits Emile to read a single book: *Robinson Crusoe*. This concession occurs well before the introduction of other reading material in Emile's adolescence. Many commentators take for granted that Defoe's novel merits exception to Rousseau's rule against books because it is about a man who interacts with his surroundings as the tutor wishes Emile to do.[2] Because Crusoe is marooned on an island and must focus on his physical survival, his story is understood as proper reading material for Rousseau's "natural" man. Defoe's novel, it seems, unlike other books, does not take Emile outside of himself. "[Rousseau] gives Emile Robinson Crusoe, who is not an 'other' but only himself."[3] On this understanding, Rousseau's rule against books in general remains intact, and *Robinson Crusoe* is explained away as an exception to the rule. One might cast Rousseau's own books in the same light, as exceptions, and thus rescue him from the charge of inconsistency. Books are permissible as long as they do not do what books usually do, which is to deprive us of an authentic experience of the world by mediating between the individual and the world.

However, Rousseau does not concede the point about the utility of Defoe's novel in a grudging or qualified manner. In fact, he introduces his discussion of the novel with the comment, "Since we absolutely *must* have books" (184; 4:454, emphasis added). The question, then, is not only why *Robinson Crusoe* is an exceptional book but why any book at all is absolutely necessary to a "natural" education. I submit that the experience of the novel is designed not to preserve Emile's asociality by encouraging him to identify with a marooned man, but rather to lay the groundwork for Emile's introduction to society, his expanded understanding of what is good, and his incipient self-consciousness. After exploring Rousseau's use of *Robinson Crusoe*, I consider Rousseau's treatment of fables and histories in Emile's education, in which the standard that Rousseau sets for his pupil parallels the standard he sets for his readers.

First, we must note the context in which Rousseau asserts that "we absolutely must have books," which underscores the significance of the remark. The discussion that immediately precedes it centers on the difficulties involved in encouraging one's pupil to develop new interests, since according to Rousseau's pedagogy all learning must result from the student's own inclination rather than from external imposition. While the tutor continues to avoid compelling Emile to do anything contrary to his own inclinations, he devotes a great deal of attention to shaping those inclinations themselves. The tension between authority and freedom in Emile's education becomes increasingly apparent, for the tutor must find a way to effect change in Emile without undermining Emile's own agency. Earlier, when the task was teaching a lazy boy to run, Rousseau posed the question, "How could I give him the desire to run without saying anything to him?" (141; 4:393). When his focus shifts from physical to intellectual pursuits, the difficulties multiply. Whereas teaching a child to run may increase his strength, thus enhancing his independence, stimulating his desire for knowledge will expand his needs by making him desire something he does not have.[4]

The desire to learn takes one outside oneself, which disrupts the self-containment that is the defining feature of Rousseau's natural man. Remaining absolutely self-contained, however, is not an option if one is to achieve self-consciousness or self-rule. The goal, therefore, is that Emile must somehow *return* to himself, which first requires that he leave himself, despite all the risks that this entails.

> In beginning this second period we have taken advantage of the superabundance of our strength over our needs in order to take us outside of ourselves. We have launched ourselves into the heavens; we have measured the earth; we have harvested the laws of nature. In a word, we have visited the whole island. Now we come back to ourselves. We are imperceptibly coming nearer to the place we dwell, only too happy on returning

there to find it still not possessed by the enemy which threatens us and which is preparing to take hold of it! (192; 4:466)

Stoking Emile's desire to learn, while necessary, thus introduces several potential pitfalls. First, the appetite for knowledge, once it is whetted, may lead to a disequilibrium between Emile's desires and his faculties and therefore threaten his happiness and freedom. Second, as noted earlier, the desire to learn can easily turn into the desire to be learned, which not only stimulates vanity but in fact leads to the desire to appear learned rather than to be learned. The tutor therefore risks inflaming Emile's amour-propre in stimulating his intellectual curiosity. This problem was addressed through his experience with the magician, as discussed in the previous chapter, which was designed to make Emile painfully aware of all that he does not know, and thus to curb his vanity. Finally, the desire for knowledge can be indiscriminate, and may lead the pupil to engage in all sorts of useless and even pernicious pursuits that are incompatible with happiness, virtue, or freedom. To avoid this tendency, the tutor furnishes Emile with a "compass" to guide his pursuit of knowledge.[5] This compass, which emerges in book III, is the question of utility, or, "What is it good for?" Clearly, Emile is being taught to judge within a very discrete and limited framework.

The question of utility is a "powerful instrument" (179; 4:446), but also a problematic one, for it implies a notion of the good, which will necessarily be conceived differently by a child than by an adult (who has foresight, among other faculties). In certain cases, the tool works perfectly: the tutor can lead Emile to see the utility of astronomy, for example, when the two are lost in the woods and hungry. Knowledge of north and south is clearly useful to a child who wants to find his way home for lunch. The key to the success of the utility principle is the ability of the tutor to see as a child sees, and thus to measure utility in a child's terms. In certain instances, however, this is impossible, and it will be necessary to alter the child's perception of the good.

To illustrate the difficulty of this task, Rousseau recalls an episode in which he needed to convince a former pupil of the utility of knowing how ink is made in order "to give [him] a taste for chemistry" (182; 4:451). The utility of ink might seem obvious to anyone who reads and writes, but Rousseau has already ruled out books. So, instead, the tutor engages in a pointless demonstration of how knowledge of alkali, which enables one to make ink, is useful because it enables one to recognize poisoned wine. Too late, he realizes that the concept of "poison" means nothing to a child who understands nothing of death. The tutor's attempt to encourage the student's inclinations in new directions is a failure. "It is easy to prove to a child that what one wants to teach him is useful; but to prove it is nothing if one does not know how to persuade him. In vain does tranquil reason make us approve or criticize; it is only passion which makes us act—*and how can one get passionate about interests one does not yet have?*" (183; 4:453, emphasis added).

A similar circularity manifests itself in *On the Social Contract*. Hilail Gildin has observed that the coming into being of the positive law that characterizes a sound political order "requires that the public spirit, which results from the enactment of certain measures, be present before they have been enacted and influence the workings of the assembly which enacts them."[6] Paradoxically, the people must be a people, a whole united by a higher bond, before it can act as a people, but it is only in acting as a people that it becomes a people. Similarly, as we have seen, Emile must be an "I," that is, he must become aware of himself as an individual, before he can encounter an other as an individual—and yet consciousness of one's identity requires an experience of an other, or at least of oneself as other.[7]

In *On the Social Contract*, this problem leads directly into the discussion of the legislator's role in attending to the preparation of the people in order that they be fit to form a sound political order. Gildin discusses the distinction between the "early" legislator, who prepares the people for lawmaking, and the later, "political" legislator. He notes that in light of this distinction, "it is puzzling to find [Rousseau] referring to Lycurgus as an example of both the first and the second kind (2.7.1, 2.7.5)."[8] But the puzzle becomes less puzzling once we discern that Lycurgus's extraordinary political acumen is less self-sufficient than it may initially appear to be. Plutarch tells us that when Lycurgus first arrived at Crete, he observed the Cretans' laws and made the acquaintance of their leaders. Plutarch's description of Thales, the most important of those leaders, is worth quoting in its entirety.

> Among the persons there the most renowned for their learning and their wisdom in state matters was one Thales, whom Lycurgus, by importunities and assurances of friendship, persuaded to go over to Lacedaemon; where, though by his outward appearance and his own profession he seemed to be no other than a lyric poet, in reality he performed the part of one of the ablest lawgivers in the world. The very songs which he composed were exhortations to obedience and concord, and the very measure and cadence of the verse, conveying impressions of order and

tranquility, had so great an influence on the minds of the listeners, that they were insensibly softened and civilized, insomuch that they renounced their private feuds and animosities, and were reunited in a common admiration of virtue. So that it may truly be said that Thales prepared the way for the discipline introduced by Lycurgus.[9]

The poet Thales prepared the way for the legislator Lycurgus; perhaps Rousseau, too, thought that poets are the unacknowledged legislators of the world. Such preparation requires attention to what Rousseau calls "the most important [law] of all, which is not engraved on marble or brass, but in the hearts of the citizens; which . . . preserves a people in the spirit of its institution, and imperceptibly substitutes the force of habit for that of authority. I am speaking of morals, customs, and especially of opinion" (*SC*, 164–65; 3:394). Clearly, some form of poetry is necessary to anchor the mores, customs, and opinions that are the primary source of these "unwritten" laws. Rousseau reveals that a legislator must attend to such preparation "in secret" and then acts in a secretive manner himself in remaining silent about Thales's role. Thales's political invisibility preserves the necessary illusion of the self-sufficient, godlike character of the legislator. In order to fully appreciate the legislator, however, one would have to see the machinations behind the illusions. Rousseau may preserve the illusion surrounding Lycurgus, but he dispels the corresponding illusion in *Emile* when he allows the reader to see the tutor's machinations, including his use of *Robinson Crusoe* and fables.

By raising the question of the utility of ink, Rousseau foreshadows the importance that books and reading can play in facilitating this necessary movement. While books tend to take us so far out of ourselves that we lose rather than find ourselves in them—or, even worse, find inauthentic selves in them—books also offer us resources that help us expand ourselves in ways that serve human happiness and freedom as Rousseau understands them.[10] Paradoxically, books both illustrate the central problem of combining integrity and change and offer a possible solution to the problem.[11]

The Trouble with Books

First, we need to understand the basis for Rousseau's rejection of reading in childhood. We begin with fables in particular. To illustrate the inappropriateness of fables for children, he analyzes La Fontaine's well-known fable of the fox and the crow to demonstrate that even such a simple tale is far from childlike in its perspective. Rousseau's diatribe against the use of fables must be understood in the context of his insistence that children, even those who seem to be precocious, are primarily physical beings. Thus the child who hears the story of the fox and the crow inevitably identifies with the fox—not because human beings are naturally crafty and vicious but simply because the child likes cheese and thus relates to the fox's desire for the crow's piece of cheese. In order to appreciate the intended moral of the story, the child would have to identify with the crow; but no one likes to be humiliated! So the child will avoid this identification. Moreover, in order to understand the trick perpetrated by the fox, one would have to appreciate the distinction between appearance and reality, virtue and vice—the very distinctions that the fable purports to teach.

Rousseau argues on similar grounds against exposing children to the study of history. History may seem more innocuous than fables because it is "only a collection of facts," but Rousseau insists that we should not assume that "the relations which determine historical facts are so easy to grasp that ideas are effortlessly formed from the facts in the children's minds." One cannot teach only facts. "If you see in men's actions only the exterior and purely physical movements, what do you learn from history? Absolutely nothing" (110; 4:348). Facts, like fables, require interpretation.

Immediately after he forbids the teaching of history, Rousseau reminds the reader that "he who speaks to you is neither a scholar nor a philosopher, but a simple man" whose "reasonings are founded less on principles than on facts" (110; 4:348). Rousseau thus extends his remarks about the complexity of reading and interpretation to his own work and the reader's capacity to understand it. If the reader must supply the interpretation to understand the "facts" he has presented, this raises the question of whether the reader is better prepared than any child to do so. Children cannot judge beyond the physical, or at least not well, but of course, in Rousseau's estimation, most adults do not judge well either.

Rousseau emphasizes that his concerns apply to most adults as well as to children—that is, his concern is not simply with a developmental stage but with the capacity for judgment—in an anecdote in which he describes a child being drilled by his governor on the life of Alexander. The boy recites the story of how a sickly Alexander drank the potion that his physician and friend, Philip, offered him, in spite of receiving a message warning him that Philip had been offered a reward for killing him. When it becomes clear that the boy thinks Alexander was brave simply because he drank a bad-tasting medicine, Jean-Jacques suspects that the child is repeating words without understanding them, although he speaks with grace. To this point, the anecdote seems simply to illustrate Rousseau's earlier claims about the inability of children to understand much of which they are erroneously "taught." But then the focus of the story shifts from the child to the adults present. After the child is finished speaking and is duly praised for his efforts, a debate ensues as to whether Alexander's action was courageous or foolhardy. The general consensus is that the act was courageous, until Jean-Jacques interjects with the comment that if in fact there was the least bit of courage or firmness in Alexander's action, the act was foolhardy. Everyone then agrees that the act was foolhardy, although they obviously do not understand the basis for Jean-Jacques's assessment. He is on the verge of explaining his reasoning when a woman sitting next to him, who has remained quiet throughout the discussion, hushes him. She tells him to keep quiet because the others will not understand him. Jean-Jacques recounts that at the time he complied and did not share his reasoning with his unsuspecting interlocutors.

However, Rousseau does *not* remain silent in response to those readers who, he imagines, would pose the question of what, exactly, he finds so beautiful in Alexander's action. He explains that it is Alexander's faith in virtue that is so impressive. Alexander approached the situation from a perspective of assuming the best rather than the worst about human nature. Alexander believed the best about Philip; only if he had any doubts about his friend's virtue would he have needed to approach the task with courage. Where there is nothing to fear, courage is not required.

Although he shares his reasoning with the reader rather than remain silent, Rousseau also makes a show of his resentment at having to do so. "If you have to be told, how will you understand it?" (111; 4:350). With these words (which he will repeat in one form or another several times throughout *Emile*), Rousseau not only associates his readers with the adults who misunderstand Alexander's story but also raises the problem of education as such: the success of an education depends in large part on what the pupil is already prepared to learn. In this way, much of *Emile* is directed against Locke's theory of the tabula rasa. Nevertheless, in the case of Alexander and Philip, Rousseau *does* tell the reader the moral of the story, even as he criticizes the reader for needing to be told. He does not simply withhold the lesson. He will be so generous only once, however. Later in book II, as he describes the kinds of games he thinks are appropriate for children, he says a few words about a particular game and then states, "This is quite enough, perhaps too much, to make the spirit of this kind of game understood. If you have to be told everything, do not read me" (137;

4:387). In books IV and V, we shall see, the lessons become even more opaque, as the reader's capacity for sound judgment is presumably improved. As I mentioned earlier, while Rousseau opens *Emile* by addressing a mother who "knows how to think" (33; 4:241) and is "tender" and "foresighted" (37; 4:245), by book V he is addressing himself to a "judicious mother" (364; 4:701). The reader's education is not only a matter of being shown the example of Emile's education but of learning to see what is good in that education, to judge it well.

Rousseau returns in book IV, when Emile is growing closer to adulthood, to the question of teaching both history and fables. When he finally introduces Emile to history, despite his earlier insistence that one cannot teach facts without interpretation, Rousseau professes admiration for Thucydides, "the true model of historians," because he "reports the facts without judging them" (239; 4:529). To understand this apparent contradiction, we must keep in mind that for Rousseau, timing is essential. In early childhood, he insists, children are incapable of judging soundly. They cannot be taught by means of fables or history because that is to put the cart before the horse, and to assume of them precisely that which you aim to teach them. When the time for studying history arrives, in adolescence, Rousseau makes clear that the point of these studies will be to learn to judge. "It is by means of history that, without the lessons of philosophy, he will read the hearts of men; it is by means of history that he will see them . . . as their judge and not as their accomplice or their accuser" (237; 4:526). To be neither accomplice nor accuser requires achieving a standpoint that is neither too dependent on the context being judged nor utterly removed. In order to produce this stance in another, or to teach judgment, one must refrain from expressing judgment and allow the child to arrive at his or her own judgment. Hence Rousseau's insistence upon unadorned facts.

Similarly, when the tutor finally allows Emile to read fables because he has entered the "age of mistakes" and will identify with the innocent, vulnerable character rather than the wicked but successful one, he adds an important stipulation. Fables are finally permissible, but with the following caveat: an explicit statement of the moral of the fable must be omitted. The issue is no longer simply avoiding the wrong interpretation; it is a matter of allowing the correct understanding to be achieved independently. A moral is not truly understood unless it is grasped despite (or because of) the ambiguity; if it is stated explicitly, there is no way it can be grasped. Rousseau's pedagogy consistently emphasizes the value of what is left unsaid over what is made explicit. "If you have to be told, how will you ever understand?" This not only tells us what

Rousseau thinks about teaching children to read; it also indicates how he himself wants to be read.

There is a strong temptation to resolve or explain the paradoxes in Rousseau's works by turning to his letters and correspondence for clarification. These works exert a siren's pull, seeming to promise direct access to Rousseau's intentions. Yet there are grounds on which to question this move, especially with regard to interpreting *Emile* in particular, given Rousseau's refusal to disclose too much.[12] If he expects the reader to do the work of teasing out his lessons—lessons that might be too complex to state simply—then looking to the correspondence to dispel all ambiguity and pin down his meaning is a little like demanding that he annex the moral to his fable. In fact, if Rousseau does annex something like a "moral" to *Emile* as a whole, something that offers a detached, reflective commentary on it, it must be the sequel *Emile and Sophie* (which I discuss in chapter 7)—but that of course is yet another fable.

The Utility of Robinson Crusoe

Although shielded from books throughout most of his childhood, Emile is given one novel in particular: *Robinson Crusoe*. At first glance Defoe's novel may seem to be an obviously appropriate choice for Emile. After all, if Emile is to learn self-sufficiency, what better teacher than a man who manages to survive alone after being shipwrecked on an island? Surely, Crusoe would be a good role model if one wanted to inculcate a lesson about considerations of utility. But to call Crusoe "self-sufficient" is misleading. He is self-sufficient neither in a physical sense nor in the sense indicated by Rousseau in book II: having an equilibrium between one's faculties and desires. Throughout his stay on the island, Crusoe is plagued by many needs that he cannot satisfy, needs that remain nascent in Emile.[13] Crusoe longs for ink in order to write, for human company, for God's forgiveness. He carries his gun everywhere, fearing the possibility of a violent death at the hand of "Savages." These characteristics highlight the fact that Crusoe is a *social* man transported into nature. We might wonder, then, at Rousseau's judgment in exposing Emile to this particular book.

Insofar as each step in the educative process requires a certain predisposition that must itself be educated, Rousseau faces a dilemma reminiscent of Plato's *Meno*. He reveals his awareness of this difficulty by imagining that his critics will ask whether "there [will] be time to learn what one ought to know when the moment has come to make use of it," and responds, "I do not know. But I do know that it is impossible to learn it sooner" (178; 4:445). Preparation seems to be required before one can begin, but how does one begin the preparation itself? Emile's introduction to sociality is anything but the radically new beginning suggested by the metaphor of a "second birth." A certain amount of preparation is required before Emile can venture into society, and this preparation is *not* simply a matter of developing immunity to negative social influences. "Thus the ideas of social relations are formed little by little in a child's mind, even before he can really be an active member of society" (193; 4:467).

Although Emile has been prevented from experiencing other worlds by means of books and reading, his own world is nevertheless expanding, in two related senses. His physical world is expanding in that his concerns will now go beyond that which immediately surrounds him, to the ends of the earth and the universe, as he begins to explore the physical and mathematical sciences. Just as important, however, his world is also expanding beyond the physical toward the moral, as the tutor prepares him for his introduction to social relations. At this point Emile is "almost [*presque*] only a physical being" (187; 4:458). The "almost" is significant, and signals that the apparently separate stages in Emile's education are not as precisely differentiated as they may seem. Emile must move forward, so to speak, without moving on to the next (moral) stage. The process of preparation involves building a bridge without crossing it, a difficult task that can be accomplished only with the aid of some of the very factors that are, according to Rousseau, quite dangerous at this stage. Emile's blossoming self-consciousness is what begins to move him beyond mere physicality and prepares him to encounter others as others. The importance of this preparation is obscured if we understand Emile's education to be strictly divided into two moments, independence followed by interdependence. While at the deepest level he does not become a social being until he experiences the birth of his sexuality in book IV, the seeds of his sociality are sown much earlier.[14] While it is at the beginning of book II that "strictly speaking, the life of the individual begins" (78; 4:301), by the end of book III Emile "has become aware of himself as an individual" (203; 4:481). It is during this transition that Rousseau makes an exception to his general rule against the use of books and permits Emile to read *Robinson Crusoe*. What is the role of *Robinson Crusoe* in fostering that self-awareness? What may appear to be a rather narrow question turns out to provide a sharp wedge into the larger questions that concern us. That is, the question of the role that a novel plays in fostering Emile's "natural" education relates to the broader issue of the role of artifice in Rousseau's over-all project, and the role of poetic illusions in fostering self-rule.

There is, of course, one major qualification in Rousseau's praise of *Robinson Crusoe*. He suggests that only parts of the novel are appropriate for Emile. "This novel, *disencumbered of all its rigmarole*, beginning with Robinson's ship-wreck near his island and ending with the arrival of the ship which comes to take him from it, will be both Emile's entertainment and instruction through-out the period which is dealt with here" (185; 4:455, emphasis added). What does Rousseau mean by "rigmarole" (*fratras*)? What precisely does Rousseau wish to excise from Emile's copy of the novel? At stake here is not simply a question of pedagogical technique; we must, as Rousseau insists, grasp "the spirit" of his examples in order to appreciate them (192; 4:465).

At least two readings are possible. The first is that Rousseau is straightfor-wardly referring to Crusoe's activities before and after his time on the island as "rigmarole" that would be kept from Emile in order to allow the figure of Cru-soe to inspire Emile to embrace his isolation. This literal reading is clearly inad-equate, however, for much of what Crusoe does and says even on the island expresses the painfulness of his isolated condition and contradicts his image as a self-sufficient man guided only by utility. Much of the time, Crusoe is as miser-able as the caricature of "civil man" that Rousseau so often criticizes. Crusoe remains a *social* man; he devotes a great deal of time over the years to plotting his return to civilization, and bases certain decisions (such as the location of his "home") on the desire to maximize his chances of being rescued, rather than with regard to a more immediate utility (such as better soil). Moreover, he is not strictly alone, since he encounters Friday halfway through the novel.

An alternative approach assumes that Rousseau would treat *all* of this as "rigmarole" and delete it from the novel before offering it—essentially rewrit-ten—to Emile.[15] But Rousseau makes it absolutely clear that Emile will read about Friday, for example, when he comments that it is important to establish Emile "on this island while he still limits his felicity to it; for the day is nearing when, if he still wants to live there, he will not want any longer to live there alone, and when Friday, who now hardly concerns him, will not for long be enough for him" (185; 4:456). If Friday "hardly" concerns him, Emile must obviously be aware of his presence, even if he proceeds for the most part to ignore him. If Emile will know about Friday, it seems, Rousseau must be will-ing to expose him to at least some of the more problematic aspects of the novel.

Even more suspect than the presence of Friday are Crusoe's fears of violent death, which are so powerful that he can hardly sleep when he first arrives on the island, and which are revived after he sees a human footprint in the sand many years after he has established his dominion there. Landing on the island after the shipwreck, Crusoe is so distraught about his fate that he is thrown into "terrible Agonies of Mind" and begins to "run about like a Mad-man."[16] It has been said that Crusoe is dominated by fear.[17] His fear stems from a foresight that is quite foreign to Emile at this point. The greatest indicator of this problem is the fact that Crusoe carries his gun everywhere, as a psychological crutch more than as a tool. Rousseau engages in some sleight of hand in dealing with this fact, mentioning only that Emile will picture Crusoe with his saber "and the rest of his grotesque equipment, with the exception of the parasol" (185; 4:455). Rousseau accomplishes a great deal with these few words. The saber raises the specter of a weapon, but it is a rudimentary weapon, unlike a gun, which is in many ways a symbol of modern civilization (and its discontents). The gun could fit into the category of "grotesque equipment," of course. It is certainly not singled out for exclusion, like the parasol.[18] But the very fact that Rousseau mentions the parasol draws attention to his silence about the gun.

Perhaps Emile will ignore the gun as easily as he ignores Friday. It is of course possible that Rousseau anticipates that, like the child who recited the life of Alexander without comprehending it, Emile will read past Crusoe's lamentations over his solitude, fears, and religious musings without absorbing them in any way. But if it were so easy to protect children from what they are unprepared to confront, then much of the project of *Emile* would be unnecessary, and there would be no harm in doing all the things that Rousseau warns against: reading fables to children, talking to them about abstract notions, and exposing them to cultural influences. They would be immune. But clearly they are not immune, and the result of their unsuitability for these experiences is not that they deflect them but that they absorb them in some distorted way, assimilating what they can in any way they can, often to their detriment. In this case, Rousseau's decision to allow Emile to read *Robinson Crusoe* seems to entail all the errors that he rails against, if only because Crusoe fears death, whereas Emile, Rousseau insists, does not yet know what death is.

I highlight these ambiguities in order to call into question the view that *Robinson Crusoe*'s function is to preserve and reinforce a very simple model of utility for Emile. As we have seen, utility is not a static concept for Rousseau, who acknowledges that a child's understanding of what is good—his framework for judging—must evolve. Defoe's novel plays an essential role in this process, precisely because of its more problematic elements. The experience of the novel does not simply maintain Emile as a physical being but also moves him beyond (or at least prepares him to move beyond) a merely physical appreciation of the world. Emile is *almost* a purely physical being, and Crusoe contributes not only to his existence as an almost purely physical being but, even more so, to his departure from it.

The novel presents many features of society as "useful." It would be hard to miss the degree to which Crusoe relies on the achievements of society to advance his own self-sufficiency. He procures many of his instruments (at least those that allow him to get started) from the wrecked ship. In fact, Crusoe makes eleven trips to the sinking ship within his first thirteen days on the island. Crusoe's survival depends upon the resources he gleans from the ship.[19] He himself does not underestimate this fact; he testifies aloud to his good luck ("an Hundred Thousand to one") that the ship had been driven so near to the shore and that he has had time to retrieve so many provisions. "What should I have done without a Gun, without Ammunition, without any Tools to make any thing, or to work with, without clothes, Bedding, a Tent . . . ?"[20] Crusoe never decides that he no longer needs the resources provided by the ship; his link to civilization is severed by necessity. As the ship sinks and disappears from view, the illusion of Crusoe's self-sufficiency is complete, the social origins of independence submerged from view rather than hovering on the horizon.

Crusoe himself never forgets his debt to the ship, commenting on his good fortune years later, and we can only conclude that his musings will help Emile (to the extent that he notices them) begin to become aware of the necessary conditions of independence. In other words, the question "what is society good for?" begins to be addressed even before Emile really knows what society is, and certainly before he can be seduced by its ills. *Robinson Crusoe* offers an effective lesson about utility not because it limits Emile's conception of the good but precisely because it alters his conception of the good, and thus provides the solution to the problems raised by the tutor's earlier attempts to teach a child to measure utility in increasingly complex terms.

Despite his initial miscalculations, Crusoe wisely chooses his provisions from the shipwreck with a view to "how I would provide for the Accidents that might happen, and for the time that was to come, even only after my Ammunition should be spent, but even after my Health or Strength should decay."[21] He may be dependent at first, but his goal is independence, and he uses the goods of society to further his independence. In this he is surely an excellent role model for Emile. But at other times he falls short in ways that Rousseau could not have missed. For example, on what will turn out to be his final visit to the sinking ship, he discovers a stash of money. His first reaction exemplifies a perspective of utility, narrowly defined. Looking at the gold and silver, Crusoe asks aloud, "What art thou good for?"[22] Crusoe may ask the "right" question here, but he certainly does not give the "right" answer, for he decides to take the money to the island, even though the weather is turning ugly, and he has to swim back to shore quickly, without taking the time to make a raft. He remarks on the extreme difficulty of his passage, due in part to the weight of the coins he carries with him. Surely, this is one instance where Emile might employ his own judgment and correct his hero, who risks his self-preservation for the sake of some useless coins. Not even Robinson Crusoe can be an authority for Emile. Emile must inhabit his own island and make his own decisions. He must be able to judge Crusoe even as Crusoe is teaching him to judge.

Years later, Crusoe comes to regret his decision to take the bag of coins from the ship; the money "had been of no manner of Value to me, because of no Use."[23] Crusoe powerfully illustrates the utility principle precisely because he initially fails to follow it, and then recognizes his mistake. In other words, the utility of the utility principle itself is made *intelligible* because Crusoe himself must actively learn it; he does not unselfconsciously embody or represent it. Emile learns from Crusoe's learning, that is, from his imperfections. With the help of a fictional character, Emile can gain experience without ever leaving the island—that is, without experiencing the real effects of such experimentation. Crusoe's independence becomes intelligible only as it comes into being. Crusoe's imperfections—indeed, his incoherence as a social man in nature— actually foster rather than inhibit the learning process that the tutor wishes to bring about in Emile. This holds true for Rousseau's education of the reader as well, inasmuch as he frequently employs the technique of contrasting Emile with examples of poorly educated children; the contrast illuminates Emile's virtues. To some degree, nature makes sense only in contrast to society, and can be known only in light of society.[24]

If this is the case, then the dimensions of Defoe's novel that appear at first glance to be unsuitable for Emile are in fact necessary to accomplish the complex goal of preparing Emile so that when he does finally confront society, he will be able to resist its corrupting effects. Thus the fact that Robinson Crusoe is not a natural man but *a social man in nature* is crucial, for it makes Crusoe acutely conscious of his natural condition, and it is for this reason alone that Emile can learn from him. Crusoe makes his solitude an object of reflection, and it is instructive for this very reason. Crusoe's self-consciousness about his isolation brings that isolation to light and makes it significant as isolation; it makes it *known*. Savage man may live alone, like Crusoe, but he could never be lonely, as Crusoe is. Savage man is like the proverbial tree in the forest that no one hears fall (until Rousseau makes us "hear" it), whereas Crusoe's self-consciousness makes him a witness to his own solitude. Emile is not intended to be a natural man in the strictest sense. He will be an "I," an individual. Emile needs an "other" in order to become a differentiated "I," but that individual must not be so "other" that he leads Emile away from himself. Robinson Crusoe fulfills this complex requirement, allowing Emile to experience the benefits of an encounter with an "other" without the risks.[25]

The Utility of Ink

It is not the case, then, that Defoe's novel just happens to fall outside Rousseau's prohibition of books; the point is that there *must* be an exception to the rule. This is why, in the final analysis, we *must* have books; adherence to the spirit of the rule against books requires exceptions to it. *Robinson Crusoe* makes manifest both the utility and the limitations of the rule. Books are absolutely necessary, in the absence of experience, in the way that an "other" is absolutely necessary.

Rousseau makes clear in many of his writings that the "I" comes into being at the point of contact with another human being.[26] The difficulty lies in preserving the integrity of that "I" and preventing it from being distorted or subsumed before it is fully formed. In other words, Emile's self must not be defined externally in the sense that it must not be shaped by prejudices, but the process of self-definition involves an inherent externality if that self is to become conscious of itself. Only then will one be capable of forming independent judgments that are not simply a conditioned reflex. While maintaining an integral self is paramount, however, the tutor must take care not to define Emile *against* others in too explicit a manner, for this is just as dangerous as defining oneself *for* others. One may take so much pride in one's independence from external society that this pride results in a different sort of dependency.[27] "Let us not go and reproduce vanity by our efforts to combat it. To pride oneself on having conquered prejudices is to be subjected by them" (201; 4:479). But if the process of self-definition involves an inside and an outside—boundaries that define not only what one is but also what one is not—then how can such a comparison be made while maintaining self-sufficiency and avoiding the temptations of vanity? Later, Emile will see himself reflected in his beloved's eyes. At this point, he needs to develop the self that will then be reflected. He needs to be a self before he can know himself. The challenge is coming to know oneself without allowing self-reflection to lead to fragmentation, amour-propre, or the "living through the eyes of others" that is characteristic of the unhappy bourgeois.

The figure of Robinson Crusoe can help Emile achieve this complex demand because Crusoe functions as both model and foil. Emile's experience of reading the novel is described in terms that suggest that he simultaneously identifies with and distinguishes himself from Crusoe.

> I want him to think he is Robinson himself, to see himself dressed in skins, wearing a large cap, carrying a large saber and all the rest of the character's grotesque equipment, with the exception of the parasol, which he will not need. I want him to worry about the measures to take if this or that were lacking to him; to examine his hero's conduct; to investigate whether he omitted anything, whether there was nothing to do better; to note Robinson's failings attentively; and to profit from them so as not to fall into them himself in such a situation. (185; 4:455)

The first part of this passage confirms the common view that Emile is meant to identify with Crusoe's example, while in the second part we see that Emile must distance himself from his hero in order to reflect on his actions and judge them. Here, Rousseau emphasizes that Emile is not simply learning to be Robinson Crusoe; he is learning to be himself. That he must grow into himself calls into question Rousseau's famous distinction between those who live outside themselves and those who live inside themselves, for while it is true that the civil man's misery is caused primarily by the fact that "we no longer exist where we are, only where we are not" (83; 4:308), it is also the case that a "wise man *knows how* to stay in his place" (84; 4:310, emphasis added). The wise man's staying in his place is a conscious choice, and it indicates an understanding of his place as well as an awareness of the context that surrounds his place. He must leave himself in order to return to himself, and in order to know *how* to stay in his place. The wise man rules himself.

Crusoe, therefore, does not represent a fixed standard to which Emile must cling in order to protect himself from being carried away by the influences of society; he represents the first step on a complex journey. And while Emile may be dependent on Crusoe for his self-definition as an individual, his ultimate goal is independence from Crusoe. Rousseau makes this absolutely clear in book IV, when Emile begins to read history. Rousseau knows that Emile will compare himself to those about whom he reads, because at that point in his life "the relative I is constantly in play, and the young man never observes others without returning to himself and comparing himself with them." Rousseau concludes that "if in these parallels he just once prefers to be someone other than himself—were this other Socrates, were it Cato—everything has failed" (243; 4:535). Because Emile's relationship to Crusoe is not one of simple identification, his experience with Defoe's novel in book III offers the necessary preparation for the further reading that takes place in book IV.[28]

Upon realizing that gold and silver are useless to him, Robinson Crusoe remarks that he would have readily traded the coins for something truly useful, like peas or beans or a bottle of ink. Crusoe's persistent longing for ink is significant, for his situation implies an answer to the question that Rousseau was at a loss to answer earlier, namely, what is ink good for? Crusoe wants the ink in order to write in his diary. This answer did not present itself to the tutor because a child who is not self-reflective would have little need for a diary. The tutor does not repeat his ill-fated lesson in the importance of recognizing doctored wines. Instead, Emile is given *Robinson Crusoe*. In beginning to appreciate the utility of ink, a child is pointed toward the discovery of the goodness of self-reflection.

This broader understanding of the utility of ink suggests that there is some irony in Rousseau's characterization of how a philosopher on a desert island might live: "He will perhaps not open a single book in his life" (167; 4:429). Perhaps. But especially if he has ever lived off the island, he is very likely to *write* a book, perhaps keeping a diary, if he has the ink to do so. We are, of course, reminded of Rousseau's own self-reflective solitude as described in *The Reveries of the Solitary Walker*. Rousseau claims in the third walk that he would have written his various books even if he had been stranded on a desert island. The *Reveries* explores the contradiction between being lost in unselfconscious reverie and consciously chronicling one's experiences of reverie.[29] It is striking that in the *Reveries* Rousseau does not explicitly mention Robinson Crusoe, for he opens the work with a description of being marooned, so to speak, and goes on to discuss in great detail the time he spent on St. Peter's Island in Lake Brienne, which in his *Confessions* he compares to Crusoe's island. The omission seems less curious, however, once we realize that Rousseau does not *need* Robinson Crusoe because at some level he *is* Robinson Crusoe, or at least, as he says several times in his *Confessions*, he is "another" Robinson Crusoe.[30] Like Crusoe, Rousseau is a social man in nature. And despite his best efforts, he is similarly unable completely to sever his ties to society. Just as Crusoe is jolted out of his solitary sense of security when he comes upon a human footprint in the sand, Rousseau comes across a factory and is jolted out of his self-contained reverie. Society intrudes upon nature; such is the legacy of human perfectibility. However, it is also true that only through the intrusion of society does nature gain the *value* (utility?) that it has for social man, because only in retrospect, in its otherness, is it knowable.

Emile absolutely *must* have books because of his lack of experience of others as others. And he needs one book in particular, not because it presents man in nature but because it depicts a man reflecting on himself in nature. Crusoe's diary is ultimately the most important part of Defoe's novel for someone like Emile. Indeed, the most instructive technical details about Crusoe's ingenious adaptation to the rigors of physical survival on the island are conveyed to the reader through his diary; even if one wanted to focus only on these technical details, the diary would be hard to overlook. This lends added significance to Rousseau's comment with regard to Emile's progress beyond the merely physical: "If I have made myself understood up to now, one should conceive how I imperceptibly give my pupil, with the habit of exercising his body and of manual labor, the taste for reflection and meditation" (202; 4:480). Rousseau seems to hope that the reader will appreciate the subtlety of how Emile's conception of what is good is extended, which extends the reader's perception as well.

There is, finally, no simple answer to the question how much of Defoe's novel Rousseau would prefer to censor, because Rousseau is deliberately ambiguous on the issue. His ambiguity is calculated to invite the reader (at least the reader who "knows how to think") to reflect on the importance of preparation, which calls into question the integrity of each maxim or formula Rousseau offers, each boundary he draws. Rousseau's insistence on shielding Emile from all that might threaten his self-sufficiency until the "proper" moment arrives conceals the impossibility of isolating such a moment, and reveals the dependence of his educational project on the introduction of those very factors *before* their ostensibly proper time. Yet Rousseau's "editing," and in particular his reference to chopping off the beginning and end of Defoe's novel, creates an illusion of self-sufficiency for his own educational project. However, the necessary role played by the "rigmarole" in all its forms is as significant in its enforced absence as Crusoe's sunken ship. Rousseau can no more create something out of nothing than Crusoe can, and he says much less than he might about the degree to which he would "edit" the novel for Emile because the questionable details are both necessary and dangerous.[31] The novel, in its problematic entirety, is both an ideal point of reference for Rousseau and a flawed example, just as Crusoe himself functions in these ways for Emile. We should keep in mind that Rousseau defends the importance of what might strike the reader as a lot of superfluous rigmarole in *Emile* when he introduces the encounter with the magician. "Here I am once again in my lengthy and minute details. Reader, I hear your grumbling, and I brave it. I do not want to sacrifice the most useful [*utile*] part of the book to your impatience. Make your decision about my delays, for I have made mine about your complaints" (172; 4:437).

The tutor has raised Emile to be self-contained—to be a socially isolated island, so to speak. But as Emile begins to explore that island, and to become conscious of himself, he must become aware of his island *as* an island. He must sense his isolation. Therein lies the utility of Robinson Crusoe's example. Emile's encounter with him simultaneously solidifies his independence by making him aware of it, and prepares him for the interdependence that will be ushered in once he matures sexually, since becoming conscious of social isolation requires that one have intimations, at least, of its opposite. That is, Emile's growing awareness of his independence will allow him to see that independence in a double perspective, both as a lack that requires companionship and as something valuable to be preserved against the worst kinds of dependence. He must see himself through his own eyes before he can see himself through the eyes of a beloved. He can judge neither himself nor others without this. While Emile's capacity for self-reflection remains incomplete, it has been stimulated and prepared, as were the people by Thales. "In general, never substitute the sign for the thing except when it is impossible for you to show the latter" (170; 4:434). A fictional "other" allows the tutor to provide Emile with the experience of an other without undermining his independence. Experience and books are not necessarily mutually exclusive.

Like Crusoe, but unlike Emile, Rousseau can be another self to himself, because he has already had the experience of others. Rousseau has experienced withdrawal from society, so he does not need to experience it vicariously through Defoe's protagonist, as Emile must do. The *Reveries* ends rather abruptly with reflections on an "other" who was crucial to Rousseau's development of a sense of self: Mme. de Warens. Had he not spent those few years with her, he says, "I would perhaps have remained uncertain about myself."[32] If he is finally self-sufficient enough to dedicate the rest of his life to conversing with his own soul, it is only as a result of his experience of himself through another, that is, a prior conversation. Thus Rousseau can do what the young Emile cannot: he can reflect on an earlier version of himself.[33] The achievement of the capacity for self-reflection is simultaneously the mark of self-sufficiency and that which reveals the impossibility of self-sufficiency. It is the mark of self-sufficiency insofar as one can be another self to oneself; however, this achievement requires another, at least in order to come into being. And if self-reflection ultimately includes reflecting on one's capacity for self-reflection, then the soul can never achieve perfect oneness, and "otherness" remains a necessary component, if only in the form of a diary.[34] It is thus no accident that the *Reveries* ends rather than begins with the discussion of Mme. de Warens, and it is no accident that the diary Crusoe writes on the island is necessarily incomplete. It is only after Crusoe returns to society that he can write the more comprehensive account of his adventures and make his solitary life an object of reflection; only then can he make a whole of his island experience. And even then, his life is not finally a whole; he sets out on further adventures. Wholeness is always mediated and incomplete insofar as it is *known*. And what is it good for, if it is not known? "Every man wants to be happy; but to succeed in being so, one would have to begin by knowing what happiness is," Rousseau states (*E*, 177; 4:444). This circularity pervades *Emile* at every level.

In promoting an illusion of self-sufficiency throughout the first three books of *Emile*, and at the same time drawing attention to the supporting conditions, as well as to the inherent unresolved difficulties (which must be simultaneously acknowledged and disavowed), Rousseau suggests the impossibility of self-sufficient projects as much as of self-sufficient individuals. Though Emile has "become aware of himself as an individual," he still believes that he is a self-sufficient whole. This self-understanding is a distortion insofar as it remains ignorant of the tutor's guiding hand. What would it mean to understand oneself as an incomplete whole?

The guiding question of Emile's early childhood education has been how to make a child wise, with wisdom defined as knowing *how* to stay in one's place. We have distinguished this conscious staying in place from the unselfconscious stasis of someone who is protected from all change by an external authority figure. Rousseau's ambition for Emile—that he become wise in this particular sense—introduces a tension between integrity and motion or change. This tension is not only inherent in the process of learning as such but is also significant for Rousseau's entire philosophical project, insofar as it raises the larger question of whether human beings can evolve as a result of their (natural) perfectibility, and yet remain—or perhaps *become*—what we most "naturally" are. Rousseau contends that man by nature is unified; he also contends that ultimately what distinguishes man from animals, even more than free will, is his perfectibility. To be human is to have integrity; to be human is also to change. *Emile* does not focus exclusively on either side of that tension but rather on the tension itself. The ultimate goal is not that Emile remain invulnerable to his own (temporary, instrumental) vulnerability, or fundamentally independent of his (temporary, instrumental) dependence on the object(s) of his desires. Rather, as we shall see in the second half of *Emile*, Rousseau suggests that the source of the soul's motion must be somehow *simultaneously* intrinsic and extrinsic to it. This understanding of the soul is therefore the counterpart to Rousseau's theory of the social contract, in which he attempts to understand human freedom such that its source is somehow simultaneously inside and outside the people, who must be *made* to be a people before they can express a general will. If there is a parallel to be drawn between the city and the soul (as in the *Republic*) for Rousseau, it is not that both are self-contained wholes (represented by Geneva and original man, respectively), but that both are simultaneously self-contained and incomplete. The most basic mark of this complexity is our self-reflection, which introduces an inescapable instability. But such self-reflection is precisely what makes self-rule over the long term possible. One becomes a more complete whole by becoming aware of oneself as simultaneously incomplete *and* whole. How this might be achieved, and how it relates to the capacity for judgment, are questions to which we now turn.

4

JUDGMENT AND PITY

From the bosom of so many diverse passions I see opinion raising an unshakable throne, and stupid mortals, subjected to its empire, basing their own existence on the judgments of others. (*E*, 215; 4:494)

The first half of Emile's education is concerned primarily with bodies in motion. First, the practical child-rearing advice of book I focuses on freeing the infant's limbs from swaddling blankets, shoes, and other unnaturally debilitating constraints. In book II, Emile learns to run and to sharpen his senses. The scientific inquiries undertaken in book III are launched by the question, "Why did this stone fall?" As he approaches adolescence, Emile has learned a thing or two about bodies in motion, and he *is* little more than a body in motion. "He has a healthy body, agile limbs, a precise and unprejudiced mind, a heart that is free and without passions" (208; 4:488). What he lacks is a soul. References to the soul are noticeably absent in book III; the soul is mentioned only in the course of Rousseau's advice to avoid any activity that might engage it.[1] But the soul (particularly the motion of the soul) takes center stage in book IV.

A revolution, no less than a "second birth," takes place at the beginning of book IV. This second birth refers specifically to the awakening of Emile's sexuality but more broadly to the birth of his soul. It is the birth of eros in its most expansive sense. Were he to lack all passion, Emile would wither as a human being. "I do not see how someone who loves nothing can be happy," Rousseau states. It is only with this "second" birth that Emile is "truly born to life" (212; 4:490) and becomes fully human. Emile develops the capacities for attachment, affection, pity, taste, spirituality, passion, and love. In other words, the birth of the soul is the birth of vulnerability. To have a soul is to have the capacity to be moved, whether by pity, gratitude, love, beauty, or reverence—all themes explored in book IV. To this point, Emile has never been moved by anything more significant than cake, having experienced only physical needs. Rousseau sets out to turn Emile into a sensitive being, into a fully human being capable of being moved in a new way that is potentially threatening to Emile's self-sufficiency and independence. The question now becomes: can Emile be moved by something (or someone) outside himself without being dislodged from himself and becoming dependent on others' opinions? Can he somehow develop the passions that make him vulnerable, yet remain invulnerable to his own vulnerability? In other words, can he allow himself to be moved, yet remain free? In establishing this paradoxical requirement, Rousseau suggests that the source of the soul's motion must be somehow simultaneously intrinsic and extrinsic to it. His understanding of the soul thus runs parallel to his theory of the social contract, in which he attempts to understand human freedom such that its source is somehow simultaneously inside (expressed in and through the popular sovereignty of the general will) and outside (insofar as the general will is guided by a godlike legislator).

Rousseau's basic goal, then, is to find a way to reconcile Emile's healthy self-love (*amour de soi*) with some degree of human interdependence—both erotic and social. He makes the social primary, delaying Emile's nascent erotic sensibility in order first to develop a more generalized sensibility that can be the foundation of a healthy sociality. The cornerstone of this development is Emile's education in pity. Throughout his works, Rousseau emphasizes the importance of mutual sympathy and fellow feeling, rather than rationality, as the essential ingredient of social cohesion. The discussion of pity in the first part of book IV of *Emile* is generally interpreted in this light.[2] Since, as Rousseau acknowledges, Emile cannot remain alone forever, the stimulation of his capacity for pity is the necessary first step in forging a healthy connection between him and the rest of humanity. Only then might a natural education be made compatible with civil society. By teaching Emile that he has *semblables*, or fellows, and by disposing him to experience good will toward these others, Rousseau seeks to reconcile our natural self-love with the requirements of social order. Our natural capacity for pity is what makes it possible to conceive of social relations that are not based primarily on power and domination.[3]

This is certainly one of Rousseau's most fundamental concerns. And yet there is more to Rousseau's discussion of pity in book IV of *Emile*—a reflective dimension that connects the capacity for pity, when fully developed, to the faculty of judgment. Emile is certainly being prepared for participation in a larger whole—and, more broadly, Rousseau is exploring the very possibility of such a whole—but this preparation consists of more than the conditioning of Emile's affective response to his fellows. Even as the tutor manipulates Emile's burgeoning passions so that they may be ordered properly, he incorporates into this stage of his educational project an education in judgment, which requires a certain measure of detachment from one's fellows. The point is not simply to become sensitive to instances of human suffering, and so to incline one positively toward one's fellow man; it is also to learn the difference between genuine and apparent human suffering—and, conversely, between genuine and apparent human happiness. The ultimate goal, in other words, is to learn to discern the truth of the human soul that hides behind the masks that human beings wear. The development of pity would thus represent not a potential hindrance to Emile's capacity for good judgment, in Rousseau's view, but rather an advancement of that capability. It would make him not only more social but also, potentially, more free.

When it comes to the physical world around him, Emile, as we have seen, is capable of judging well—that is, both independently and accurately. His faculty of judgment is firmly grounded in the senses, as is appropriate for a primarily physical being. Because his questions and interests are confined to his physical existence, he can rely on himself to seek answers independently. Therefore, within these boundaries, Emile is capable of exercising independent judgment, for he has "a precise and unprejudiced mind, a heart that is free and without passions" (208; 4:488). In other words, because he remains a self-contained whole (maintained by the tutor), and because his world is a simple, self-contained whole of bodies in motion, he can base his judgments on a clear and unwavering standard. As he begins to move into the realm of human relations and morality, however, more complex forms of judgment are called for. Emile's ability to engage this emerging complexity depends upon the birth of his soul; but at the same time this birth ushers in a new vulnerability that both threatens and enhances his capacity for judgment—with regard not only to his fellow human beings but also to himself. His nascent sensibility thus changes his relationship to others and also to himself.

"So long as he knows himself only in his physical being, [Emile] ought to study himself in his relations to things. This is the job of his childhood. When he begins to sense his moral being, he ought to study himself in his relation with men. This is the job of his whole life" (214; 4:493). This lifelong task is to be undertaken in stages. We see this not only in the transition from generalized compassion in book IV to a particular erotic attachment in book V but also in Rousseau's treatment of compassion itself. What begins as an education in feeling develops, as we shall see, into an education of reflection and judgment, "for the truth of sentiments depends in large measure on the correctness of ideas" (227; 4:512). Rousseau invites us first to consider the role of pity in fostering healthy sociability, and then its role in fostering sound judgment.

Pity and Sociability

Rousseau begins his discussion of the development of Emile's moral sense by making sure that Emile's incipient passions do not distort his relations with other people. "As soon as man has need of a companion, he is no longer an isolated being. His heart is no longer alone. All his relations with his species, all the affections of his soul are born with this one" (214; 4:493). The most prominent and dangerous among these affections of soul is amour-propre, which, in Rousseau's view, drives all social interaction in civil society. It is the root of all unhappiness, unfreedom, and vice in civil society. Rousseau's larger project is to help us to conceive of social interaction founded on something other than amour-propre. But while sociability may be possible without amour-propre, erotic attachment is not. "One wants to obtain the preference that one grants. . . . To be preferred, one has to make oneself more lovable than another, more lovable than every other, at least in the eyes of the beloved object" (214; 4:494). This presents a problem for Rousseau's argument that sociability follows from sexual maturity. Since one's "first glance at one's fellows" is motivated by the desire to be preeminent in the eyes of the beloved, "emulation, rivalries, and jealousy" will be the inevitable result (214; 4:494). The possibility of fraternity or equality among human beings is dashed. Therefore, erotic awakening must be delayed as long as possible. Rousseau attempts to anchor justice in pity rather than reason in order to circumvent the problem (identified in the *Second Discourse*) of having to make Emile "a philosopher before making him a man" (*SD*, 96; 3:126). But in so doing he creates another difficulty: he must make Emile a man before making him a *man*, that is, a gendered individual.

There is a certain natural order to the birth of the passions, and the birth of amour-propre should be the last step. When it develops too early, it perverts all the other passions. Rousseau offers a finely detailed account of how the physical longings awakened by puberty give birth to a host of threatening passions. Specifically, the desire to be loved leads one to seek to make oneself lovable— *more* lovable than others, who now become rivals. In other words, the desire for love becomes the desire for preeminence. "He who senses how sweet it is to be loved would want to be loved by everyone" (*E*, 215; 4:494). Thus is amour-propre born. The competition stimulated by amour-propre not only sows the seeds of social inequality, as each seeks to elevate himself at the expense of others, but also destroys the individual's capacity for good judgment, as he comes to see himself through others' eyes. "From the bosom of so many diverse passions I see opinion raising an unshakable throne, and stupid mortals, subjected to its empire, basing their own existence on the judgments of others" (215; 4:494).

Although Rousseau delays inflaming Emile's adolescent passions as long as possible, he makes clear that his purpose is not to suppress the development of these passions but only to delay them. At this stage in life, nascent sexuality and the competition and self-consciousness it engenders make the development of amour-propre unavoidable, Rousseau insists. Too often it takes hold too early, because children have been warped in some way by their upbringing. This is not the case with Emile, whose development follows nature's timetable. Moreover, Rousseau contends, the passions are naturally good; God himself would never wish to annihilate them (212; 4:490–91). With this comment Rousseau challenges three other conceptions of human freedom and morality: the Christian, the Stoic, and that of modern philosophy. All three, to different degrees and in different ways, encourage a kind of absence of passion, whether because passion is tainted by original sin, or because it is a threat to one's stoical detachment,[4] or because it is an obstacle to purely cognitive rationality. Rousseau counters that well-ordered passion can be good and is compatible with (and even essential to) human freedom and morality.

The adolescent's nascent erotic sensibility is to be delayed not by means of "an artful untruth" but by "nature's ignorance" (219; 4:500). Although Rousseau cannot prevent the development of Emile's new feelings, he can thwart any awareness on Emile's part of what these feelings are about. Rousseau contrives to stall his pupil in a curiously liminal state of desiring without knowing what precisely he desires (220; 4:502). Lacking a specific object, Emile's "desire" can be directed at the whole of humankind, and equality and fraternity thus become possible. "The blood ferments and is agitated; a superabundance of life seeks to extend itself outward. The eye becomes animated and looks over other beings. One begins to take an interest in those surrounding us; one begins to feel that one is not made to live alone. It is thus that the heart is opened to the human affections and becomes capable of attachment" (220; 4:502).

Emile's heart must be opened in this way because as he enters this phase of his education he is still thoroughly self-interested, oblivious to the needs, experiences, or emotions of others. This is hardly unique among children, Rousseau adds. "Indifferent to everything outside of himself like all other children, he takes an interest in no one. All that distinguishes him is his not caring to appear interested" (222; 4:505). Emile's indifference is healthier than feigned interest, but the indifference must be overcome, replaced with a generalized sensibility that is nevertheless compatible with healthy self-love. "The first act of his nascent imagination is to teach him that he has fellows [*semblables*]" (220; 4:502). The birth of this awareness of others must be accompanied by the sentiment of pity for them, for "we are attached to our fellows less by the sentiment of their pleasure than by the sentiment of their pains" (221; 4:503).

We are moved by pity only "by transporting ourselves outside of ourselves and identifying with the suffering animal, by leaving, as it were, our own being to take on its being." To produce this effect, the educator must "offer the young man objects on which the expansive force of his heart can act—objects which swell the heart, which extend it to other beings, which make it find itself everywhere outside itself—and carefully to keep away those which contract and concentrate the heart" (223; 4:506). These objects or examples must be carefully selected. "Do not put the seeds of pride, vanity, and envy in him by the deceptive image of the happiness of men." Whereas the sight of a happy man arouses envy and spite, the sight of a suffering man has the opposite effect. "Pity is sweet because, in putting ourselves in the place of the one who suffers, we nevertheless feel the pleasure of not suffering as he does" (221; 4:504). Pity flourishes insofar as it is pleasant, and is therefore compatible with our natural self-love.

It takes an act of imagination to put oneself in another's place.[5] "Thus no one becomes sensitive until his imagination is animated and begins to transport him out of himself" (223; 4:506). Whereas elsewhere Rousseau derides imagination as a major source of human ills, here he indicates that when properly directed, imagination can be a salutary force. Pity both takes us out of ourselves and brings us back to ourselves. Even while feeling another person's pain, we take pleasure in our own absence of pain. If pity were limited to empathetic identification, Rousseau would be unable to explain why we do not simply flee from the feeling the first time we experience it, since self-preservation dictates that we turn away from what is painful. The experience of identification with another person's suffering would then have the effect of turning us away from our fellows. By causing Emile to experience a pleasant return to himself, the tutor hopes to achieve two objectives at once. Pity will ensure that Emile never desires to harm another, and that he never desires to leave himself, or to live outside himself, as civil man is inclined to do. Paradoxically, however, since pity is the key to this latter development, Emile must leave himself (identify with another) in order to desire never to leave himself. The pleasure at escaping the suffering of another requires that we believe that we *could* suffer as he does; only in the shadow of this possibility do we feel relief at having escaped it. "One pities in others only those ills from which one does not feel oneself exempt" (224; 4:507). Pity is not an automatic or generic response to another person's suffering but is based on some judgment that we make about that suffering and its meaning.

This is most strongly reflected in the third of the three "maxims" Rousseau offers in regard to pity. While the first maxim states that we pity only those who are less happy than we, and the second states that we only pity in others those ills from which we do not feel exempt, Rousseau adds a third, which stipulates that "the pity that one has for another's misfortune is measured not by the quantity of that misfortune but by the sentiment which one attributes to those who suffer it" (225; 4:508). Rousseau's point is that we tend to feel pity to differing degrees for different people, depending upon our subjective judgment of the extent of the person's suffering. We may not pity a sheep as he unwittingly faces his slaughter, insofar as we believe that his fate is suited to him, and because he is unwitting. But when it comes to human beings, Rousseau explains, distinctions based on social status inevitably and erroneously color our reactions to perceived pain, causing us to pity a king's suffering more than a peasant's. This tendency must be countered. "To the man who thinks, all the civil distinctions disappear" (225; 4:509). Emile must be taught to pity and feel connected to all human beings without regard to class or status, which interfere with the ability to judge individual cases of suffering with any acuity.

How is this universal perspective to be achieved? One cannot be shown the whole at once. Rousseau insists that pity is aroused not by the abstract idea of human suffering but only by direct exposure to specific instances of suffering. In fact, Rousseau counsels educators to use very few examples, very carefully, for maximum impact. Although he wants Emile to understand that suffering is the basis for extensive human commonality, he will *not* show Emile the whole world suffering. To do so would harden rather than sensitize him (231; 4:517). He will show him a few select instances of suffering and allow Emile to make the leap between these particular examples to the idea that suffering is the universal human condition. It is not entirely clear how Emile will manage to do this, since Rousseau insists repeatedly that his pupil will rely only on direct sensory experience, and that he lacks abstract ideas. Yet in order to achieve the perspective to which Rousseau's education aspires, Emile must extend a salutary sensibility to a wider expanse of humanity by extrapolating from the significance of particular examples. He must therefore learn to reflect on them, and to do it well.

To be sure, Rousseau's treatment of pity initially emphasizes the role of fellow feeling in forging social cohesion, and thus the first step in Emile's moral education connects him to his fellows universally and without (arbitrary) distinctions (between rich and poor, etc.). Arbitrary distinctions based on status and wealth produce social disharmony. However, as the discussion of pity progresses, it becomes clear that Emile is in fact learning to make *real* distinctions. He is taught to distinguish among individual lives (judging which are truly happy and free), as well as to discern the difference between legitimate and illegitimate social orders, judging "the consideration which is due them according to justice and reason" (236; 4:525). Of course, given that so few individuals are happy or free, in Rousseau's view, and so few political orders legitimate, there is the risk that Emile will condemn every example he encounters. On the one hand, Rousseau does not want Emile to be taken in by the false appearances that surround him; on the other hand, he does not want Emile to despise humanity in all of its deformity. He is training Emile to see humanity by looking at human beings who have ceased to be human in that they are empty vessels defined by opinion and prejudice. But while this is a "reality," so too is the reality that is occluded by this distortion. Emile must not just see things for what they are but must apprehend them in light of what is missing. "Let him see that all men wear pretty much the same mask, but let him also know that there are faces more beautiful than the mask covering them" (237; 4:525). This is less about being moved by a spectacle than it is about becoming reflective and learning to judge.[6]

Rousseau calls for a similarly reflective perspective from his reader as well, even with regard to his own teachings. In introducing his three maxims about how to nourish a child's nascent sensibility, he notes that his goal is to summarize his preceding reflections "in two or three maxims which are precise, clear, and easy to grasp" (223; 4:506). He sets off each maxim from the surrounding text with the subheadings "First Maxim," "Second Maxim," and "Third Maxim." Considering his effort to enumerate these maxims and his claim that they are "precise, clear, and easy to grasp," the fact that he refers to this grouping as "two or three" maxims is somewhat puzzling. Why the ambiguity? Are we to infer that these maxims may be less clear and distinct than they first appear? To be sure, the third maxim differs from the first two in explicitly emphasizing the role of judgment in the development of pity. Whereas the first two maxims address the affective response of the observer to suffering, the third addresses the cognitive appraisal of the suffering victim's status. One is reminded of Rousseau's repeated demand that the reader move beyond his explicit formulas to grasp their underlying principles. These principles are not, it seems, reducible to a defined set of maxims, for he concludes his presentation of the "maxims" by emphasizing the indefinite over the definite: "This is the spirit of the method which must be prescribed" (226; 4:510). In other words, even when his advice seems most concrete and straightforward, Rousseau reminds the reader that his educational project is not a matter of subsuming particular situations under universal rules but of intuiting the spirit of his method. There is no way around the need for judgment.

Pity and Reflection

If we understand pity strictly in terms of a pleasurable identification with another's physical suffering, Emile's education in pity seems perfectly consistent with his status as a primarily physical being. However, because pity has a reflective dimension that is critical to its proper functioning, the conditioning of pleasure and pain is not sufficient. Whereas pity is said in the *Second Discourse* to be a movement of the soul "anterior to reason" (*SD*, preface, 95; 3:126), in *Emile* this anteriority characterizes only the first movement of pity.[7] Rather than emphasize the unreflective apprehension of (or the direct identification with) human suffering, Rousseau emphasizes the importance of the memory of that experience, as filtered through the pupil's reflections on it. "It is not so much what he sees as his looking back on what he has seen that determines the judgment he makes about it" (*E*, 231; 4:517). In fact, Rousseau indicates that a primitive human being would not be capable of the response he is calling forth in his imaginary pupil. Referring to Emile's newly felt reactions to "the sounds of complaints and cries," he notes that if the boy "had remained stupid and barbaric, he would not have [these new movements]; if he were more learned, he would know their source. He has already compared too many ideas to feel nothing and not enough to have a conception of what he feels" (222; 4:505). In this characterization, pity and the judgment that it requires occupy an intermediate position between the nonrational and the rational.[8]

The reflective dimension of pity not only makes it possible for Emile to connect the individual examples of suffering that he witnesses to a broader notion of common human suffering—in other words, to connect him to his *semblables*—but also to make important distinctions among human beings. For Emile's education in pity, as I have shown, is as much an education in human differences as in human commonality.[9] This tension pervades the very notion that Emile has *semblables*. What could it possibly mean to say that Emile resembles other human beings if he is a unique specimen among the corrupted and deformed multitude? Rousseau presents pity as an impulse that does not (or ought not to) discriminate, especially insofar as Emile is encouraged to identify with all fellow human beings without regard to social status. Yet, only a few pages later, Rousseau urges educators to portray human beings to their pupils "such as they are—not in order that young people hate them but that they pity them and *not want to resemble them*" (236; 4:525, emphasis added). This involves a judgment. The trick is to observe the spectacle of human folly from the proper distance. Observe "too closely" and the pupil will see "nothing from the good side," and soon "the general perversity will serve him less as a lesson than as an example" (237; 4:525–26). At the other extreme, the study of humanity becomes abstract and theoretical; the tutor would end up lecturing the pupil instead of allowing him to form his own judgments. Rousseau announces that he has a solution that will "remove both of these obstacles at once" (237; 4:526), which is to introduce Emile to the study of history. This will allow Emile to observe human beings from a healthy distance; he will be able to "see the stage without ever being able to act on it" (237; 4:526).

What becomes clear as Rousseau's discussion of history progresses, however, is that the point is not simply to observe various spectacles that transpire on the stage of human history in order to avoid similar pitfalls, but rather to come to see the stage *as a stage*. It is for this reason that Rousseau prefers biographies, for example, which can, at their best, get "inside" a life, over histories, which catalogue the actions and events from an external perspective. "I would prefer to begin the study of the human heart with the reading of lives of individuals" (240; 4:530). Ultimately, the goal is for Emile to come to appreciate the distinction between "inside" and "outside," and to see that the outside is very often misleading. In other words, he must come to recognize that the masks that human beings wear *are* masks, and that the spectacle of human activity is just that—a spectacle. "Think of [Emile] at the rising of the curtain, casting his eyes for the first time on the stage of the world; or, rather, set backstage, seeing the actors take up and put on their costumes, counting the cords and pulleys whose crude magic deceives the spectators' eyes" (242; 4:532).

Whereas the ordinary spectator is likely to be taken in by stories about the exploits of human beings pursuing illusory goods, Emile, we are told, is not deceived. Once again, Rousseau makes this discernment seem both very easy and very difficult. Emile, he explains, will initially be surprised by what he sees, and then become "indignant" at seeing "the whole of humankind its own dupe, debasing himself in these children's games. He will be afflicted at seeing his brothers turn into ferocious animals because they do not know how to be satisfied with being men" (242; 4:532). In other words, he is prone to pity the human beings who chase after false happiness, and who are not wise enough to know how to stay in place. He is not tempted to imitate their example, because he himself is not prone to the unnatural passions and prejudices of most human beings. He judges others always against his own example, and has been conditioned to feel his own situation as preferable to that of others. Moreover, through the tutor's prudence and selectivity in choosing his readings, he will be provided with examples in which false or misguided heroes come to an unhappy end. An unhappy ending, in itself, functions as a cautionary tale, and also elicits a reaction of pity rather than admiration or envy.

To this point, Rousseau has suggested that Emile's proper response to these examples of human foolishness is highly predictable. His exposure has, after all, been restricted to narratives in which the worldly hero comes to an unfortunate end. However, Rousseau goes on to remark that unhappy endings cannot be relied upon to teach the lesson Emile needs to learn. "All conquerors have not been killed; all usurpers have not failed in their enterprises; several will appear happy to minds biased by vulgar opinions" (242; 4:533). It is therefore necessary that Emile pity not only those who ultimately fail but also those who appear to succeed by conventional standards. In other words, the pain suffered by the triumphant conqueror is not easily discernible because he appears successful, but this is precisely what Emile must come to appreciate. This goal cannot be achieved simply by conditioning his responses by means of painful and pleasant stimuli. In fact, this phase of his education is only superficially about being exposed to suffering and conditioned by the pleasure and pain that this exposure brings. More fundamentally, his education is aimed at seeing suffering that masquerades as happiness for what it is, in order to be able to discern genuine happiness, which is not always apparent on the surface. Someone who appears to be suffering may in fact be happy, and someone who appears happy may be deeply troubled. "We judge happiness too much on the basis of appearances; we suppose it to be where it is least present" (229; 4:515). Properly understood, pity is not simply the experience of being moved by the spectacle of human suffering; it is the ability to discern the difference between spectacle and reality. What is being honed, in other words, is not only Emile's sensibility but his faculty of judgment. "It is difficult to find a viewpoint from which one can judge his fellows equitably" (237; 4:526).

By controlling Emile's exposure to human suffering so that he always senses his own situation as preferable to that of others, Rousseau has guaranteed that he is free of envy. But he has introduced a new difficulty. Pity may be the cornerstone of healthy social cohesion, inasmuch as it works against the vanity that fuels inequality and strife, but pity can also contribute in its own way to the development of vanity. To the degree that Emile's affective response is automatic and unreflective, it might lead him to believe (erroneously) that his superiority is somehow innate. Why should he believe otherwise, if his situation is consistently preferable to that of others? The only way to preserve the positive dimension of pity and to reduce its negative impact is to cultivate Emile's ability to stand back from both his own example and that of others in order to reflect on them without easy recourse to a clear calculus for determining their relative merits. What is required, in other words, is an exercise of judgment, not the unreflective application of a fixed standard—Emile's own example—to each and every case. While Emile has, of course, been trained to judge others against the superior standard set by his own situation, Rousseau goes on to make clear that this is only a first step; Emile must also come to reflect critically on the standard he himself sets, even as he applies it. This is the next and most important step in his education in pity.

Pity and Self-Reflection

Rousseau is confident that his pupil will make consistently sound judgments about his fellow human beings because his field of vision and range of experience are so controlled that he has no opportunity to make bad judgments about them. Restricted to encountering other human lives that are obviously inferior to his own, he will remain both content with himself and uncorrupted in his judgments and sensibilities with regard to others. Rousseau acknowledges, however, that there is one potential pitfall to this highly controlled method, and it is that Emile may show poor judgment with respect to himself. The problem is not that he might turn away from himself to pursue the false happiness promised by ambition and riches—he feels his own contentment too strongly for that—but that he might misunderstand *why* he is so content.

Emile has been conditioned to experience his own lot as pleasant and superior to other ways of life. Since he sees himself as a standard against which all other human beings fall short, he is likely to develop a sense of pride in his status. This is the potential source of his self-misunderstanding. The reader, of course, sees that Emile is what he is only because the tutor is controlling every aspect of his situation. The reader is privy to what goes on "backstage," or the "cords and pulleys" (242; 4:532). In other words, the reader sees that Emile is an incomplete whole. However, Emile may believe that he is a self-sufficient whole, since his subjective experience of illusory self-sufficiency is part of what produces the contentment that allows him to prefer himself to all others. He "will be tempted to honor his reason for the work of yours and to attribute his happiness to his merit. . . . In congratulating himself, he will esteem himself more, and in feeling himself to be happier than [other men] are, he will believe himself worthier to be so" (245; 4:536–37). He would be gravely mistaken. This is the "error most to be feared." To combat it, Rousseau advises a two-step process that further conditions Emile's responses (using painful experiences of humiliation) and also develops his awareness of his own limitations.

Insofar as he "prefers his way of being, of seeing, and of feeling to that of other men, Emile is right. But if he thus believes himself to be of a more excellent nature and more happily born than other men, Emile is wrong. He is deceived. One must undeceive him" (245; 4:537). Rousseau's focus shifts from ensuring that Emile is not deceived by the "cords and pulleys" behind the lives of his apparently happy (but actually miserable) fellow human beings to ensuring that he is not deceived about himself. As we have seen, Emile's way of being, seeing, and feeling does, according to Rousseau's criteria, elevate him above his fellows, so the pleasure he takes in returning to himself and pitying others is not unjustified. But if this pleasure is accompanied by pride, all is lost. Rousseau attacks this problem in three steps. First, Emile must be humbled, so as to squelch his pride and make him acutely aware of his vulnerability. Second, he must come to see his tutor as possessing a superior wisdom that he himself lacks. Finally, he must come to appreciate his own situation in a new light. Only then will he be able to judge others both sensitively and accurately.

Emile must be humbled: the humiliation that he experienced at the hands of the magician in book II is to be "repeated in countless ways" (245; 4:537). As he is fleeced and abused by various charlatans and opportunists—all arranged by the tutor, of course—he begins to sense his weakness and his dependence on his older and wiser teacher. A tutor should warn the pupil about mistakes before he falls into them, but never reproach him afterward. Instead, he should offer the consolation that countless others have made the same mistakes. In this way, "you correct him by appearing only to pity him; for, to him who believes he is worth more than other men, it is a most mortifying excuse to be consoled by their example" (247; 4:540).

By repeatedly humiliating Emile in this way, the tutor further conditions him to associate pride with pain—a necessary counterpart to his conditioned association of pity with pleasure. But to rely on that earlier tactic would suggest that one might take the same approach with one's pupil in adolescence as in childhood. Yet Rousseau has indicated that Emile's "second birth" requires that the tutor change his method (215; 4:494). Moreover, while a simple repetition of the earlier experience may further condition Emile to associate pride with pain, it will not suffice to "undeceive" him with regard to himself. Thus the tutor does *not* in fact simply "repeat in countless ways" the earlier experience, but rather alters it in one significant respect. Whereas previously the tutor allowed himself to be reprimanded by the magician, and therefore experienced the humiliation along with his pupil, he now stands apart and observes Emile's failings from a safe distance, offering pity and consolation. The effect is to make Emile sense not only his vulnerability to the same weaknesses he observes in his fellows, but also the gap between himself and his tutor. The pupil should not, at this stage, "suppose an understanding as limited as his own in the master and the same facility at letting himself be seduced. This opinion is good for a child who, knowing how to see nothing and compare nothing, takes everyone to be on his level." Emile's confidence in his tutor ought to be based on his recognition of the tutor's "authority of reason" and "superiority of understanding" (246; 4:539).

Emile's new awareness of the gap between his tutor and himself helps him to sense that he, like most average people (who are, in fact, his *semblables*), is vulnerable to making mistakes. This is in keeping with Rousseau's goal of having his pupil feel connected to his fellow man. Recognition of this gap also helps to solidify the tutor's hold over his pupil as they enter the dangerous period of adolescence. Finally, and perhaps most important, it represents an important step in the development of Emile's own independent judgment. As Emile develops an appreciation for his tutor's superior reasoning and understanding, he prepares to recognize his own superiority vis-à-vis his fellows— not simply "tasting" it as pleasant but truly "knowing" it on a more rational level. Emile must at some point reconcile his sense that all men are *semblables* with a new discernment of, and appreciation for, genuine distinctions of merit.

Rousseau explicitly connects the question of finding a legitimate perspective from which to judge one's fellow man to the question of finding a legitimate perspective with regard to oneself.

> I show from afar—for I also do not want to say everything—the roads deviating from the right one in order that one may learn to avoid them. I believe that in following the one I have indicated, your pupil will purchase knowledge of men and of himself as cheaply as possible, and that you will put him in a position to contemplate the games of Fortune without envying the fate of its favorites, and to be satisfied with himself without believing himself to be wiser than others. You have also begun to make him an actor in order to make him a spectator; you must finish the job; for from the pit one sees objects as they appear, but from the stage one sees them as they are. To embrace the whole, one must move back to get perspective; one must come near to see the details. (249; 4:542)

To "finish the job" of developing the pupil's correct perspective on the world and on himself, one must help him achieve a vantage point that combines the virtues of distance and proximity. This is both a philosophical problem for Rousseau and a practical one, as his recommendations throughout this stage of Emile's education vacillate between encouraging his pupil to connect with his fellows and remain detached from them. This is not simply a function of the need for Emile to be both social and independent; it is also, Rousseau suggests, a prerequisite of a certain kind of knowledge ("of men and of himself"). This necessary if paradoxical combination of distance and proximity is reflected in Rousseau's oft-quoted statement about what is required in order to observe men well: "a great interest in knowing them and a great impartiality in judging them. A heart sensitive enough to conceive all the human passions and calm enough not to experience them. If there is a favorable moment in life for this study, it is the one I have chosen for Emile" (244; 4:536).

This sensitive detachment or detached sensitivity is the mark of Rousseau's ideal of good judgment. It recalls the opening passages of book I, in which he criticized both *les sages* for their speculative detachment and the tender mother for her overbearing attachment. Rousseau stakes out a similar middle ground when it comes to knowing human beings. "It is not philosophers who know men best. They see them only through the prejudices of philosophy, and I know of no station where one has so many. A savage has a healthier judgment of us than a philosopher does" (243; 4:535). However, even the savage's judgment is ultimately deficient (just as, in book I, the tender mother required correction). "My pupil is that savage with the difference that Emile, having reflected more, compared ideas more, seen our errors from closer up, is more on guard against himself and judges only what he knows" (243–44; 4:535). It is by allowing Emile to see human errors "from closer up" *and* by having him stand back in order to make comparisons that Rousseau strives to correct the perspective of both the philosopher and the natural savage.

Emile and the Reader

Rousseau anticipates that his readers will find his prescriptions for Emile's education in pity too gloomy, and will wonder how a young man can be happy when exposed to so much human suffering. Rousseau defends his method by pointing out, "I promised to make him happy, not to appear to be. Is it my fault if you, always dupes of appearance, take it for reality?" (227; 4:512). The question that Rousseau insists must be posed with respect to humanity as a whole—what is true happiness?—is a question that the reader must pose with respect to Emile, even as we judge humanity against the standard Emile sets.

Ignorance of the deepest form of human suffering and ignorance of the most genuine form of human happiness are two sides of the same coin. Rousseau fears that his readers can appreciate neither, since most people tend to focus on mere appearances, and neither the most profound suffering nor the most profound happiness appears on the surface. Rousseau notes that there is a type of human suffering ("moral suffering and inner pains," as opposed to physical pain or material deprivation) that only very sensitive individuals are able to see. Such sensitive souls are rare. "There are people who can be moved only by cries and tears" (227; 4:511). The ability to discern the highest reaches of human happiness is similarly rare. "We judge happiness too much on the basis of appearances" (229; 4:515). The reader who is quick to assume that

Judgment and Pity ✳ *101*

Emile's exposure to human suffering will make him gloomy and morose misunderstands not only how pity operates with regard to others' suffering but also the nature of human suffering. In short, such a reader makes the mistake of reading only the surface.

Although the reader was asked to judge Emile on an earlier occasion, at the end of book II, in that instance Rousseau suggested that Emile be judged in comparison to other children. In book IV he takes a different approach. In order to make the hidden, internal dimension of the human experience visible to his superficial readers, Rousseau does not appeal to actually existing children; instead, he creates an imaginary pupil against whom Emile is to be judged. He does not leave it up to the reader to look around, for the reader may be fooled by appearances. Instead, Rousseau introduces a thought experiment, which entails the comparison of two pupils: the one he has been describing (Emile) and the one that his readers should have in mind when they object to his description. Only when the question of the relative merits of these two pupils has been resolved can we know, Rousseau says, "whether I have gone astray" (254; 4:550).

> Let us take two young men, emerging from their first education and entering into society by two directly opposite paths. One suddenly climbs up to Olympus and moves in the most brilliant world. He is brought to the court, to the nobles, to the rich, to the pretty women. I assume that he is made much of everywhere, and I do not examine the effect of this greeting on his reason—I assume that his reason resists it. Pleasures fly to him. . . . You take him to be satisfied; but look at the condition of his soul. You believe he is enjoying himself; I believe he is suffering. (227; 4:512)

On what basis does Rousseau claim that this most celebrated and privileged young man is unhappy? He makes manifest the unhappiness that may be invisible to the casual observer, pointing out that such a lad is likely to worry constantly about whether someone else has more rewards than he. The lad must be wracked with unfulfilled desires for "multitudes of alleged goods which he did not know, and most of which, since they are only for a moment within his reach, seem to be revealed to him only to make him regret being deprived of them" (228; 4:512–13). To be sure, this calls to mind Rousseau's many references to the distinctive misery of one whose desires outstrip his faculties. But here his formulation is also strikingly reminiscent of the argument Socrates makes in Plato's *Republic*, and specifically of the thought experiment that frames Socrates's entire dialogue with Glaucon and Adeimantus.[10] Socrates is asked to prove that, despite appearances, the unjust man is actually miserable. He ultimately rests his argument on a view of the tyrant as tortured day and night by his unquenchable desire for more.[11]

Rousseau, too, paints a picture of a miserable tyrant. "He covets everything; he is envious of everyone. He would want to dominate everywhere. Vanity gnaws at him. The ardor of unbridled desires inflames his young heart" (229; 4:514). It is a rather superficial picture that he paints, however. Whereas Socrates goes to great lengths to probe the depths of the tyrant's soul, Rousseau looks to his facial expressions. He contrasts the "impertinent, sugary and affected" look on the face of the young tyrant, "which displeases and repels plain people" (230; 4:515), with the serene expression on his own pupil's face, which others find endearing. Rousseau seems to assume not only that the state of one's soul is reflected in one's external appearance (an argument he makes in other works as well), but also that negative social consequences will befall the tyrant and positive ones will befall the fresh-faced innocent. His argument therefore reverses the dynamic that frames the *Republic*'s inquiry into justice, in which the unjust man gains external rewards and the just man is a social pariah. In light of Rousseau's complaint that we judge happiness too often on the basis of appearances and his critique of those who identify suffering only with perceptible pain, this is bizarre. Can Rousseau really believe in his own simpleminded assertion that a person's character can be divined from his facial features and external bearing? Does he really think that the outside always reflects the inside? Is this Rousseau at his most optimistic about the possibility of "transparency" without "obstruction?"[12] He has just finished pointing out (echoing Glaucon) that appearances are often misleading, and reminding us that he promised to make his pupil truly "happy, *not* to appear to be" (227; 4:512). If assessing true happiness were as easy as looking at someone's face, the entire argument of the *Republic* (and that of *Emile* as well) would be superfluous.

Rousseau's recourse to the facile possibility of divining human character from facial features has to be read against his recurring references to the complexity of judging. His defense of physiognomy (the subject of serious debate in the eighteenth century)[13] occurs in the context of a larger discussion about how difficult or even impossible it is to judge another human being's internal state at all. The ability to discern the most profound human happiness, as well as the most profound human suffering, he says, is extremely rare. He advises the reader not to judge too hastily, and observes that the worldly man is often "whole in his mask" (230; 4:515). He even criticizes an acquaintance who once mistook an Englishman for a German elector on the basis of his physical bearing. So, on the one hand, Rousseau suggests that seeing into another human soul is easy, but on the other he suggests that it is exceedingly difficult. How are we to reconcile these radically opposed claims?

Rousseau's description of Emile's debut in polite society, at the end of book IV, provides some clues. Despite having spent his childhood in relative isolation from human beings other than the tutor, Emile fares very well when introduced into bourgeois social circles. Rousseau's account of this sounds two very different notes, in succession, continuing the pattern I have traced throughout the narrative. At first, Rousseau emphasizes just how easily and perfectly Emile will fit in. "Far from shocking others, Emile is quite willing to conform to their ways—not to appear knowledgeable about social practice or to affect the airs of an elegant man; but, on the contrary, he does so for fear of being singled out, in order to avoid being noticed. He is never more at ease when no attention is being paid him" (336; 4:666–67). Emile acts as everyone else does, but for completely different reasons—the *right* reasons. His politeness is genuine, whereas his peers are frauds. But what distinguishes him from his peers remains invisible. On the outside, both behave politely. "Do not deceive yourself about his comportment, however, and do not try to compare it to that of your young charmers" (336–37; 4:667).

A subtle shift occurs in Rousseau's rhetoric as the differences between Emile and others begin to manifest themselves. Rousseau now maintains that these differences will be discernible, but not problematic. People see that Emile differs from them, as would "a likable foreigner," but they will pardon him because the "difference will be noticeable without being offensive." Not only will they pardon him; they will accept and even like him. However, "they will like him without knowing why." Similarly, "no one will vaunt Emile's intelligence, but he will be gladly taken as a judge among intelligent men" (339; 4:670). At first glance, this might seem to express Rousseau's fervent wish that what is good will naturally hold sway as long as it is readily apparent. However, it also signals a certain defect in the reception Emile receives. If people like and respect him "without knowing why," then they do not understand him. They begin to see what had been unseen, but they see without insight. In fact, they are like Emile himself, who prefers himself to others without fully understanding why his lot is better. Emile's example moves them but fails to enlighten them.

Rousseau expects more from his readers. Readings of *Emile* that suggest that Emile's example ought to appeal to the reader's passions in order to incline them toward virtue[14]—that is, as something to be attracted to rather than thought about—imply that the reader, too, is expected to find Emile likable "without knowing why." But it is important to note that Rousseau asks the reader to judge his pupil a *second* time in book IV, and the progression from the first to the second opportunity elucidates the standard to which Rousseau holds his readers (and toward which he moves them). That standard includes knowing the *why*. The initial, facile argument about the connection between happiness and physiognomy reflects the fact that the reader's judgment is still ill formed and tends to operate superficially; the reader does not yet see as Rousseau sees. Most people, Rousseau contends, can only appreciate "cries and groans" of suffering, rather than internal turmoil, and still judge happiness on the basis of appearances. His observations about Emile's merry appearance and the tyrant's worry lines may be designed to prompt the reader to conclude that Emile is happy by providing simple images—pure types—making it easy for us to judge but also giving us standards that might guide the more complex judgments that he calls for later. For readers who take the surface to be the only reality, this move might be necessary. But it is not Rousseau's only or final move. When he leaves behind his sugary-faced tyrant and asks the reader a second time to judge his pupil, the issue is not so much *whether* he is happy, but *why*, on what basis. This invitation to judge occurs immediately after Rousseau's discussion of the proper use of fables, which are appropriate at this age only if one omits the moral. When he then invites the reader to assess his pupil yet again, Rousseau follows his own advice and omits stating the conclusion that the reader ought to draw.

Anticipating (as he has several times) his readers' incredulity, Rousseau now conjures up a reader who denies that a young man like Emile could ever exist. This imagined reader goes one step beyond the earlier imagined reader in not simply questioning whether Emile could be happy but whether he could exist at all. Rousseau confronts this imagined skeptic by observing that anyone who says such a thing is like someone who "den[ies] that there was ever a big pear tree because one only sees dwarf pear trees in our gardens" (254; 4:549). He goes on to defend his method by stating that he bases his claims on observation, and as little as possible on reasoning. "I found myself not on what I have imagined but on what I have seen" (254: 4:550). By this he does not mean that he actually observed Emile (or someone like him) but that he is basing his claims about Emile on his observations of human beings. Having spent a life observing them, he "eliminated as artificial what belonged to one people and not to another, to one station and not to another," and "regarded as incontest-

Judgment and Pity ✄ 105

ably belonging to man only what was common to all, at whatever age, in whatever rank, and in whatever nation" (254; 4:550). In other words, he subtracts all particularity, so as to come up with a universal abstraction. He challenges our pear tree not by pointing to another tree but by abstracting from all others and pointing to the abstraction.

It is on the basis of such an abstraction that Emile is to be judged. "Now if in accordance with this method you follow a young man from childhood *who has not received a particular form* and who depends as little as possible on the authority and opinion of others, whom do you think he will most resemble, my pupil or yours? This, it seems to me, is the question which must be resolved in order to know whether I have gone astray" (254; 4:550, emphasis added). Instead of comparing Emile to the average young man and assuming that Emile's virtues will be readily apparent, as he did earlier, Rousseau now invokes a third young man against whom the first two can be judged. Like Emile, this young man relies as little as possible on the authority and opinion of others, but unlike Emile, he has no particular form. His lack of precise articulation is consistent with Rousseau's principle of leaving the most important lessons unexpressed. Of course, as soon as one tries to picture such a young man, one cannot help but give him a form, and of course he looks suspiciously like Emile. Rousseau never quite does away with the chimeras that incline us to judge well, but he also distances us from them, creating a space in which judgment comes into play.

Rousseau's analogy of the pear tree suggests that he needs something like the Platonic idea of an Emile, just as one would need the Platonic idea of a pear tree against which to judge the many dwarfs. The Platonic model further illuminates Rousseau's strategy. We might say that earlier, when appealing to the superficiality of facial expression, Rousseau treated his readers as lovers of sights and sounds; he now treats them as philosophers. But his treatment highlights the ambiguous status of Emile as a model: he is a particular that points to the form, but he is not the form itself. That is, Rousseau presents Emile as a standard against which his readers can judge their own particular lives and children and ideas about what is natural and possible for human beings, but Emile is a particular. He is not a universal rule that can be applied objectively. This in-betweenness is inherent in the very nature of judging, which by definition functions in the absence of a universal rule or precept. Emile must be a particular so that readers can see him, for they will not be moved by an abstraction (just as Emile will not be moved by lectures about suffering, only by images of suffering). Rousseau is thus critical of those who "persist in imagining only what they see" (253; 4:549). And yet he is at pains to avoid severing the imaginary from the reality before our eyes.

Having presented us with a particular, how can Rousseau prove the universal validity of his particular? He makes us "see" Emile as a young boy, and as a result we cannot help but read into him all of our expectations about young boys. So even as Rousseau makes us see Emile, he must simultaneously make his pupil difficult to see (or "alien" to his readers' eyes), or else we will either conform him to our prejudices or consign him to "the land of chimeras" (253; 4:549). This is the challenge for any author who wishes to be understood and therefore speaks in the prevailing vocabulary, but with the goal of transforming the prevailing vocabulary. Emile must be recognizably human but at the same time alter our sense of what it means to be human. It is by treading this fine line between the actual and the chimerical that Rousseau hopes to sensitize his readers to see the real in the ideal and the ideal in the real. It is in that space, which neither attaches itself to some abstract criterion of validity nor collapses into mere opinion, that judgment operates.

5

PIETY AND AUTHORITY

It is especially in matters of religion that opinion triumphs. (*E*, 260; 4:558)

We began with a political problem: while Rousseau's political theory holds out the promise of genuine democratic freedom, the means by which he proposes to secure this freedom seems to undermine that very freedom at its core. In his discussion of religion in book IV of *Emile*, this problem resurfaces in a new register. On the one hand, Rousseau purports to offer the Savoyard Vicar's profession of faith as a "model for how to reason with one's pupil," with a view to encouraging the pupil to form his own judgments in matters of faith rather than accept received dogmas. On the other hand, as many commentators have noted, despite this characterization of the Vicar as a radically independent thinker, his profession of faith ultimately amounts to a rather conservative teaching in the service of conventional morality. Peter Emberley, for example, suggests that the Vicar's speech functions as a noble lie meant to "inspire virtue by portraying a simulacrum of virtue, dazzling in its charm and beauty and capable of alluring men away from vice."[1] Allan Bloom seems to confirm this assessment in claiming that the Vicar's teaching "is too conventional to satisfy anyone who thinks."[2] If this is correct, then Rousseau subverts independent judgment even as he extols its importance, by deploying a salutary illusion designed not to provoke thought but to condition a "correct" response.

But even if we take Rousseau's praise of the Vicar at face value and focus on the Vicar's reliance on his inner conscience rather than external influences, this difficulty is not resolved but only deferred. Others have addressed the question of whether Rousseau held the views that the Vicar expounds and intended them to stand as his own statement of faith.[3] That is not my purpose here, for Rousseau tells us that he has transcribed the profession of faith "not as a rule for the sentiments that one ought to follow in religious matters, but as an example of the way one can reason with one's pupil in order not to diverge from the method I have tried to establish" (313; 4:635). Of course, this distinction between reason and sentiment is precisely the problem of the profession of faith. Moreover, earlier in book IV, in the context of Emile's education in pity, Rousseau says that following his method means following the spirit of that method, and that this spirit cannot be reduced to any single example. We must look beyond the Vicar's words, then, to discern the spirit of Rousseau's method here.

To that end, it is worth noting that there are two revelatory moments in book IV: the Vicar reveals himself to the young Jean-Jacques, and the tutor (the adult Jean-Jacques, though there is narrative slippage here) reveals himself to Emile. In addition to these two models, Rousseau gives us two examples of students responding to the revelation. Ultimately, we learn more about Rousseau's position on cultivating independent judgment in the face of absolute claims of authority from the interaction between the two interlocutors in each scene (and from comparing the two scenes) than from the Vicar's profession of faith alone. This is yet another instance in which Rousseau offers two examples or occasions for a particular lesson and requires a greater exercise of independent judgment in the second round.

Moreover, the profession itself is not one uninterrupted speech but rather two, separated by a brief interlude. That this famous speech has two distinct parts is not surprising, given the many divisions (and subdivisions) in *Emile* that I have already discussed. The task is to reflect on how the two parts work together. The first part concentrates on the interior dimension of the Vicar's religious experience, and the second on the external manifestations—creeds, doctrines, and so on. In the first part, the Vicar disputes the notion that reason can settle theological questions. Reason can take him as far as natural religion and no further. "I have done what I could to attain the truth, but its source is too elevated. If the strength for going further is lacking to me, of what can I be guilty? It is up to the truth to come nearer" (294; 4:606).

In the second part, reason resurfaces when the Vicar appeals to it in order to challenge revelation and doctrinal dogmatism. Reason ultimately leaves us with no solid basis for making, and acting on, moral decisions, for it leaves the most serious questions too open. At the same time, the dogmatic and parochial quality of organized religion is too closed. It supports morality but discourages thinking. The Vicar seeks a middle ground between these two poles. "Proud philosophy leads to freethinking as blind devoutness leads to fanaticism. Avoid these extremes" (313; 4:633–34). Although it has been said that Rousseau replaces reason with sentiment, I argue that in book IV he presents reason and sentiment as necessarily connected in the activity of judging for oneself what and how one ought to believe. Just as the earlier discussion of pity raised the question of how one might be moved by the suffering of others and yet remain free, Rousseau's treatment of religious education explores the question of how one might be both piously devout and genuinely free.

Living under the empire of opinion, most human beings base their own existence on the judgments of others. Emile's education has been an effort to avoid this subjection so that he may remain free from that kind of servility. Not surprisingly, then, when it comes to matters of faith, Rousseau insists that his pupil is not to be indoctrinated into a particular religious tradition but rather put in a position to exercise independent judgment. Whereas most children are raised, by accident of birth, in whatever religious tradition their parents happen to subscribe to, this is not an option for Emile—not only because he is an orphan but because he is not raised to accept anything on the basis of received tradition or authority.

> But we who pretend to shake off the yoke of opinion in everything, we who want to grant nothing to authority, we who want to teach nothing to our Emile which he could not learn by himself in every country, in what religion shall we raise him? To what sect shall we join the man of nature? The answer is quite simple, it seems to me. We shall join him to neither this one nor that one, but we shall put him in a position to choose the one to which the best use of his reason ought to lead him. (260; 4:558)

Ultimately, however, Rousseau suggests that the answer is not quite so simple—or, rather, that the goal is simple enough to identify, but challenging to reach. What does it take to inhabit such a position? How does one arrive there? Rousseau is quite clear about what such an education should *not* be. He is, for example, highly critical of Locke's approach to religious education in early childhood, because it assumes that children have the capacity for abstract thought, which Rousseau denies. "Locke wants one to begin by the study of spirits and later go on to that of bodies. This method is that of superstition, of prejudices, and of error" (255; 4:551). To a child's mind, a spirit can "cry out, speak, flutter, and make noise." In other words, children imagine a spirit as a body. This is not an innocent mistake that is easily corrected with age but a foundation for future prejudice and error of the sort that is susceptible to exploitation and corruption. "As soon as people are accustomed to say words without understanding them, it is easy to make them say whatever one wants" (256; 4:552). Thus Emile, who is educated to think independently of opinion and prejudice, will have no religious instruction until he is much older than is typical. Even at fifteen, we are told, Emile "did not know whether he had a soul" (257; 4:554).

The proper age for religious instruction should, Rousseau insists, be determined by the developmental pace of the pupil's capacity for abstract thought. He assures us that Emile will arrive at abstract questions on his own, "when the progress of his enlightenment leads his researches in that direction" (259; 4:557). But Rousseau never explains how an inclination toward such speculation might naturally arise. Indeed, he emphasizes how difficult it must be for human beings to ascend from sensible objects to abstractions, since we provide "almost no hold" for abstract notions:

> To arrive at them we must either separate ourselves from the body—to which we are so strongly attached—or make a gradual and slow climb from object to object, or, finally, clear the gap rapidly and almost at a leap, by a giant step upward of which childhood is not capable and for which even men need many rungs especially made for them. The first abstract idea is the first of these rungs, but I have great difficulty in seeing how anyone got it into his head to construct it. (255; 4:551)

On the one hand, then, Rousseau rejects the notion that children should be exposed to religious instruction from an early age in the hope of cementing their piety as they mature; instead, they must be allowed to follow their own developing inclination to raise the questions to which religion offers answers. On the other hand, he suggests that it is highly unlikely that a child raised according to nature, who is primarily a physical being, will arrive at such a point independently. When forced by his own argument to address the question of where religious sensibility comes from, Rousseau draws a direct connection between one's appreciation of the beauty of nature (which causes one to wonder about its author) and the turn toward the divine. But he also raises doubts as to whether Emile would make this connection, asking, for example, "how can [Emile] be touched by the beauty of nature's spectacle, if he does not know the hand responsible for adorning it?" (169; 4:432). It appears that while an appreciation of nature's beauty is necessary to develop an appreciation of divine authorship, the reverse is also the case. Where to begin?

Rousseau suggests that the experience most likely to move someone to wonder about its creator is the experience of being in love, which disposes one to see nature in romantic terms and thus to marvel at its beauty. The Savoyard Vicar's description of how he can ascend rationally to a conception of natural religion thus applies only to someone who, like himself, has experienced erotic love, not an innocent like Emile. One might wonder, then, how it is that Emile's mind might, of its own accord, turn in the direction of theological speculation, having never heard any discussion of God, and having never been in love.

Allan Bloom notes this difficulty as well. "But how can a purely sensual being such as man even have abstract thoughts? Rousseau presents the movement from sensibility or sensuality to abstract thought as a kind of miracle."[4] Clearly, the advent of puberty introduces sensual longings, but Rousseau insists that these changes remain on a physical level, a far cry from the erotic sensibility necessary to ignite a divine quest. "A long restlessness precedes the first desires; a long ignorance puts them off the track. One desires without knowing what" (220; 4:502).[5] We are told that Emile must be educated in compassion and in religion before he receives an erotic education and develops the kind of imagination that might appreciate the beauty of nature. He is therefore still very much a physical being when Rousseau introduces the subject of religion, and not likely to raise the kinds of questions that would give rise to thoughts about God. This is perhaps one reason why we do not witness this important moment in Emile's education.[6] Instead, Rousseau recalls a story about his own religious education, that is, the education of one who had already been exposed to many dogmas and religious disputes (as well as many sexual encounters). But we are given no explanation or illustration of how to begin a religious education ex nihilo.

It is in the context of this larger, vexing question about the "natural" progression of the capacity for theological speculation that Rousseau turns to the subject of religious belief and practice. In other words, his discussion is driven not only by the question of what to teach a child about the divine but also by the question of how human beings move from the particular to the abstract. If Emile is to be made to love the highest things—that is, if he is to be able to judge on the basis of anything other than vulgar utility—this issue must be addressed. And insofar as Emile is to be more than a mere product of his conditioning—if he is to be genuinely free—Rousseau's exploration of this issue necessarily entails the question of what it means to make one's standard of judgment one's own.

Reasoning About the Limits of Reason

The profession of faith offers an account of how one might be moved to reflect on the question of the divine in a way that accords with our natural independence, but it begins from an altogether different beginning point than that represented by Emile. The profession concerns the education and conversion of the Savoyard Vicar, whose first encounter with religion did not grow out of an experience of the beauty of nature but came in the form of the traditional religious education that he received as a young boy. The Vicar describes how he first received a faulty religious education and was then saved from its ill effects. His ascension of the rungs of the ladder of natural theological speculation comes only after a more parochial religious education. He moves not from the absence of an idea of God to some particular idea of God but from a parochial idea of God to a new understanding of God as reflected in nature. Thus the profession does not answer Rousseau's question about how one constructs the first rung on the ladder of human inquiry into the divine. Rather, it suggests (like the discussion of education in general in book I) that a beginning must be made before a beginning can be made. Moreover, we are told, the Vicar had fallen away from the church; his predilection for unmarried girls had left him in ruin. His ascent follows a descent, and this fact about him conditions his reasoning about the limits of reason.

The profession of faith opens with an account of how the Vicar arrived at his present condition. Having fallen into "that frame of mind of uncertainty and doubt that Descartes demands in the quest for truth" (267; 4:567), the Vicar first turns to the philosophers for answers, but he finds only vain posturing and disputation. Like Descartes, he resolves to turn to his natural inner light to settle his doubts and ascertain the truth. What he means by "inner light," however, is complex, and a better understanding of this concept will in turn clarify the relationship between sentiment and reason in Rousseau's thought.

Like Descartes's *Discourse on Method*, the profession of faith begins with an account of the author's formal education and his decision to turn away from it in order to reason independently. Both texts employ metaphors of illumination extensively. Both profess to offer a method of right reasoning, and each method yields four principles. But while the Vicar begins where Descartes begins ("in that frame of mind of uncertainty and doubt that Descartes demands in the quest for truth"), he then continues in a sharply different direction. Descartes's first principle is that he will accept nothing as true that does not present itself to his own mind as clearly true. Rousseau's Vicar, by contrast, vows "to accept as evident all knowledge to which in the sincerity of my heart I cannot refuse my consent" (270; 4:570). His formulation may invite us to draw a stark contrast between the two philosophers: Descartes knows he exists because he thinks; Rousseau knows he exists because he feels. However, before accepting this characterization, we must consider carefully what, exactly, Rousseau means by the notion of "sincerity," since it is on this that the distinction between them turns.

Certainly, for Rousseau, sincerity stems from conscience, and conscience is something felt. As a general rule, the Vicar states that he will yield to conscience rather than to reason. But as soon as he brings this rule to bear on the particular task of questioning his own sensations, he is led to affirm that his "rule" of "yielding to conscience more than reason is confirmed by reason itself" (272; 4:572). Is this an abdication on the part of reason, or is reason the ultimate arbiter? As the Vicar goes on to describe the proper functioning of the *lumière naturelle,* he seems to require not that sentiment disregard reason but that reason and sentiment operate in tandem. At every turn, as he articulates each article of faith, the Vicar brings both reason and sentiment to bear on his conclusions. The limits of reason are always stressed, but reason is always brought to bear upon the question at hand. In justifying his view of the immortality of the soul, for example, the Vicar acknowledges that this view is based on his presumption that moral order, which does not exist in a world in which the unjust prosper, must be restored in some form of an afterlife. The alternative—the possibility that the unjust prosper and go unpunished—is unbearable to him. He finds the presumption of an afterlife consoling. But then how can his presumption be distinguished from mere prejudice, or wishful thinking? "Since this presumption consoles me *and contains nothing unreasonable,* why would I be afraid of yielding to it?" (283; 4:590, emphasis added). Similarly, his first article of faith, which posits that matter is moved by will, "contains nothing repugnant to reason" (274; 4:576–77). Reason cannot be relied upon to settle the matter, or to provide an unshakable metaphysical foundation. Since it cannot apprehend the whole, it cannot confirm the ultimate truth of the Vicar's sentiments. However, it still retains veto power, although it cannot provide positive standards on its own.

After laying out his four articles of faith, the Vicar concludes that he has deduced all that he needs to know "from the impression of sensible objects and from the inner sentiment that leads me to judge of causes according to my natural lights" (286; 4:594). Whereas Descartes's inquiry into the question of God's existence begins with his decision to close his eyes and ears, here the inner sentiment is stimulated by sensory input. The Vicar makes his profession while beholding a beautiful natural landscape. But beauty, and the sentiments it arouses, is only part of the story. The inner sentiment *motivates* the process of right reasoning (i.e., according to one's natural lights); it *leads* the Vicar to judge but is not itself sufficient for judging well. The Vicar opens not only his eyes and heart but his intellect as well. "The greatest ideas of the divinity come to us from reason alone. View the spectacle of nature; hear the inner voice" (295; 4:607). The senses, conscience, and reason are all in play.

What Descartes takes as axiomatic (that he is persuaded by reason) Rousseau sees as having an origin. We might say that the profession of faith (like Rousseau, throughout *Emile*) seeks to reveal the "backstage" workings of reason—the cords and pulleys. This parallels Rousseau's political critique of Hobbes and others who take civil man, as a static concept, to be the beginning point of an inquiry into human nature. Rousseau seeks to show the movement that produces the condition from which his predecessors begin, to show the coming into being of their point of origin. Whereas, in the *Second Discourse*, he demonstrates that civil man (with his vanity-driven rationality) has an origin, in the profession and throughout *Emile* he demonstrates that the proper exercise of reason also has an "origin" of sorts (although he vacillates on the question of whether reason or conscience is analytically and experientially prior). Thus Rousseau, like Descartes, can argue that truth claims ought not to be accepted by any authority other than the inner light of the individual, and yet he can also maintain that the inner sentiment is fundamental to the "inner light," which is complex rather than narrowly rational.

Specifically, the Vicar seems to be asking: why is it that I am moved to affirm certain arguments and not others? Here we can detect Rousseau's most serious challenge to Descartes, who seeks to expunge the messy complexity of being human for the sake of achieving certainty. As many of his careful interpreters have noted, in his works Descartes stops short of explaining exactly how or why one is moved to affirm as true the clear and distinct ideas apprehended by the intellect. Judgment, for Descartes, is an act of will, which affirms (or denies) the ideational content that the understanding supplies.[7] Descartes affirms as true any perception that is both clear (present and accessible to the attentive mind) and distinct (sharply distinguished from all other perceptions). The challenge lies in explaining the move Descartes makes from seeing something distinctly to affirming it as true. Moreover, he waffles on the question of whether the will *automatically* affirms clear and distinct ideas. He holds that he cannot help but affirm clear and distinct ideas. Freedom of the will requires that assent not be automatic, but at the same time Descartes suggests that clear and distinct ideas virtually *compel* assent. The operation of such affirmation has been much discussed, with some, such as Bernard Williams, concluding that Descartes's "theory of assent itself requires a step which cancels out the notion of assent."[8]

The most pointed, explicit critique of Descartes in *Emile* is that he "formed heaven and earth with dice, but he was not able to give the first push to these dice or to put his centrifugal force in action without the aid of a rotary motion. . . . Let Descartes tell us what physical law made his vortices turn" (273; 4:575). Although this criticism centers specifically on Descartes's failure to provide an account of the motion of the universe, it also applies to his failure to provide an adequate account of the motion of the soul as it seeks to understand the universe it inhabits. For example, in the preface to the *Meditations*, Descartes states that he wishes to be read only by those who have the ability and desire to meditate seriously with him.[9] He indicates that it is a demanding and laborious process. He does not, however, engage the question of how one is moved to desire to meditate as he does. How is this ability developed? Where does this desire come from? The ability is presumably developed by his *Discourse on Method*, which offers a model of "right reasoning." The origin of the desire to meditate seriously on serious issues, however, is more ambiguous. Descartes says of himself in the first part of the *Discourse* that he "always had an especially great desire to distinguish the true from the false."[10] To Rousseau, who was acutely aware of how this desire can be corrupted by amour-propre and degenerate into the desire to appear to know rather than actually know, Descartes's assumptions about the pre-given quality of this desire would have to seem insufficient. From the perspective of *Emile*, Descartes seems to forget the origins of his own questions.[11]

Descartes distinguishes between two kinds of motion: the kind linked with the body (the animal spirits moving us, discussed in the *Passions*), and the kind that is self-generated by the nature of the will itself. If the will allows itself to be moved erroneously, that is a problem, but at the same time it must be moved by clear and distinct ideas. The conditions under which this can happen, in Descartes's presentation, are conditions of stillness: a quelling of turmoil, of the mind. Thus Descartes focuses on removing the obstacles to the proper exercise of reason (prejudice, sensation); he offers, in other words, a negative program. He does not address explicitly the positive requisites of the correct motivation of the will in affirming truth.

Indirectly, then, the "positive" education of book IV of *Emile* supplements not only Rousseau's own "negative" education in books I–III but also what Rousseau sees as Descartes's merely negative education. Both philosophers seek to root out the sources of the corruption of reason. But whereas Descartes focuses on what gets in the way of seeing the truth, Rousseau also concerns himself with what moves one toward seeing the truth (as opposed to staying still). As the Vicar points out, human beings are not made to remain in the turmoil of doubt. In his view, one either lapses back into old opinions out of laziness or moves toward the truth. Whence the will—the fortitude—to move forward? More precisely, whence the desire that Descartes requires of his reader in the preface to the *Meditations*? "I should never advise anyone to read it excepting those who desire to meditate seriously with me, and who can detach their minds from affairs of sense, and deliver themselves entirely from every sort of prejudice."[12] Descartes believes that prejudices get in the way of the proper exercise of reason; but by characterizing his *Discourse on Method* as a story or "fable,"[13] he implies a need to prejudice his readers in favor of reason. Either he too understands the necessity of fables, or he exemplifies the philosophical practice that Nietzsche describes as bad faith (i.e., assuming that reason is autonomous) and demands that we renounce in the name of intellectual honesty. Rousseau's attempt to articulate a complex dynamic between reason and sentiment is less vulnerable to this charge inasmuch as it does not treat reason as simply autonomous. Neither does it exhibit the countertendency to treat reason as thoroughly pernicious or simply irrelevant.

At stake in the Vicar's profession of faith is ultimately the motion of the soul, and on this point Rousseau takes his bearings not only from Descartes but also from Plato—specifically from the *Phaedrus*, a dialogue that takes place in a beautiful natural setting that similarly sets the discussion in motion. And just as the young Jean-Jacques says to the Vicar at the end of the first part of his speech, "You have told me only half of what I must know" (294; 4:606), the young Phaedrus similarly complains when Socrates stops midway through his first speech.[14]

Socrates responds to Phaedrus's protests with his "palinode," a speech in which the soul is depicted as a combination of two horses and a charioteer. The dynamic between the passionate dark horse and the rational white horse is what produces the motion of the soul. Socrates describes an arduous process that involves both straining toward the beloved and retreating in a protracted tug-of-war between the parts of the soul. This account is more suggestive of self-motion, but it is hardly a smooth and steady motion. Indeed, all motion is initiated by the unruly passionate horse, whose eager pursuit of the beloved is what makes it possible for the lover to get a good look at the beloved's beauty. The dark horse is so insistent that the charioteer and white horse end up "yielding and agreeing to do whatever is commanded" (*Phaedrus* 254b). Only at that point, after they approach the boy and gaze at his beautiful face, is the charioteer's memory carried toward the essence of the beautiful. Socrates's account of the lover's response to the beloved's face includes even more advancing and retreating, until "*at last* it actually happens that the lover's soul follows the darling with awe and a sense of shame" (254e, emphasis added). After the lover remains by the side of the beloved "over time," in the gymnasium and elsewhere, a spring gushes over him, and the waters enter into him and nourish his wings (255c–d). Both lover and beloved are altered and enriched by this experience, as the stream of love flows back and forth between them. Moreover, the unruly horse reemerges as a force to be reckoned with (255e–256a), and must be actively reined in by the noble horse and charioteer. "If these moderate forces prevail, the couple moves toward a regimented life and love of wisdom" (256a).

What is particularly striking in Socrates's description of the process of capturing the beloved is that all of this activity leads *toward* a love of wisdom, which turns out to be an effect as much as a cause. And the desire for the particular beloved, who is no longer conflated with the essential beauty of which he is a reminder, never disappears. The psychic disharmony that eros can induce in the soul—the struggle between the charioteer and horses, or reason and passion—while successfully managed, is never simply resolved into a static condition. Not only are both passion and reason necessary in Socrates's account, as for Rousseau, but even the dark horse seems amenable to reasoning. He grudgingly assents to the entreaties of the rational horse and charioteer that "the attempt should be deferred to another time" (254c). Contrast this image with Descartes's comment that in order to commence his process of right reasoning, he will first let his passions (like a wild horse) run their course until they are spent, and then his faculty of reason will take charge. What Descartes presents as a logical progression, Rousseau (with Plato) understands as a perpetual tension.

Because his goal is to counter the prevailing view that grounds all that is distinctively human in reason alone, the Vicar tends to stress the necessity of conscience to reason rather than the reverse. As Rousseau makes clear in the two *Discourses* and other works, reason is an insufficient ground for morality. His objection is motivated partly by his democratic sensibilities: he refuses to believe that a human being would have to be a philosopher before being a man. He also objects that what passes for reason tends to be merely the narrow calculation of self-interest. In the profession of faith he has the Vicar voice some of the implications of this tendency:

> It is said that everyone contributes to the public good for his own interest. But what then is the source of the just man's contributing to it to his prejudice? What is going to one's death for one's interest? No doubt, no one acts for anything other than for his good; but if there is not a moral good which must be taken into account, one will never explain by private interest anything but the action of the wicked. It is not even likely that anyone will attempt to go farther. (289; 4:599)

The Vicar's formulation calls to mind book II of Plato's *Republic*, where Glaucon asks Socrates to show him why one ought to be just (rather than simply seem just). As Glaucon sees it, all the persuasive arguments are on the side of injustice rather than justice. Yet Glaucon, who is able to articulate a persuasive argument in favor of injustice—an argument he finds so persuasive that he presents it as a model for Socrates to follow in praising justice—remains unpersuaded (he claims) by that very argument. His request (which motivates the rest of the argument of the *Republic*) that Socrates provide him with an argument to support what he wants to believe—that justice is good in itself—illustrates the Vicar's point. What can account for Glaucon's refusal to consider the question settled by the many persuasive arguments he has heard? At the end of the profession of faith, the Vicar refers to the central importance of the "hope of the just." It is this hope that motivates Glaucon and provides the motivation for rational inquiry into the question of justice. Without it, it is not "likely that anyone will attempt to go farther" than common opinion. But this hope is hardly a rational expectation, given the prevalence of injustice; it is something more akin to faith.

Reason and Sincerity

Rousseau's ideal of sincerity is often presented as privileging inner sentiment at the expense of reason. For example, Roger Masters states that Rousseau "ultimately replaces reason by sentiment."[15] Similarly, Melzer, in his analysis of what he terms Rousseau's "religion of sincerity," argues that the Vicar is "convinced of the inadequacy of reason," and therefore "replaces truth with sincerity as the ground for salvation."[16] Understanding inner sentiment as an alternative to reason—*replacing* reason—Melzer doubts its legitimacy as a foundation for religious belief. On this understanding of sincerity, the Vicar's arguments "make no serious attempt to distinguish the inner sentiment from a kind of wishful thinking."[17]

Without a doubt, the Vicar's speech emphasizes sincerity and inner sentiment (conscience), and it certainly strives to expose the inadequacy of human reason for settling theological disputes. But reason does not drop out of the Vicar's religious teaching altogether, displaced by sentiment. Rousseau's response to Descartes is, I have shown, much more complex than a simple argument for the opposite extreme. Just as the first part of book IV reveals a rational dimension of pity, the profession of faith reveals an intimate connection between inner sentiment and reason. In large part, the critique of reason in the profession is a critique of the vanity that tends to motivate its exercise. And just as there are healthy forms of amour-propre,[18] there is for Rousseau a correct method of reasoning about religious questions, one in which reason and sentiment function in a complex dynamic. Rather than simply privileging sentiment over reason, the Vicar's profession elaborates a more comprehensive model of reasoning in which the individual's reasoning leads him to appreciate the limits of his own reason and its dependence upon inner sentiment, which is in turn reinforced by reason. Reason and conscience, in the Vicar's presentation, presuppose, reinforce, and check each other.[19]

Whereas the first part of the profession of faith downplays the role of reason in matters of faith, in the second half of his speech the Vicar insists that faith should rest on one's own reason and not on the claims of authority. He scorns appeals to miracles, inspiration, and revelation and defends human reason against such appeals. He challenges *all* authoritative claims—even his own—as he seeks to restore reason to its rightful, limited role. He has shown that one's heart must be in the right place before one's mind can reason well; he now goes on to suggest that one can know whether one's heart is in the right place only by critically examining it by means of reason. Commentators tend to focus on the first part of this sequence—on the fact that Rousseau's psychology emphasizes the need for sentiment or passion to motivate reason, which can never act independently. The second part—which, paradoxically, identifies reason as critical to the proper development of that same motivation—tends to be overlooked.

One exception is Ronald Grimsley, who characterizes reason's role as helping us "to perceive and understand more clearly the object of our fundamental feeling."[20] Rousseau repeatedly stresses the necessity of reasoning about the objects of our sentiments, even in the context of Emile's education in pity, where he states that the "truth of sentiments depends in large part on the correctness of ideas" (227; 4:512). Rousseau echoes this claim in the stance that he himself takes in the preface to *Emile,* when he states that he distrusts his own sentiments (34; 4:242).

Even as the Vicar urges his young listener to seek the truth independently and "sincerely," he suggests that sincerity is achieved not by conscience (or inner sentiment) alone but by subjecting all that they have been taught by authority figures to the examination of both "conscience *and* reason" (297; 4:610, emphasis added). Thus Melzer is correct that the profession of faith espouses a religion of sincerity, but he underestimates the complexity of Rousseau's understanding of sincerity, which draws on the senses, conscience, *and* reason. Allan Bloom's reference to "sensitive reasoning" comes closer to capturing this complexity.[21] The term is promising, yet Bloom's analysis of the details of the Vicar's speech says little about how this rehabilitated reason remains a form of reason. Instead, in Bloom's presentation (as in Melzer's), the Vicar does little more than substitute feeling for thinking; Bloom describes the Vicar's method of reasoning as "the logic of the heart *rather than* the logic of the mind."[22] Similarly, Bloom characterizes conscience, which guides man's freedom, as a sentiment, a "felt" expression of the universal, or "generalized pity or compassion."[23] But, while conscience certainly is all of these things, its proper function entails a rational, reflective dimension.

Rationality is deemphasized in the Vicar's discussion of metaphysical questions in the first half of his speech precisely because it is in such matters that reason is most likely to prevail as an unquestioned final arbiter and thus to overstep what Rousseau sees as its proper bounds. This point is consistent with Rousseau's own remarks in several places to the effect that human reason cannot settle the most profound metaphysical questions. In this arena, the Vicar (perhaps too readily) accepts precepts that he finds comforting, as long as they contain nothing repugnant to reason. Although his profession of faith denies the possibility of a purely rational metaphysics, it is not thoroughly *anti*rational. In the second half of his speech, in which the Vicar addresses religious orders and practices, reason resumes a prominent role, because the discussion concerns a realm in which reason has not generally been allowed sufficient place—the realm of tradition, revelation, and dogma. Taking the two parts together, we see that the Vicar challenges the authority of *both* reason and tradition in order to make room for the exercise of independent judgment.[24] Part of what it means to exercise this judgment, however, is to acknowledge the Vicar's own partial dependence on these very things. That is, his attack on reason in the name of conscience relies on reason to check his inner sentiment, and his subsequent attack on organized religion culminates in the admonition to return to the religion of one's childhood. These are not contradictions but reflect Rousseau's understanding of the mutual interdependence of reason and sentiment in the exercise of judgment.

Still, the fact remains that the Vicar concludes by urging his young listener to return to the religion of his childhood and practice it with sincerity, which may leave us with the impression that ultimately the Vicar (and perhaps Rousseau, who certainly shared the Vicar's distrust of metaphysical speculation)[25] cares more about preserving conventional morality (while curbing fanaticism) than about encouraging independent judgment. His one correction of conventional religion strives to make it more tolerant of others on the grounds that all religions are equally dogmatic. One might argue that he challenges conventional authority only to capitulate to it in the end, albeit in a more gentle and tolerant form. This capitulation reflects, at least in part, the Vicar's discomfort in the face of metaphysical uncertainty. He seeks peace, unity. He seems willing to back off from rigorous intellectual scrutiny in order to preserve his own tranquility, as well as social tranquility, through the affirmation of conventional morality.

To the degree that this account accurately captures the Vicar's position, it suggests that the profession of faith—despite the reaction of Rousseau's contemporaries—is actually quite conservative. Peter Emberley has argued that the Vicar is much more conservative than Rousseau himself. Raising the question of what purpose, then, the Vicar's speech serves, Emberley argues that it offers a more palatable and realistic alternative to the radically independent perspective Rousseau attributes to Emile, which is not suitable for most individuals or societies.[26] The profession of faith, then, would be a digression from the "true" teaching of the work in which it appears, a second-best teaching that adds little or nothing to our understanding of the serious philosophical dimensions of *Emile*. Allan Bloom's remark that the Vicar's advice "is too conventional to satisfy anyone who thinks" would confirm such an assessment.[27]

Certainly, there is evidence to support this view. At times the Vicar recoils against the uncertainty that results from his critique of both revelation and reason, and tries to "annihilate" his reason. He preaches virtue to his fellows and strives to strengthen their faith in "the truly useful dogmas every man is obliged to believe" (309; 4:628). This support of "useful dogmas" may be taken to mean that the philosophical pursuit of truth is ultimately set aside for the sake of the people's moral health. "While waiting for greater enlightenment, let us protect public order" (310; 4:629). But, while he supports the notion of "useful" dogmas for the sake of public order, he arrives at this apparently conservative stance only by means of exposing those dogmas as just that—as ungrounded. He affirms them as socially necessary rather than as simply true. This is a radical departure from the *internal* (parochial) perspective of any sect, which claims an absoluteness that the profession affirms only *after* subjecting it to critical scrutiny. Thus if we take into account not only where the Vicar ends up but also how he gets there, we see that while the profession reinforces certain prevailing forms of authority, it *alters the terms on which that authority is legitimated*—a simultaneously conservative and radical project. In making clear the reasons why religious teaching and public order ought to be protected, the profession of faith supports belief systems that, on their own terms, discourage questioning and reflection, and at the same time teaches that questioning and reflection are necessary to supporting them properly and sincerely. If we take seriously the Vicar's critique of both "blind devoutness" and "proud philosophy," then there must be some difference between blind devoutness and practicing one's inherited religion with sincerity.

If I am correct that for Rousseau sincerity requires making an effort to examine one's beliefs in light of both conscience and reason, then the advice to "return" to one's father's religion is less conservative than it seems. It calls for another version of the demand made at the end of book II: that a truly mature adult (as opposed to the childish civil man) must learn to see as a child sees. Is it possible to do so without becoming child*ish?* Rousseau affirms that it *is* possible and helps us to better understand the distinction. Making a conscious choice to return to the religion of one's childhood is fundamentally different from never leaving at all, never putting oneself in a position to choose. In the *Second Discourse*'s dedication to Geneva, Rousseau claims that his status as one who has fallen away is precisely what enables him to see clearly what the Genevans ought to do to preserve the goodness of their political order. If he could choose his birthplace, he would choose Geneva. This is the result of neither ingrained prejudice nor purely rational deliberation, but is generated by a form of deliberation in which both his heart and his head are engaged. That his heart is engaged in this process does not, in Rousseau's view, detract from its being deliberative; rather, it animates that deliberation.

The Vicar's abandonment of theoretical speculation does not reduce his position to "blind devoutness." Neither is his concluding admonition to "know how to be ignorant" (313; 4:633) an affirmation of unexamined prejudice; it entails making a conscious choice, after surveying the options, to return to a childhood religion and practice it with sincerity. The ultimate goal, then, seems to be a middle ground that partakes of piety as well as philosophy. The interesting question is not which side Rousseau finally chooses (since this would mean ignoring the attention he gives to the opposite extreme) but how he recasts the alternatives. One of his goals is to curb fanaticism, which he seeks to achieve not by making people less devout but rather more devout, or devout in a different, deeper way. At the opposite pole, his goal is to curb "freethinking philosophy," which threatens morals, not by annihilating philosophy per se but by reclaiming it on new terms. Throughout *Emile*, the idea of learning how to be ignorant is an admonition not to retreat but to grow. It is not a turning away from philosophy but a rehabilitation of philosophy to make it more Socratic, less dogmatic. The relationship between these two dimensions of the Vicar's teaching is similar to the relationship (and tension) between the Socrates of the *Apology* (questioning all authority) and the Socrates of the *Crito* (defending the authority of the law). One is not simply subsumable by the other.

I do not deny that, on one level, the profession of faith advocates conventional morality, but my reading suggests that this is not its only, or even its primary, function. The profession operates on multiple levels, and the Vicar is not ultimately Rousseau's model of judgment with regard to matters of faith. All that the Vicar ultimately blots out for himself in his effort to "annihilate" his reason is not blotted out for the reader. Just as the lessons of *Emile* cannot be reduced to the figure of Emile, the teaching of the profession cannot be reduced to the figure of the Vicar; he does more to stimulate the proper reflective attitude than to exemplify it. Recall Rousseau's claim that he presents the speech as a model of *how* to reason with one's pupil. The Vicar invites his young interlocutor to judge him: "I have told you my reasons for doubting and for believing. Now it is for you to judge" (310; 4:630). The Vicar emphasizes repeatedly that his young listener must not accept his profession of faith unquestioningly but must make his own judgment. The appeal seems to work: at the end of the Vicar's first speech Rousseau tells us, "He was moved, and so was I. I believed I was hearing the divine Orpheus sing the first hymns and teaching men the worship of the gods. Nevertheless I saw a multitude of objections to make to him" (294; 4:606). The Vicar is as moving as Orpheus (the subject of the illustration for book IV), whose music moved men and even rocks and trees, and yet his young listener can see "a multitude of objections." In the interaction of the two characters, and in the doubleness of the response the Vicar elicits, Rousseau conveys the complexity of his understanding of the proper response to any "profession" or revelation. One can be moved but simultaneously reflect on one's experience of being moved. This is the only way that human beings—who are not unmoved movers—can achieve self-motion. We do not have to achieve godlike autonomy in order to be free. We can be human—vulnerable, needy, incomplete—and still in some sense free.

Emile and the Author of His Being

I have suggested that the profession of faith raises the question of how to be both pious and free. I have also noted the significance of Emile's displacement by the young Jean-Jacques and have raised the question of how the exchange between the flawed Vicar and the flawed young man might be applicable to the relationship between the (seemingly) perfectly wise tutor and the perfectly innocent Emile. In the exchange between Emile and the tutor that immediately follows the profession of faith, in which the tutor reveals himself to Emile as the "author" of his education, these two questions come together with striking force.[28] In a different sort of profession or revelation, Emile learns about the author of *his* being, who is Jean-Jacques, and the question of whether he is going to be merely obedient and virtuous or genuinely free takes center stage.

Although the tutor has delayed the development of Emile's sexuality as long as possible, "the true moment of nature comes at last. It must come. Since man must die, he must reproduce in order that the species may endure" (316; 4:639). Before delving into the details of how to manage the pupil's sexual longings, Rousseau notes that because the pupil is no longer a child, the educator must speak to him in a new way. "When, by the signs of which I have spoken, you have a presentiment of the critical moment, instantly abandon your old tone with him forever" (316; 4:639). Rousseau's account of how this new tone ought to differ from the old one draws on the language of freedom and the language of subjection at once. On the one hand, the character of the educator's authority must change. To this point, the tutor has governed Emile's behavior by manipulation. "He had to be constrained or deceived in order to obey you" (316; 4:639). Such measures are unsuitable for a pupil on the threshold of adulthood. At the same time, Rousseau insists, this transition is so fraught with peril that complete abdication of the educator's authority is unthinkable. A young man flooded with intense new passions is in no condition to be left to himself; this is the moment "when he least knows how to conduct himself, and when he makes the greatest slips" (316; 4:639). Yet precisely because the pupil is under the influence of such strong passions, it is impossible to exert any direct control over him. The educator is thus caught between the equally problematic alternatives of attempting (and probably failing) to exercise direct control over the pupil and exercising no control at all—as Rousseau puts it, one can be a tyrant or an accomplice. Both approaches are doomed to fail.

Thus a new kind of education is needed in order to move educator and pupil beyond this impasse. This particular transition, like so many other episodes in *Emile*, has two parts. That is, Rousseau gives two responses to the crisis of authority generated by this stage of adolescence. On the one hand, he explains that because the teacher cannot reason with his pupil at this stage, he must work with the language of the heart. He appeals to the eloquence of the ancients, who knew how to use "the language of signs" to capture the imaginations of their peoples in order to secure their obedience indirectly. Moderns, Rousseau laments, "no longer have a hold over one another except by force or by self-interest" (321; 4:645). The sublimation of Emile's sexual longing must be accomplished, then, by working through his imagination to orient his longing properly. Rather than stifle the imagination, the goal earlier in childhood, the tutor now seeks to direct it. Thus without directly constraining or deceiving his pupil, the tutor can nevertheless exert tremendous influence over him. Direct rule is replaced by indirect rule; this might be characterized as either Rousseau's genius or his danger, depending upon one's point of view. From either perspective, Emile's autonomy is in some significant sense compromised.

Despite these divergent assessments of the import of Rousseau's turn to indirect rule, what both perspectives overlook or downplay is that there is a second dimension to Rousseau's response to the "tyrant versus accomplice" impasse. He not only draws upon the ancient mode of deploying signs to enchant his pupil in new ways; he also suggests that a form of disenchantment is appropriate.

> Surrounded by ever growing perils, [Emile] is going to get away from me no matter what I do. At the first occasion—and this occasion will not be slow in arising—he is going to follow the blind instinct of the senses. The odds are a thousand to one that he is going to be ruined. I have reflected on men's morals too much not to see the invincible influence of

this first moment on the rest of his life. If I dissimulate and pretend to see nothing, he takes advantage of my weakness. Believing he deceives me, he despises me, and I am the accomplice of his ruin. If I try to straighten him out, it is too late; he does not listen to me anymore. . . . Therefore I have only one reasonable course to take—to make him accountable to himself for his actions, to protect him at least from the surprises of error, and to show him openly the perils by which he is surrounded. Up to now I have stopped him by his ignorance; now he has to be stopped by his enlightenment. (317–18; 4:640–41)

To be sure, this "enlightenment" should not take the form of dry speeches; there is still a role for the ancient language of signs. Moreover, the revelation ought to have the effect of establishing an equality of sorts between the tutor and pupil. The tutor must become the pupil's confidant. This will allow him to maintain some influence—the influence of friendship rather than of an authority figure. This can be achieved only if the tutor refrains from scolding or pulling rank. "You can be sure that if the child fears neither a sermon nor a reprimand on your part, he will always tell you everything" (319; 4:642). And such openness is closely linked with innocence—or, at least, secrecy and shame are linked with corruption. We should recall that in book I Rousseau insisted that an educator should be as young as a wise man can be, so as to create the smallest possible age gap between teacher and pupil. This reflects Rousseau's concern for equality and his ambivalence about the exercise of authority. Yet, as we have seen, the real gap between pupil and teacher is vast insofar as the tutor is virtually omniscient, and the pupil thoroughly innocent. Initially, then, the insistence on some semblance of equality was a rather empty gesture. Now, however, Rousseau intimates that a more substantive equality is possible. Instead of striving to bring the tutor down to the level of the pupil (if only in age), he seeks to elevate the pupil. Perhaps Rousseau sees a genuine, self-conscious, mature freedom as indeed possible.

What, then, is the relationship between this call for candor and enlightenment, on the one hand, and the call for charming language to capture the imagination, on the other? Does Rousseau gesture toward the possibility of genuine, self-conscious freedom and at the same time sacrifice that freedom in favor of the more secure course of manipulating the passions and imagination? Or can these two impulses be reconciled in some way? I think that they can, and that Rousseau's commitment to freedom is not sacrificed for the sake of virtue. To see this requires that we attend to Rousseau's language as he moves from one discussion to the other. After claiming that Emile must be "stopped by his enlightenment" and explaining the need to become the pupil's confidant, Rousseau tells his readers that this does not entail a single conversation "held at random," as they might erroneously conclude, for "what one says means nothing if one has not prepared the moment for saying it" (319; 4:643). Once again, Rousseau distinguishes between the lesson to be imparted and the preparation required for the lesson to take effect, preparation in which the imagination plays a vital role. But the lesson itself cannot be reduced to the response elicited by the manipulation of imagination and thereby the passions. Rousseau compares Emile at this fragile stage to a "somnambulist, wandering during his slumber," who, "in the slumber of ignorance, escapes perils that he does not perceive." "If I awaken him with a start," Rousseau adds, "he is lost. Let us first try to get him away from the precipice; and then we shall awaken him" (319–20; 4:643).

Thus, while it is tempting to conclude that Emile is moving not toward greater freedom but toward more deeply internalized dependence on his tutor—one that *appears* as independence precisely because it is so deeply internalized—this internalized dependence, achieved through manipulation of the passions by means of the imagination, is only half of the story. "I shall *begin* by moving his imagination," says Rousseau (323; 4:648, emphasis added). Initially, the tutor appeals exclusively to Emile's sentiment rather than his reason—that is, he appeals to Emile's sentimental attachment to his tutor and lifelong friend. He also appeals to divine authority, bringing "the Eternal Being, who is the Author of nature, to testify" to the truth of his speech and taking him "as judge between Emile and me" (323; 4:648). Revealing all that he has done for Emile over the course of his life, the tutor professes his unwavering attachment to his pupil and his deep investment in Emile's choices. He tells Emile that there is no conflict between his own interest and the young man's happiness—the two coincide in a beguiling image of perfect wholeness and harmony. The goal is to touch Emile deeply, in order to move him to take his commitment to obeying the tutor seriously. The tutor goes on to claim that if Emile's education proves to be a failure, the tutor's life's work will be for naught. Shedding tears, he tells Emile, "If you frustrate my hopes, you are robbing me of twenty years of my life, and you are causing the unhappiness of my old age" (323; 4:649).

Naturally, Emile is moved, and he responds by pledging eternal obedience. "I want to obey your laws; I want to do so always. This is my steadfast will" (325; 4:651–52). Unlike the young fugitive who interrupts the Vicar and sees a multitude of objections to his profession of faith, Emile does not even hesitate when confronted by his tutor's revelation. Rousseau indicates, however, that Emile's response is insufficient. Immediately following Emile's profession of undying obedience, the tutor admonishes him. "Young man, you make difficult commitments lightly. You would have to know what they mean in order to have the right to undertake them. . . . Take your time and give me mine for thinking about it." He then explains to Emile how to go about such reflection. "You are in a position to see the motives of my conduct in all things. To do so, you have only to wait until you are calm. Always begin by obeying, and then ask me for an account of my orders. I shall be ready to give you a reason for them as soon as you are in a position to understand me, and I shall never be afraid of taking you as the judge between you and me" (326; 4:652–53). Once again, Rousseau suggests that even a *correctly* passionate response must be subjected to the critical reflection of reason. We see a clear transition from God as the judge (which amounts to deferring to authority) to Emile as the judge— that is, to the ideal of becoming one's own judge.

Thus, while the first step is to begin by moving the pupil's imagination, this is *only* the first step. The tutor demands more than blind obedience from Emile; he demands meaningful consent, or obedience grounded in full and conscious understanding of what is at stake. This parallels the Vicar's advice to return to the religion of one's childhood in full appreciation of its virtues and limitations. The two parts of the tutor's speech parallel the two parts of the Vicar's profession of faith inasmuch as the first appeals to emotion rather than to reason, whereas the second restores the critical role of reason. This pattern, repeated throughout *Emile*, suggests that only when the pupil has been brought to the first point can the next step be taken. And it *must* be taken; Emile's pledge of eternal obedience does not bode well for the possibility of self-rule. If his education were to end here, we might be tempted to conclude, with Ruth Grant, that "in Rousseau's view self-consciousness is simply not a necessary requirement for freedom. Rather, through manipulation and deception, freedom and virtue together are purchased at the price of a highly developed rational self-consciousness."[29] Insofar as Emile might govern himself at all (rather than operate on automatic pilot, so to speak, thoroughly determined by his education), his activity is purely negative: to conserve, to prevent change, to maintain stasis. He may know *what* he is and *how* to preserve it, but unless he knows *why* he should do so, he is not fully choosing to be himself.

Emile fails to question the image that is revealed to him even after the tutor tells him that he must. The tutor's revelation to Emile of the "cords and pulleys" behind his education simply replaces one image with another. Emile accepts the latter without question; he never demands an accounting of the tutor's reasoning. But Rousseau artfully connects this revelation with another, the Vicar's profession of faith, which provides an example of a young man who *does* question his teacher's reasoning. We are told that he sees a multitude of objections to the Vicar's "revelation," although we not told precisely what those objections are. He explains that he plans to meditate on the Vicar's speech and will seek to judge it by his own inner light. Perhaps we are not told his specific objections so that we may judge the speech for ourselves. In any case, in light of the standard set by the young Jean-Jacques, Emile falls short in his response to his tutor's revelation. But the reader is shown both responses.

It is only after the tutor's departure (in the unpublished sequel to *Emile*) that Emile questions his own education—at which point the tutor is not around to answer. This silence, this refusal to say everything, is precisely what creates the conditions for freedom and wisdom. It remains to be seen what Emile does with that freedom, a question I take up in chapter 7. At this point, what we are shown is that there are always two steps to each stage of Emile's education; the first appeals to his conditioning (that is, to his passions) and the second to his (nascent) independent reasoning. The two moves, in combination, are characteristic of Rousseau's education of judgment.

Passion, Reflection, and Judgment in Matters of Taste

It is not only in matters of religion that opinion triumphs (260; 4:558), according to Rousseau. In societies marked by social inequality, "fashion stifles taste, and people no longer seek what pleases them but seek rather what distinguishes them." When this happens, "the multitude no longer has judgment of its own. It now judges only according to the views of those whom it believes more enlightened than itself. It approves not what is good but what they have approved" (340–41; 4:672). As in matters of religion, there is a tendency to defer to authority. Pieties are observed. Having pursued the question of what it would mean to judge for oneself with regard to religion, Rousseau turns, in the final pages of book IV, to the question of taste. Once again, his lesson is not presented in reference to Emile. Rather, in a brief discourse on taste, Rousseau offers himself as a model for how to reflect on what moves us, at least on the simple level of what gives us pleasure.

Emile presumably has good taste, since he has been conditioned to have it. We recall that earlier in his education he was presented with the choice between a gourmet meal and a simple peasant picnic; he chose the picnic. Emile already has the inclination to prefer simple and healthy pleasures to decadent ones. When he is exposed to the literature and academic chatter of his day, he is in no way impressed; he "casts a glance at all this, then leaves it never to return" (344; 4:678). Clearly, from Rousseau's point of view, Emile's instincts are well formed. Yet Rousseau puts Emile to the side and substitutes his own example in making his case for simplicity. If Emile has the same inclinations as Rousseau, why must he be put aside? Rousseau tells us that Emile's heart is too pure to serve as a model in matters of taste. This is not simply because Rousseau believes that his readers are corrupt and thus too far removed from Emile's example to appreciate him; Emile, Rousseau says, cannot serve as an example "for anyone" (344; 4:678). I have suggested that this is the case because Emile chooses well but still has almost no understanding of *why* he is right. His correct response is simply instinctive. Because his faculty of judgment is incomplete, his example is insufficient to illuminate "the reasons" for choosing simple pleasures over luxuries. By the same token, however, precisely because his inclinations are so well conditioned, his example plays a necessary (if ultimately insufficient) role in educating the reader's faculty of judgment. It orients us so that we are then receptive to thinking through the reasons.

To be sure, throughout his discussion, Rousseau contrasts the sophisticated tastes of elites with the "simplicity of taste that speaks straight to the heart" (342; 4:675). He goes on to argue that even if he were rich, his taste would incline him toward the simple pleasures in life. However, this is not a romantic defense of simplicity. It is simultaneously a defense of complexity insofar as Rousseau defends the conscious choice of simplicity in full recognition of a complex field of possibilities. That is, by discussing his own case rather than that of his pupil, Rousseau offers a model of someone who consciously and actively chooses the simplicity that characterizes Emile's happiness. Emile is happy with simplicity, one might argue, because he doesn't know any better. Rousseau's own example thus supplements Emile's in the same way that the Vicar's does: it depicts someone moving *toward* the goal, rather than occupying the desired state effortlessly and flawlessly.

Rousseau engages in a thought experiment to explore the kind of life he would live if money were no object. He believes that he would differ from other rich men "by being sensual and voluptuous rather than proud and vain" (345; 4:678). He would not live in a palace but in a simple abode. He would remain himself, despite the change in his circumstances. Because of his lack of affectation, he would have true friends and true mistresses, for "neither a friend nor a mistress can be bought" (349; 4:683). He would choose to live with a group of these friends in a wholesome village somewhere. These friends would be people like himself, "who love pleasure and know something about it" (351; 4:687). These are not cultural innocents whose simple traditions and virtuous, tightly knit communities assure them a pleasant and happy existence, but those who know how to be happy. Despite their sophistication, however, Rousseau and his friends would blend easily into the life of the village, participating in all of the practices of the local peasants. "Becoming villagers in the village, we would surrender ourselves to throngs of diverse entertainments" (351; 4:687). In a manner that calls to mind his earlier claim of how easily Emile's more conventional peers will accept him, Rousseau claims here that the locals will accept him as one of their own. For example, they will not make fun of him when he speaks to them about such things as agriculture. They will chat with him over a bottle of wine and feel no envy or ill will toward their rich neighbor, for the difference between them is hardly discernible.

I say it is *hardly* discernible because, at the same time, the difference between them *must* be discernible to the reader if the similarity between them is to register or mean anything significant. And, once again, a shift occurs in this section of Rousseau's narrative, bifurcating it. Whereas the first half emphasizes the perfect assimilation of Rousseau and his band of fellow hedonists to the life of the village, the second half introduces a necessary contrast. Rousseau's fantastical riches finally take on some significance, as he raises the question of whether he will engage in *the* outdoor activity that serves as the mark of the wealthy. "'Up to this point everything is marvelous,' I will be told, 'but what about the hunt? Is one really in the country if one does not hunt?' I understand. I only wanted a little farm, and I was wrong. I assume that I am rich; therefore I must have exclusive pleasures" (352; 4:688). Once again, the reader is presumed to be unconvinced by the first part of Rousseau's account. The reader will not believe that he is rich—that is, he will seem too much like the peasants—unless he hunts. "Very well," says Rousseau, and proceeds to imagine what this requirement will do to his fantasy. He spins a tale in which he (once again like Socrates's tyrant in the *Republic*) is made miserable by fear, insecurity, and, ultimately, loss of independence, all caused by his extensive material possessions and, especially, his need to secure enough land to support the hunt. He finally asserts that the only way to reclaim his happiness would be to open the hunt to everyone in the village rather than keep it exclusive. Inequality, which civil man takes to be the best enhancement of pleasure, is shown to be a hindrance to pleasure.

Rousseau characterizes his readers as blinded by "illusion, chimera, [and] foolish vanity," and seeks to educate them about the difference between true and apparent pleasures. He proceeds in part by providing them with an image of an idyllic pastoral existence, but also by annexing to that image a reflective discussion of the alternative sets of assumptions that would account for the image's seductive pull or lack thereof. The two parts of his discussion correspond to the two examples he gives of good taste: Emile and himself. Emile, who "feels" the things Rousseau has said about pleasure but does not "know" them (354; 4:691), serves as an unreflective model to (re)condition the reader's inclinations, whereas Rousseau's own example does that and more. It includes a reflective dimension that does more than produce a certain effect; it seeks to stimulate understanding of *why* that effect is desirable and good.

This passage elucidates Rousseau's claim that Emile's tastes are too pure to serve as an example for anyone. Like the Vicar, Rousseau is flawed, and it is for precisely this reason that Rousseau twice displaces Emile with these other examples. Mistakes are as necessary as idealized images to Rousseau's education. The images may strike us as good, and may move us in the right direction, but it is only by considering them in contrast to flawed alternatives that we may come to see why they are good. This is consistent with Rousseau's characterization of human wisdom as a combination of feeling and knowing. "Do we, then, want Emile to love the truth; do we want him to know it?" (252; 4:547). Loving the truth is a necessary orientation that causes one to seek knowledge of it. In the early educational stages, Rousseau insists, it is better to feel without knowing than to know without feeling, which is no knowledge at all. "For if he does not feel it, how will he ever know it?" But the goal is ultimately for Emile to know as well as to feel. For Rousseau, feeling is a *necessary but not sufficient* condition for knowing. Wondering whether Emile is too easily moved by the noble images to which he has been exposed, Rousseau counsels, "Be a sensitive man, but also a wise one. If you are only one of the two, you are nothing" (344; 4:677).

In book II of *Emile* Rousseau defines wisdom as knowing how to stay in one's place. Certainly, Emile must feel, he must be moved, without allowing himself to become "too moved" (344; 4:677). But there is more to the second half of his education than an extension of stoicism. What Rousseau does not state explicitly—since, as he repeatedly reminds us, he does not want to say everything—but what permeates his entire narrative is that one must know not only *what* one's place in nature is and *how* to stay there, but also *why*. Love of a virtuous woman will help to keep Emile in his place, at least insofar as it will keep him from falling away from himself into corruption. But Rousseau's goal for his pupil is not stasis but wisdom. Insofar as Emile will love a particular virtuous woman named Sophie, or wisdom, Rousseau intimates the possibility that he will become not only moderate but wise—that he will not only stay in his place but learn how and also why. Ultimately, Emile must take charge of the motion of his own soul, which does not mean an absence of longing but developing a reflective attitude toward the ideals and images that condition his longings. The task of his social/moral education is not simply the provision of salutary standards against which to judge the world around him, but the ability to reflect on those standards and make them truly his own. This is what it will ultimately mean for him to learn to love Sophie, or to become a lover of wisdom.

6

JUDGMENT, LOVE, AND ILLUSION

Love has been presented as blind because it has better eyes than we do and sees relations we are not able to perceive. (*E*, 214; 4:494)

On the surface, Rousseau's discussion of love in book V of *Emile* seems focused principally on the cultivation of virtue and has little to do with the cultivation of judgment. Rousseau's earlier rhetoric about the importance of Emile's thinking his own thoughts disappears, replaced by a concern with directing his pupil toward a healthy sociability and preventing sexual debauchery. "I shall make him moderate by making him fall in love" (327; 4:654). Emile falls in love with a woman named Sophie who exists as an idealized poetic construction in his imagination long before he meets her in person. The lure of this imaginary love object makes Emile moderate by making him "disgusted with those that could tempt him; it suffices that he everywhere find comparisons which make him prefer his chimera to the real objects that strike his eye" (329; 4:656). Thus one wonders whether he is exercising independent judgment or simply reacting on the basis of his conditioning, manipulated by his attachment to a salutary illusion.

One could argue that the image of an idealized beloved functions as a "compass," guiding Emile's judgment just as the standard of utility functioned earlier in his education. But there are significant differences that suggest that Emile is not simply trading one standard for another. In book III, Rousseau presents his pupil as capable of determining for himself the utility of this or that object. To be sure, the example of Robinson Crusoe shapes Emile's understanding of utility, but Emile does not apply Crusoe's standard uncritically. He is expected "to examine his hero's conduct" and take note of his failings. "The surest means of raising oneself above prejudices and ordering one's judgments about the relations of things is to put oneself in the place of an isolated man and to judge everything as this man *ought to judge of it* with respect to his own utility" (185; 4:455, emphasis added). Emile does not simply take Crusoe's judgments for his own. Furthermore, as he moves from judging "the relations of things" to making judgments about people and social relations in book IV, Emile is similarly required to reflect on the images his tutor parades before his eyes.

When it comes to the idealized image of Sophie, however, it is less clear whether Emile ever achieves any measure of critical distance. First, we must notice that when Emile meets Sophie in person and hears her name for the first time, he does not even begin to judge for himself whether she is the Sophie of his dreams but simply looks to his tutor for confirmation. Furthermore, as their relationship progresses, Sophie manipulates Emile's affections and rules him indirectly, in much the same way that his tutor did earlier. And while Rousseau insists that Emile preserve some modicum of his former independence by taking a break from Sophie in order to "learn to bear her absence" (448; 4:823), Emile resists strenuously and must be "dragged away with difficulty" (450; 4:826). In other words, he must be forced to be free. When the tutor finally reunites the lovers, he tells Emile, "Sophie is your governor from now on," and advises Sophie in secret about how to manage Emile's affections. Thus, although his love for Sophie is ostensibly supposed to complete Emile's internalization of the external authority upon which he has depended for so long, he still needs a legislator figure to preserve his carefully constructed state. All of this invites skepticism toward Rousseau's claims that Emile is his own man. Emile may be free of the unhealthy social dependency that characterizes civil society, but he hardly seems self-governing. Rousseau's confidence in his pupil's judgment, which he expressed so forcefully in the first four books of *Emile*, seems to wane as Emile approaches adulthood.

We are left with the question: does the relationship between Emile and Sophie represent the pinnacle of Emile's education in judgment and achievement of freedom, or does it circumvent the risks of judgment by substituting illusion, manipulation, and the deepest conditioning of the passions in order to produce an illusory freedom? I have shown that throughout *Emile* Rousseau's shaping of Emile's judgment cultivates his ability to be simultaneously seduced by and critically detached from the chimeras that are necessary to sustain human happiness and freedom. Rousseau's treatment of erotic love is the capstone of this education precisely because it deals explicitly with these chimeras and their role, indicating the importance of a middle ground between salutary enchantment by poetic ideals and utter disillusionment. Emile, however, is not the best representative of this middle perspective; Sophie surpasses him in this respect.[1] In the character of Sophie, Rousseau offers a model of judgment that does not simply complement Emile's (furthering his development at the expense of her own, as some have argued), but stands alone as an alternative model for the reader, who is the primary target of the education developed in *Emile*. What is notable about Sophie's character is not primarily how she governs Emile, but how she governs herself and her relationship with Emile. She is both influenced by illusions and poetic ideals and detached from them, perpetually negotiating this fragile tension. Thus book V is the apex of Rousseau's pedagogical project not because it finally resolves the tensions in Emile's earlier education but because it exposes those tensions, contrasting Emile's dependence on his guiding chimeras with Sophie's more complex perspective, which seems to suggest that she is, despite her legal and social dependence, more genuinely *free* in her exercise of judgment. However, Rousseau's exploration of the education of judgment does not end with Emile, or with Sophie, or even with the whole of *Emile*, but continues in the unpublished sequel to *Emile*, *Emile and Sophie, or The Solitary Ones*, which I consider in due course. Insofar as the relationship between Emile and Sophie, itself a poetic idealization, dissolves in the sequel, *Emile and Sophie* offers a vantage point from which to reflect critically upon that idealization—taking us full circle to the preface of *Emile*, in which Rousseau asks that his project be judged.

Rousseau's Feminine Ideal

Book V begins not with the details of the relationship between two particular individual characters, Emile and Sophie, but with a general discussion of relations between the sexes. In other words, we do not begin with the image of Sophie in particular but with "woman"—an abstraction. Rousseau first attempts to distinguish the sexual sphere from the whole person. "In everything not connected with sex, woman is man. She has the same organs, the same needs, the same faculties" (357; 4:692). When it comes to sexual reproduction, "each contributes equally to the common aim, but not in the same way" (358; 4:693). Rousseau will emphasize the differences between the sexes for the rest of book V. This does not mean, however, that we should ignore his initial claim about their commonality, a claim that is in no way necessary to the argument for sex-based education other than to delineate its boundaries. Rousseau suggests at the outset that the differences between the sexes do not negate their common humanity. This is our first indication that Sophie's education must not only differ from but must also share a common core with Emile's.[2]

Rousseau begins with physical differences between the sexes but quickly moves on to moral and intellectual differences. The issue of physical attractiveness provides the transition. Rousseau attributes to young girls a love of adornment and concludes from this ostensibly "natural" fact that women are meant to develop attractiveness as men are to develop strength. He then moves from physical appearances to speech and conduct, charging that women ought to worry more than men about the effect of their words and behavior. "Man says what he knows; woman says what pleases" (376; 4:718). Instead of asking, "what is it good for?" (the question of utility that guides Emile as a child), young girls should pose the question "what effect will it have?" and concern themselves above all with how they are seen by others. "It is not enough that they be estimable; they must be esteemed. It is not enough for them to be pretty; they must please. It is not enough for them to be temperate; they must be recognized as such" (364; 4:702). Rousseau extends this concern for reputation to conclude that "opinion is the grave of virtue among men and its throne among women" (365; 4:702–3).

Such statements have led many to conclude that Rousseau in no way intends to apply to women his general standards of wholeness—at least not the self-sufficient wholeness that fosters moral and intellectual autonomy. Women seem to be deprived of such autonomy, their speech and conduct dictated by convention rather than by self-governance.[3] Thoroughly dependent upon the opinions of others, they do not think their own thoughts and seem incapable of exercising independent judgment. But Rousseau provides us with clear evidence that this is not at all his intention. First, despite the distinction he draws between masculine knowledge and feminine taste, he gives the substance of men's speech and women's speech a common core: "The truth ought to be the only element common to their discourse" (376; 4:718). The rule of saying what is pleasing should be subordinate to the rule of saying what is true.

Furthermore, Rousseau backs away from his remarks about women's dependence on public opinion: "Perhaps I have said too much about it up to now. To what will we reduce women if we give them as their law only public prejudices? . . . A rule prior to opinion exists for the whole human species. . . . It is important, therefore, that [women] cultivate a faculty that serves as arbiter between the two guides. . . . That faculty is reason" (382; 4:730). Rather than make women thoroughly dependent on public opinion, Rousseau criticizes existing educational practice on this very point. "Far from opposing in any way the empire of public prejudices over their minds, you have fed these prejudices!" In contrast, he counters, "When I say I want a mother to introduce her daughter into society, I make the supposition that she will make her daughter see it as it is" (388; 4:739). This is the same goal that Rousseau attributed to Emile's education in pity, which was designed to teach him to judge his fellow men as they truly are, not according to the masks they wear. Here, however, Rousseau does not spell out the method for achieving this clear-sighted perspective.

It is simply inaccurate, then, to say that Rousseau seeks to deprive women of their capacity to judge or to reason as moral agents, or simply enslaves them to public opinion. Just as Emile's education entails that he move past his complete dependence upon his tutor's authority in order to become capable of exercising independent judgment, Rousseau's description of feminine education includes a similar transition. "Finally, the moment comes when they begin to judge things by themselves, and then it is time to change the plan of their education" (382; 4:730). Instead of remaining dependent upon the opinion of others, a young woman "becomes the judge of her judges; she decides when she ought to submit herself to them and when she ought to take exception to them" (383; 4:731). This judging stance involves a double perspective. A young woman's education must not trap her into slavish dependence on public opinion, but she must always take public opinion into account. "As soon as she depends on both her own conscience and the opinions of others, she has to learn to *compare* these two rules, to reconcile them, and to prefer the former only when the two are in contradiction" (383; 4:731, emphasis added). In other words, she must exist both inside and outside the opinions of others. As Penny Weiss puts it, "Saying [that Sophie] is to prefer the dictates of conscience to those of opinion *only* when the two disagree amounts to saying she is to prefer conscience *whenever* the two conflict, and, further, implies that her conscience is always active and critical."[4]

Weiss goes on to argue, however, that the unresolved friction Sophie experiences between the two commitments ultimately undermines the familial wholeness that such integrity is intended to foster. But there is a positive aspect to this friction, or tension. Let us return to the dictate that Sophie must exist

Judgment, Love, and Illusion ❄ 139

both inside and outside the confines of public opinion. It requires a certain degree of self-consciousness to compare internal and external dictates, and then to choose when to follow and when to lead. The difficulty of comparing and choosing is an important theme in the sexual politics of *Emile*, in several ways. First, comparison is necessary in order to fall in love at all. "One loves only after having judged; one prefers only after having compared. . . . This choosing, which is held to be the opposite of reason, comes to us from it" (214; 4:494). Moreover, this comparison takes place not only among prospective beloveds but also between any prospective beloved and the *image* one has of an ideal beloved. Both sexes engage in this process of comparing, judging, and choosing. The reader, too, compares and judges several times throughout the earlier books, as Rousseau conjures up various "alternative" pupils (mostly spoiled young men) against whom Emile might be compared and judged—and now between Emile and Sophie as alternative models of how judgment might be exercised. In fact, as he concludes his account of how Sophie's parents encourage her to choose a husband, Rousseau appeals to the reader's capacity for choice: "I proposed to say in this book all that can be done and to leave to the reader the choice—among the good things I may have said—of those that are within his reach" (406; 4:763).

Comparing Sophie and Emile, we notice significant differences in how *they* compare and judge. Of the two, Sophie exhibits a greater degree of independence in choosing her mate. The tutor, of course, cannot ultimately dictate Emile's emotional response to Sophie, but he does everything in his power to control it to the greatest extent possible. "I would have refused to raise [Emile] if I had not been the master of marrying him to the woman of his choice—that is, of my choice" (407; 4:765). Emile carries around the image of his ideal beloved for quite some time before he actually meets Sophie. Although he must compare the Sophie he finally meets to the image of Sophie in his head, his method of comparison suggests a rather anemic capacity for exercising independent judgment. First, the choice is made rather easy for him, since Sophie shares the name of his ideal beloved. Even so, he looks to the tutor for confirmation that this is in fact *the* Sophie (414–15; 4:776). In contrast, Sophie chooses her own criterion and decides when it has been met. She draws her image of the ideal mate from Fenelon's *Adventures of Telemachus*, and, eyes lowered, she looks to no one (not even to her mother) to confirm that her Telemachus "has been found" (415; 4:777).

Fenelon's novel, we are told, "fell into her hands by chance [*par hazard*]" (410; 4:769). Whether Rousseau is being ironic or straightforward, we are given no indication that Sophie was told that Telemachus would be the perfect man for her. She appears to have made this decision herself, for she recognizes Telemachus's virtue. Moreover, she recognizes similarities even though Telemachus and Emile do not share the same name. Interestingly enough, when Emile is given the same book to read, later in book V, there is no indication that he recognizes any similarity between himself and Telemachus, or between Sophie and Eucharis (although Sophie's father compares her to Eucharis, as does Sophie herself, more than once). The association of Sophie and Eucharis is somewhat curious insofar as Telemachus does not marry Eucharis but weds Antiope, whom he meets later in the story, after he extricates himself from Eucharis's grip despite her wiles. Sophie's confidence in the face of a script so unfavorable to her already indicates that she maintains a certain distance from the very images that inspire her. Sophie is not simply following the script; she hopes to bring about a different ending, one that allows for a combination of the charms of Eucharis and the wifely appeal of Antiope.

Given how Rousseau describes the initial encounter between Emile and Sophie, we cannot avoid the conclusion that Rousseau's model woman is a more independent thinker than her model husband. There is, of course, one significant caveat to this conclusion, for Sophie's independence is precisely what Rousseau expects her to conceal from Emile. The paradigm for the kind of feminine dissembling that Rousseau encourages here is prefigured in his earlier discussion of men's and women's physical differences: while men are physically stronger, he says, women exaggerate their weakness in order to manipulate men into using their strength to women's advantage. He extends this model to other differences. Overall, Rousseau expects women to be stronger, smarter, and more independent than they let on. This suggests that their moral and intellectual self-sufficiency is tainted by self-censorship or dissembling. The question that lingers goes to the heart of the feminist debate with Rousseau: why does Rousseau encourage women to maintain the appearance of subordination? And does this not contribute to their actual subordination?

This question must be addressed from several angles. Joel Schwartz explains it in terms of a balance of power. Women are expected to rule men indirectly, while men rule women directly.[5] But direct (publicly sanctioned) rule will always be more powerful than indirect rule. Moreover, direct rule allows for coherence between an individual's self-understanding and the understanding that he or she projects to others and that others recognize. Indirect rule, by contrast, requires a division between appearance and reality, and divides an individual's experience of both the world and the self. Thus even if the exercise of indirect rule provides women with some measure of power, it still compromises their wholeness. Are we to conclude that Rousseau expects women to have a perpetually divided self, showing one face to themselves and another to others, suspended in the unhappy divided state that characterizes civil society and that Rousseau seeks to correct for men at the expense of women's happiness? This would be extremely problematic (and unjust) on Rousseau's own terms. But this assumes that wholeness is indeed Rousseau's standard, and, as we have seen, throughout *Emile* Rousseau distances the reader from the ideal of wholeness (as embodied in natural man, for example), drawing attention to its character as a chimera—a good and perhaps a necessary one but a chimera nonetheless. Sophie extends this pattern in two ways. Her ambiguous status with regard to the whole of the ostensibly seamless complementarity of the sexes calls into question the whole of the family or marital relationship, and her ambiguous status with regard to her own self-consciousness calls into question the standard of wholeness for the individual.

Certainly, in Rousseau's presentation, feminine dissembling plays a role in maintaining the family unit, just as the tutor clandestinely preserves Emile's subjective wholeness and the legislator forms the political community. But in Sophie's case there is an important difference. Unlike the tutor and the legislator, Sophie is not separable from the whole that she governs; she is a part of that whole. The division inherent in the self-consciousness of women is therefore not separable from the family of which they are a part, which is itself divided. It is therefore doubtful that Rousseau intends the family to adhere to the standards of wholeness that shape his characterizations of the model political community. Weiss and Schwartz, observing that Rousseau intends family life to prepare men for civic participation, assume that the family must be a form of community in which the individual experiences no conflict between his or her own interest and the common good. However, it may be that the friction that remains between the part and the whole is precisely what makes the family so pivotal for Rousseau. The family may be the one example he can find where that friction has a positive rather than a negative effect on human happiness, insofar as a happy marriage based on freedom and affection (and not only on duty) is Rousseau's goal. The goal of family life would then be the successful (healthy) deployment and maintenance of the self-consciousness that accompanies amour-propre. If this is the case, then the fact that Sophie experiences this tension more acutely than Emile suggests that her education is neither inferior nor merely complementary to Emile's education.

Emile must take one step beyond the balanced equilibrium of self-identification when he falls in love with Sophie. New desires are born in him, but the tutor simply transfers Emile's amour-propre onto one person before it can extend any further. It is a controlled, mediated disruption of the equilibrium of faculty and desire that characterized his happiness until that point, and the forming of a new equilibrium on a new plane. Sophie, however, must take a step and a half, because she has to be aware of the nature of amour-propre and know how to guide it; she must understand the character of the whole she is responsible for maintaining. For example, early in their courtship, Sophie challenges Emile to a race. She runs more quickly than he expects,[6] and this arouses his vanity by presenting him with a public challenge. But as they approach the finish line, she slows down. When he sees that his victory is secure, he stops, lifts her over the finish line, and declares her the winner (437; 4:807). According to Rousseau, in a perfectly ordered relationship, it is impossible to tell who was the actual winner. But who governs this order? It is Sophie, who understands and controls amour-propre, and who therefore orders and is not simply ordered.

Amour-propre is both dangerous and necessary.[7] The family unit requires it, and moderates it, but does not ultimately do away with the risk it poses. Feminine dissembling is meant to disguise this paradox, not simply to hide brains behind a pretty face in order to preserve a husband's illusion of superiority. While it might disguise the paradox in practice, however, Rousseau's treatment of it in fact exposes it for the reader, whose education then resembles Sophie's more than Emile's insofar as the reader, too, is shown the "cords and pulleys" behind Emile's education. Just as the reader must be seduced by Emile's example but also critically detached from it, Sophie must be both inside and outside the whole that is formed by her relationship with Emile. In order to maintain the illusion on which that relationship rests, Sophie must not be simply taken in by it. She therefore cannot be reduced to the illusion, which is the error commentators fall into when they underestimate the self-consciousness dictated by Sophie's education. Sophie has been characterized as a "perfect spectacle, fashioned to be looked at without a dangerous reciprocal gaze."[8] In this view, she is thoroughly passively constructed. "Women are, for Rousseau, sources of natural illusion," according to Tracy Strong. "They thus play the same role in relation to the polity that the 'noble lie' did in Plato."[9] But, as we have seen, Sophie self-consciously wields this tool and therefore cannot be reduced to the tool. If all that is meant by this critique is that Rousseau constructs and wields her, as a character in his book, then of course this could be said of any character, including Emile. If, rather, the charge is that Sophie is thoroughly constructed by social norms of femininity, in the service of preserving a certain heterosexual social order, then the characterization is overdrawn. Sophie is *not* reducible to an object of the male gaze; she gazes back, she governs, and she judges.

It is thus not surprising that the tutor presents Emile to Sophie using terms with political overtones and identifying her role with his own: "Today I abdicate the authority you confided to me, and Sophie is your governor from now on" (479; 4:867). As noted above, however, what distinguishes Sophie from the tutor and the legislator is that she is part of the whole that she is trying to maintain. The lawgiver in the *Social Contract*, for example, is a foreigner, as Bonnie Honig's self-described "gothic" interpretation emphasizes. According to Honig, Rousseau (like a gothic heroine) casts about desperately for a "rescuer"—in this case, a solution to the problem of paternal power—and comes up with the foreign lawgiver who conveniently departs when his work is done. A foreigner, Honig argues, has an insulating detachment from the "particular intrigues at work" in a particular community. That is, "foreignness models founding virtues such as objectivity, disinterestedness, and impartiality, while also symbolizing a denaturing self-alienation that life under law enacts and requires." Thus Rousseau's "solution" comes at a price: it "positions citizens in a relation of heteronomy that is deeply at odds with Rousseauvian legitimacy."[10]

Sophie offers an alternative "solution" to the dilemma that Honig identifies by offering a different model of rule. Certainly, her example confirms that some degree of self-alienation is inescapable, but whereas the legislator is *thoroughly* alienated from the political community, Sophie's position is more complex. Her education must prepare her to exist both inside and outside herself and the "whole" that she governs. This education therefore cannot simply be complementary to the education that her male counterpart receives; it must both comprehend and transcend it. Only then will Sophie be able to stand back from the relationship in order to govern it. Only then will she be able to be the "judge of her judges," deciding when to submit and when to lead. *Choosing* when to submit and when to lead is hardly the mark of an individual deprived of moral or intellectual autonomy. But neither does it add up to perfect autonomy. Sophie is not only governing her husband; she is governing herself as well, and she is governing the relationship, of which she is a part. This dynamic also distinguishes the family from both the wholeness of an independent soul and the wholeness of the community prescribed in the *Social Contract*. Unlike natural man and citizen, Sophie can step back from the "whole" of her experience to reflect on it. Yet, unlike the legislator, she is also "inside" the whole she is governing. Hers is a partial detachment. She shares with the legislator (and the tutor) the ability to discern and manipulate the difference between image and reality, to engage in noble lies, for the sake of maintaining a "whole." Unlike them, however, she must ultimately maintain the whole from the *inside*. This is a challenge of a different order. The legislator is immune to the illusions he weaves; but if Sophie is to fall in love, she cannot simply be immune. Therefore, Sophie is an alternative not only to natural man and citizen but to the legislator as well.[11] And because she is an integral part of the whole that she maintains, its character is also altered. The capacity to judge is not restricted to the alienated figure of the legislator but incorporated into the whole that is governed (partially) from within.

Sophie's Necessary Imperfection

We are well into book V before we actually meet Sophie, Rousseau's example of education for women. Rousseau treats his readers in the same way that he treats Emile, seducing us with an idea of Sophie—an image of the "ideal" woman—before introducing her to us. We are thus invited to judge for ourselves, keeping in mind the tutor's remark in presenting the image to Emile: "Doubtless there is such a woman and in the end we shall find her, *or at least the one who is most like her*" (328; 4:656, emphasis added). Along with Emile, the reader is forewarned that there may be a gap between the real Sophie and the ideal Sophie. Fortunately, the reader is given much more information about Sophie than Emile receives, and is in a better position to see the image of Sophie as just that—an image that she herself cultivates. For her part, Sophie seems to understand from the outset that Emile both is and is not Telemachus. Her affection for Emile seems to grow over time, as he reveals himself to her through his choices, statements, and behavior, whereas Emile is smitten with Sophie from the moment he learns her name. At stake is the ability to maintain a critical distance from the ideals that guide us. By reflecting on what moves us, we are not simply moved but attain some measure of self-direction.

At first, Sophie seems the perfect incarnation of the education that Rousseau has just described for women in general. She is graceful, tasteful, moderate, and talented. Her mind is able and solid without being brilliant or profound. She is pleasing and polite without engaging in flattery. Above all, Sophie loves virtue. We meet Sophie's parents as they inform her that the time has come for her to choose a husband. They encourage her to make her own choice in the matter and, while they give her general advice, do not seek to influence her decision.[12] Her happiness is all that matters to them, and they advise her that "perfect happiness is not of this earth, but the greatest unhappiness, and the one that can always be avoided, is being unhappy due to one's own fault" (400; 4:700). Sophie is being trusted as an agent of her own happiness in a way that Emile was not. His tutor denied Emile this agency so that he would *feel* free. Sophie is expected to *be* free (in the moral sense), even as she feels and is acutely aware of the constraints she faces as a woman (public opinion). In fact, her parents suggest that in such matters she ought to disregard public opinion and choose the mate who makes her happy, just as they are disregarding common practice in allowing her to choose her husband. "If the whole world should blame us, what difference does it make? We do not seek public approval. Your happiness is enough for us" (401; 4:758).

In book I of *Emile* Rousseau defines happiness as perfect equilibrium between one's desires and one's faculties, and the aim is to maintain this equilibrium as closely as possible. Such perfect equilibrium is in tension with the self-consciousness that is necessary to maintain it independently, and Emile's tutor thus maintains his state of mind externally, through a great deal of art. But the understanding of happiness that Sophie's parents articulate emphasizes personal responsibility and active reflection rather than static equilibrium. The point is not that Sophie, as a woman, is to be denied the possibility of "perfect" happiness, but that her parents' perspective uncovers a difficulty in that initial formulation. If happiness is to be maintained internally rather than externally, a certain degree of self-consciousness is necessary, which disrupts the perfect equilibrium of faculty and desire. That is, to be a *truly* self-sufficient whole is to be a divided whole. Sophie, who is raised by her parents and not by a tutor, must exist inside the whole that makes up her happiness in order to experience it authentically, and yet, in order to be free, she must somehow be able to stand outside it, holding it together, playing the role of the tutor to herself. Here we have another version of the double position that Sophie is expected to inhabit with regard to both public opinion and the marital relationship.

Rousseau raises the question of how Sophie will respond to her parents' speech. He says that he trusts that her good judgment will prevail and she will make a good choice. He then digresses on the subject of whether Sophie is real or imaginary. Ostensibly in order to convince skeptical readers that Sophie is not an imaginary being, he proceeds to tell the story of "a girl so similar to Sophie that her story could be Sophie's without occasioning any surprise"

(402; 4:759). There are now two Sophies in the story. This is not surprising, given the dual role that Sophie must play. In more than one sense, Rousseau splits Sophie in two.

Rousseau tells us that the girl like Sophie is taken out into society to look for a mate but keeps coming back empty-handed. Her parents wonder what is wrong, and she explains that she sees many attractive men, but none whom she loves in her heart. Her mother presses her to explain further, and the girl throws a book on the table, *The Adventures of Telemachus*. She explains that she loves Telemachus as a model of virtue and can find no one to meet the standard he sets. "I do not seek Telemachus. I know that he is only a fiction. I seek someone who resembles him." Her parents laugh and try in vain to reason with her. "Sophie also had her own reason and knew how to turn it to account. How many times she reduced them to silence by using their own reason against them" (405; 4:762).

Rousseau can barely bring himself to finish his story. There is no man in existence good enough for this Sophie! He asks himself whether he should describe the unfortunate ending, in which the girl is led, in effect, to her grave instead of the altar, and he chooses not to go on. Abandoning the tragic story line of the girl like Sophie and returning to the original Sophie, he simply explains that the example was intended to show that "in spite of the prejudices born of the morals of our age, enthusiasm for the decent and the fine is no more foreign to women than to men, and that there is nothing that cannot be obtained under nature's direction from women as well as from men" (405; 4:763). That women as well as men can love the noble is not an issue for Rousseau; what is at stake is how one relates to noble ideals.[13] In this, the "original" Sophie is more instructive, not because she is a more realistic or less tragic model, held to a lower standard, but because she is held to an even higher standard. She is expected to love the noble in a more complex way than the girl like Sophie, for whom it is all or nothing. The more ordinary Sophie is similarly guided by poetic ideals (specifically, *Telemachus*) but responds with neither blind enthusiasm nor despair and disillusionment. She is not as fooled by illusions as Emile is, but she is also not as impervious to them as the girl like Sophie, who knows that Telemachus is only a beautiful fiction but cannot romanticize any of her actual suitors enough to resemble him, or to see any beauty in them at all.[14]

Sophie's imperfection, in the form of her divided soul, is both inevitable and necessary, and it allows her to accept imperfection in turn. She chooses the real over the ideal, and yet her "realism" is not capitulation to what is common, or what passes for "real" among those who, in Rousseau's view, are so prejudiced or corrupt that they can no longer see what is truly real or natural. She can appreciate Emile; while it takes an image like Telemachus to help her in this, she does not assimilate Emile to Telemachus. Her double vision can encompass both men. She exists simultaneously "inside" and "outside" the illusion that inspires her, neither fully bewitched by it nor utterly detached. She thus exhibits the complex spectatorial stance that Rousseau introduced in book IV when he expected Emile to be able to observe both the action on the stage and the "cords and pulleys" behind the stage.

As we have seen, because Sophie must understand the nature and complexity of interdependence in order to direct and maintain it, she must be able to stand back from it. It requires a certain degree of detachment to manipulate Emile's affections as Rousseau says Sophie does, for example, by provoking his jealousy. "The generous Sophie, exciting his love by giving him some moments of alarm, will know how to regulate them well and to compensate him for them" (431; 4:799). But while she must be able to stand back from the relationship for the sake of the whole, she must also be able to step back into it if she is to experience love herself. This is the difference between Sophie and the girl like Sophie. Both Sophies conceive of an image that they can love. It is not the case that the girl like Sophie loves more passionately than Sophie does. In fact, paradoxically, she is more detached, *too* detached. The girl like Sophie is so acutely aware of the distinction between image and reality that she cannot fall in love. Her detachment is the flip side, or even the by-product, of her excessive passion. The girl like Sophie cannot allow herself to submit to a whole that is not perfect, and therefore she remains perpetually "outside," a condition that Rousseau presents as tragic. In order to avoid such a tragedy, Sophie must exist both inside and outside her relationship. She must combine passion and detachment, rather than vacillate wildly between them, like Emile. In the contest between reason and sentiment, Rousseau emphasizes sentiment but never discounts reason—for either sex.

But if only Sophie and not Emile were able to stand back from the relationship, a radical emotional and moral inequality would corrupt their bond, and their relationship would be more like that of ruler and ruled than a partnership based on equality and mutual affection. Therefore, we must ask how Rousseau attempts to balance the relationship on this issue. On the one hand, we could say that he balances out Emile's psychological dependence on Sophie with Sophie's legal and economic dependence on Emile.[15] But since Rousseau does not even address this form of women's dependence (taking it for granted, surely), it is hard to imagine that he is incorporating it seriously into his analysis. Rousseau does in fact deal with the issue of balance, but in another way. He makes it clear, first of all, that Sophie does not want a malleable weakling for a husband. "Sophie did not want a lover who knew no law other than hers" (439; 4:810). She seeks a man whose self-rule parallels her own; only then can he freely commit to her. She does not seek to rule tyrannically, either directly or indirectly.

Emile does indeed establish his ability, or at least his intent, to stand back from the relationship. He misses an appointment with Sophie because he is detained helping an injured man on the way to her house. She is angry when he and the tutor arrive the next day, which upsets Emile, but he swallows his fear and announces, "Sophie, you are the arbiter of my fate. You know it well. You can make me die of pain. But do not hope to make me forget the rights of humanity. They are more sacred to me than yours. *I will never give them up for you*" (441; 4:881, emphasis added). Sophie, who had been withholding her answer to his marriage proposal, now embraces Emile and agrees to marry him. As much as she wants and needs to govern him, she wants him to be more than her subject; he must be a self-ruling and virtuous man. He must merit her love. Emile's declaration appears at first to demonstrate such independence of mind. Yet we must wonder at Sophie's enthusiasm for Emile's proclamation. He has demonstrated that he can stand back from their relationship, but he has also presented that distancing as an irrevocable commitment. As long as the inside and outside are not in conflict, he can handle both, but as soon as there is a conflict, he will *automatically* choose the outside; he will "never" give up his principles for her. He will not judge; he has internalized a rule and will apply it indiscriminately. He has prejudged, just as he fell in love with Sophie before he even met her. This is a far cry from the subtle discernment that Rousseau invites us to expect from Sophie.

Shortly thereafter, Emile fails to live up to his arrogant proclamation. When it comes time to leave Sophie to travel and learn more about the rights of humanity, Emile must be dragged away from her. The high drama of the scene reminds us of the story of the girl like Sophie, who also had to be dragged—but in the opposite direction, toward a mate rather than away. Emile appears at first glance to be the complete opposite of the girl like Sophie; but in their self-defeating extremes, Emile and the girl are in fact counterparts in their respective attachment and detachment, two sides of the same coin. Emile believes that his governing ideal is thoroughly captured by the particular Sophie, while the girl like Sophie sees no trace of her idealized Telemachus in the particular suitors she encounters.

Whereas Emile is either completely inside or completely outside their relationship, alternatively engulfed or detached, Sophie hovers on the cusp. He inhabits one alternative or the other, by turns. She, by contrast, inhabits a different and more complex perspective altogether, one that is as tenuous as it is promising.[16] That Sophie is aware of the need to be *both* inside and outside, to be both self-consciously detached and unselfconsciously committed, however, does not mean that this ceases to be a challenge for her. The "feminine" education that Rousseau sets forth in *Emile* does not resolve the tension he perceives in human existence; it exposes that tension. I am not arguing that he turns the feminine on its head so as to portray it in a positive rather than a negative light; rather, he turns it inside out so that we can see the internal tensions that drive human relationships. The attempt to mitigate these tensions is not without its risks, which may only fully come to light in the sequel, the subject of chapter 7. It is only in *Emile et Sophie* that the two characters have the opportunity to exercise judgment in the absence of any guidance from the tutor.

One might argue that both Emile and the girl like Sophie are superior to Sophie insofar as they seek to transcend the realm of particulars and becoming in order to approach something like the Platonic ideas. Rousseau advises Emile that it is futile to form permanent attachments "on this earth where everything changes [and] everything passes away." Instead, he should attach his heart "only to imperishable beauty" (446; 4:820). This certainly sounds as though he is turning Emile toward something like the philosophical idea of the beautiful. If so, we should expect him to reject Sophie in light of this ideal, for she has her share of imperfections, and in any case whatever beauty she possesses is necessarily transitory. "Except for the single Being existing by itself, there is nothing beautiful except that which is not" (447; 4:821). In other words, just as the girl like Sophie can love only the Telemachus who does not exist, Emile cannot be expected to love the real Sophie if he is truly attached only to imperishable beauty. The imperishable beauty to which he is attached, however, is not the abstract *idea* of beauty but a particular poetic construction of an idealized woman. In other words, as others have observed, Rousseau modifies Plato by replacing the ideas with ideals—that is, poetic ideals, which are more suitable for an ordinary individual.[17] These ideals do not have the same degree of permanence or universality as the Platonic ideas, but they are nevertheless a step above the vicissitudes of public opinion and decaying morals. And they may hold the promise of an even higher transcendence; Rousseau's choice of the name of *Sophie* for Emile's beloved intimates that such poetic ideals may function as stepping-stones to wisdom in the spirit of Socrates's presentation of

Diotima's ladder of love in Plato's *Symposium*—or at least the achievement of adequate second-order wisdom suitable for ordinary human beings rather than the rarest or highest types.

What complicates this promise of ascent, however, is that Rousseau plainly admits that the poetic constructions that he proposes to guide this elevation are illusions. Insofar as he seeks to attach his pupil—and his readers—to such illusory ideals, Rousseau can be accused of countering ignorance not with truth but with a different sort of ignorance, rooted in a beneficent mystification, or a kind of noble lie. How, then, does Rousseau understand what it means not just to love, but to love wisdom (*Sophia*)? In others words, how are we to understand the possibility of transcendence intimated in Rousseau's discussion of love in light of his insistence that love necessarily involves illusion? And how can judgment possibly be guided by love, if love is grounded in nothing but illusion?

Love and Illusion

According to Rousseau, love necessarily involves illusion, and his account of the relationship between Emile and Sophie—and between them and the reader—is fundamentally an exploration of the relationship between these illusions or chimeras and reality. "And what is true love itself if it is not a chimera, lie, and illusion?" Rousseau goes on to suggest that love is so fundamentally dependent on illusion that when the "magic veil" of illusion falls away, "love disappears" (329; 4:656). Many readings of *Emile* take this to be Rousseau's final word on love— that love is nothing but illusion, and that disenchantment must necessarily follow love's enchantment (just as all good political orders must eventually decay). And yet there are indications throughout the text that invite us to take Rousseau's question, as a *question*, seriously. In other words, what *is* love, what might it be, if it is not merely chimera, lie, and illusion? Can love be grounded in truth? Can love's illusion be followed by anything other than disillusionment and collapse— can it grow into something genuine rather than merely illusory?

Although Rousseau certainly emphasizes the role of illusion in love, he also introduces additional considerations that suggest that while love necessarily involves illusion, is cannot simply be reduced to illusion. In fact, what book V ultimately shows is that love requires an awareness of the distinction between the illusory beloved and the actual beloved, while keeping both in view. Rousseau hints, from the start of Emile and Sophie's relationship, that this partially detached perspective is the goal. When he first introduces the idea of Emile's ideal beloved (in book IV), Jean-Jacques draws attention to the distinction between the image and the reality. "We shall not easily find her perhaps. True merit is always rare. . . . Doubtless there is such a woman and in the end we shall find her, *or at least the one who is most like her*" (328; 4:656, emphasis added). From the outset, the tutor indicates that the "real" Sophie will resemble her ideal image but should not be expected to embody it fully.

Emile remains, as yet, blissfully unaware of any gap between illusion and reality when it comes to his beloved Sophie, and throughout the early stages of their courtship the tutor seems to encourage his pupil to remain in this enchanted state—and also encourages Sophie to use her feminine wiles to preserve the illusion as long as possible. However, just as there is a moment of "awakening" in book IV with regard to Emile's understanding of the underpinnings of his own education, as we saw in the previous chapter, Emile also has an awakening with regard to his passionate attachment to Sophie that begins when the tutor insists that he leave Sophie for two years of travel. While Emile resists and feels ready to commit to Sophie, Rousseau suggests that there are several reasons for this separation. First, Emile must learn the duties of citizenship, and he therefore needs a wider experience of the world and an expressly political education. Second, he must learn to bear Sophie's absence. He must not become so attached to her that he allows his happiness to become subject to the vagaries of fortune. It is in this context that the tutor advises Emile to attach his heart only to imperishable beauty. By remaining free of attachments to transient particulars, one might avoid the pain and misery of experiencing the inevitable losses that occur in every human life. This focus on the imperishable guides Emile's political education as well, insofar as he is provided with universal (imperishable) principles of political right to guide him as he encounters a multitude of flawed political systems during his travels. Emile's education in politics thus parallels and supports his education in love.

There is, however, a third, more fundamental reason for Rousseau's demand that Emile take a break from his beloved, one that bears upon both his erotic and his political education. Referring to this first part of his speech as a "preamble" (446; 4:820), the tutor explains that the two-year separation will test Sophie by determining whether she lives up to the image she projects. "You want to marry her not because she suits you but because she pleases you—as though love were never mistaken about what is suitable, and as though those who begin by loving each other never end by hating each other" (447; 4:822). Although the tutor has suggested earlier that love must end when the "magic veil" of illusion falls away, he now raises the possibility that these two moments may not be exhaustive—that one might move beyond the illusions to come to a deeper and truer appreciation of the beloved's character. The tutor insists that Emile seek this knowledge, which is attained only over time, before committing to Sophie. "Will you wait to know each other until you can no longer separate?" (448; 4:822). The "test" is more than a test of Sophie's virtue (her chastity). "It is not her virtue I am putting in doubt," the tutor tells Emile, "it is her character. Does a woman's character reveal itself in a day?" He tells Emile that he must get "a deep knowledge of her disposition" (447–48; 4:822). The separation of the lovers is not primarily about loosening Emile's attachment to his beloved but about allowing his knowledge of her to deepen by making it less conditioned by illusion. Insofar as Rousseau's objective is to maintain Emile's freedom, this involves both managing his attachment and managing his relationship to the illusion that motivates that attachment.

This perspective differs markedly from the kind of erotic longing that Aristophanes describes in Plato's *Symposium*, in which lovers long to fuse together to become a single whole. Given the rhetoric of complementarity that Rousseau uses in introducing his discussion of feminine education in book V, one might expect to see in the subsequent relationship of Emile and Sophie an Aristophanic model. Allan Bloom, for example, argues that book V chronicles a quest for one's other half and a seamless melding together. "There is no war between the sexes here, and each desires the other for the sake of wholeness."[18] I have argued, in contrast, that although Rousseau sees true love in just this way in its beginnings, this does not exhaust his view of the possibilities for what love is or can be. As the relationship between Emile and Sophie develops, Rousseau indicates the possibility of another sort of whole, one in which attachment and detachment are properly balanced.

This possibility is also anticipated in the advice that the tutor later gives Sophie about how to preserve love over the long term. Although the tutor encourages Sophie to stoke Emile's passion for her by means of occasional coquettish refusals, he also reminds her that the effect of her beauty, and her caprices, will eventually wane, and gives her the following advice: "When you stop being Emile's beloved, you will be his wife and his friend. Then, in place of your former reserve, establish between yourselves the greatest intimacy. No more separate beds, no more refusals, no more caprices" (479; 4:866). In both of the tutor's speeches, we are pointed toward the possibility that love can continue once the magic veil of illusion falls away, and so toward the possibility that one might truly love another person—that is, love the truth of another person,

Judgment, Love, and Illusion ※ 153

finally knowing their real character—rather than merely the image one has constructed.

Rousseau's explicit warnings about the need for genuine understanding—first to Emile, when he insists that Emile travel before committing to Sophie, and then to Sophie, in predicting that passion will cool—are positioned as bookends vis-à-vis the carefully crafted image of the seamless union of the lovers. These warnings encroach upon that illusion and call attention to the limits of the apparent seamlessness of their union. The self-understanding of passionate love is that it is eternal, an illusion that Rousseau certainly encourages but also dispels insofar as he warns that the relationship exists *in time*. As "asides," the warnings are both part and not part of the love story, which simultaneously reinforces the illusion of eternity and subtly undermines it by introducing the temporal nature of all things human, including erotic love. Eternity and concrete historicity come together in Rousseau's vision of a love that is discovered anew and freely expressed each and every day. This is the goal of his admonition against feelings of entitlement on the part of either partner. A marriage that makes love into a duty in an attempt to protect love from the unpredictability of day-to-day existence substitutes an ersatz eternity for a genuine one, which must be constructed anew each day. Paradoxically, it is by grappling with the challenges of time, growth, and change, rather than avoiding them, that one is best equipped to learn to stay in place, which is what Rousseau often says the "wise" man knows how to do. If love can point us toward wisdom, it is in this indirect way, and it is a partial, distinctively human wisdom.

Emile's political education is similarly structured. Rousseau arms his pupil with an imperishable calculus against which he can measure and judge all existing (transient, flawed) political orders. Emile is told that he should search for a place to settle down with Sophie on the basis of a political ideal based on the principles articulated in Rousseau's *Social Contract*. If he locates a regime that lives up to this standard, he will have found "true happiness"; if not, he will at least "be cured of a chimera" (457; 4:836) and can resign himself while remaining safely aloof. Once again, at first glance the goal seems to be to attach oneself to the imperishable—in this case, eternal principles of political right—in order to arm oneself against despair. However, just as the presentation of eternal love incorporated considerations of time, Rousseau's discussion of political right balances abstract principles with concrete considerations of place, which suggests a more complex and nuanced goal.

Emile *is* provided with an absolute standard against which to judge the political system and laws of each country he visits, and Rousseau's presentation of this standard has the appearance of absolute universality and precision. "Before observing, one must make some rules for one's observations. One must construct a standard to which measurements one makes can be related. Our principles of political right are that standard" (458; 4:837). Rousseau goes on to discuss sovereignty, the general will, and the relationship between the sovereign, the magistrates, and the government. While the arguments in support of these principles unfold along more or less the same lines as in the *Social Contract*, here Rousseau claims a much greater degree of precision. For example, while he passes over many specifics very briefly, he devotes considerable attention to the rule of "continual proportion" that should govern the balance of power between the sovereign, magistrates, and government. The point of this rule is that as the state grows or shrinks, the size of the government relative to the size of the people should grow or shrink proportionately. The example Rousseau provides—that of a state composed of ten thousand citizens—suggests that the size of the government should always be the square root of the size of the sovereign. Rousseau presents this formula as one that is neatly applicable to a state of any size, and he insists that "these rules are incontestable" (465; 4:846). Here he gives no indication that this rule has any limitations or qualifications.

However, in discussing the rule of continual proportion in the *Social Contract*, book III,[19] Rousseau includes numerous caveats that warn the reader against expecting a literal application of the formula. He notes, for instance, that the ratios under discussion "are measured not only by numbers of men, but more generally by the amount of activity," which is much less precisely calculable. He adds that it is impossible to provide an exact formula because factors such as climate and soil affect the equation. Furthermore, he expresses concern that he not be ridiculed for providing an overly neat and tidy formula when he intends something more flexible. Christopher Bertram thus concludes his detailed analysis of this section of the *Social Contract* with the following observation: "It would seem to follow from all this that Rousseau believes that while the 'square root' formula gives us a rule of thumb for the appropriate size of government, this can never be mechanically determined and will vary greatly depending on these further factors." Bertram adds that it is "part of the art of the lawgiver" to make the necessary determinations and judgments within a particular political community.[20]

This helps us to make sense of the absence of any mention of the legislator in *Emile*'s summary of the principles of the *Social Contract*, since the point of Emile's education is to get him to the point where he has no need of a legislator. He should be able to exercise judgment himself.[21] Thus the summary of the *Social Contract* Emile receives provides a standard against which he might evaluate existing political orders. I have argued, however, that the pattern Rousseau repeats throughout *Emile* is to encourage critical distance from each guiding standard that he furnishes, in order to cultivate genuinely independent judgment. Why, then, does he present these general rules as "incontestable?"

In fact, Rousseau *does* indirectly qualify the apparent seamlessness of the relationship between his universal political principles and the particulars of political life in *Emile*, just as he emphasizes the limits of the timeless model of love. Before articulating his principles of political right, he begins by observing that that "the science of political right is yet to be born, and it is to be presumed that it will never be born." He concedes that Montesquieu came closest to creating such a science but stopped short by focusing only on "the positive right of established governments." Montesquieu "was careful not to discuss the principles of political right." "Nevertheless," Rousseau continues, "whoever wants to make healthy judgments about existing governments is obliged to unite the two" (458; 4:836). Rousseau does not simply say that such a science has not yet been born but also that it will *never* be born, which suggests that a perfect reconciliation of abstract principles and particular circumstances is impossible (even for the venerable Montesquieu). The claim that one is nevertheless obliged to unite the two in order to judge suggests that one is obliged to *strive* to unite them; one must think them together, however imperfectly. That they cannot be perfectly or seamlessly united may be what makes a science of political right impossible, but at the same time it makes judgment both possible and necessary.

Moreover, as he approaches the conclusion of his discussion of political principles, Rousseau remarks that he would not be surprised if his pupil were to have "the good sense" to interrupt him in the middle of all of this reasoning to object that "someone might say that we are building our edifice with wood and not with men, so exactly do we align each piece with the ruler!" Rousseau would counter that "right is not bent by men's passions" and would encourage his pupil to examine what men have built on such impressive foundations. "You will see some fine things [*de belles choses*]!" (467; 4:849). By indirectly drawing attention to the limits of a human, as opposed to a natural, science, and at the same time maintaining that this illusory precision will enable one to see some beautiful or fine (rather than strictly true) things, Rousseau conforms here to the pattern we have seen throughout *Emile*, deploying a seductive image of perfection in order to inspire a salutary attachment to the "right" ideals. And he continues the pattern we have seen by following this image with a speech that dispels the illusion of perfection: Emile is finally asked to choose where he would like to settle with Sophie, and Emile, having absorbed this education in the "science" of political right, announces that it makes no difference to him where he lives, since all existing political orders will hamper his independence. He has, it seems, attached himself to imperishable principles, to the exclusion of any particular attachments (apart from Sophie). "Give me Sophie and my field—and I shall be rich," he declares. This may seem to reflect the freedom of an "abstract man," but Rousseau's immediate response draws attention to the difficulty that Emile's formulation implies: "A field which is yours, dear Emile! And in what place will you choose it?" (457; 4:835). There is no abstract or universal field; a field must be somewhere in particular.

Reproaching Emile for this "extravagant disinterestedness" (473; 4:857), Rousseau offers a strong corrective that is reminiscent of his critique of philosophical indifference in book IV. Although he approves of Emile's assessment of the corruption of all existing orders, he challenges the young man's understanding of the implications:

> If I were speaking to you of the duties of the citizen, you would perhaps ask me where the fatherland is, and you would believe you had confounded me. But you would be mistaken, dear Emile, for he who does not have a fatherland at least has a country. . . . Do not ask then, "What difference does it make to me where I am?" It makes a difference to you that you are where you can fulfill all your duties, and one of those duties is an attachment to the place of your birth. Your compatriots protected you as a child; you ought to love them as a man. (473–74; 4:858)

Rousseau draws attention here to the particularity of place, as he did with regard to time in the context of love, thus transcending the all-or-nothing framework of idealism versus disillusionment, both of which foster complete detachment from the existing social order. Emile must return to the cave, but he is not returning as a philosopher-king; he is returning as a man—a man who is neither utterly "abstract" nor defined by civil society. If he has gained wisdom, it is a distinctively human kind of wisdom that keeps in view both the ideal and the reality. For Rousseau, only a double perspective that encompasses both can distinguish what is real from fantasy. Mistaking fantasy for reality, or vice versa, is the error of those, like Hobbes, who look at civil man and believe they are seeing natural man (*SD*, 102; 3:132). This double perspective is consistent with

Judgment, Love, and Illusion ✳ 157

Emile's education in pity, which sought to inculcate a perspective from which he could judge his corrupted fellows without despising them. "Let him know that man is naturally good; let him feel it. . . . But let him see that society depraves and perverts men." If he loses sight of human goodness, he will "say to himself that if man is thus, he himself ought not to want to be otherwise" (*E*, 237; 4:526). In other words, man both is and is not "thus," or as he is found in civil society. If Rousseau consistently weaves together beautiful ideals with sobering caveats, this is why. His engagement with this tension is consistent across even the apparently divergent "negative" and "positive" segments of Emile's education. Just as one must see the child in the man and the man in the child, as he argues in book I, one must see the ideal image in existing conditions in order to see what is (in the sense of what actually exists) and also what could be (in the sense of what is truly real). This parallels the double sense of the "natural" as something both profoundly lost and yet always available to us. By attaching Emile to his country, while keeping in view both its imperfections and the perfection of the ideal that exists "only in men's hearts," Rousseau facilitates not blind attachment to either but partial detachment from both.

7

JUDGMENT AND THE POSSIBILITY OF PARTIAL DETACHMENT

All those perfect people are neither touching nor persuasive. (*E*, 334; 4:664)

Immediately after finishing *Emile*, Rousseau began working on a sequel, *Emile et Sophie, ou Les Solitaires*, which remained incomplete at the time of his death in 1778. The work consists of two letters from Emile to his absent tutor. In the first, Emile describes the events that led to the dissolution of his marriage to Sophie and laments the psychic pain that he has experienced as a result. In the second (unfinished) letter, Emile relates that he has become a new man, entirely free of his former attachments and reminiscent of the "abstract man" of book I of *Emile*. No longer a husband, father, or citizen, he travels the world until his ship is attacked and he is sold into slavery, eventually becoming the overseer of other slaves and an adviser to the Dey of Algiers. Rather than lament this turn of events, Emile announces that he is freer than ever before, and he attributes this achievement to his excellent education.

The existence of a sequel, even an unfinished one, means that Emile's story does not end with *Emile*, and therefore raises questions about what it might mean to understand Emile's education as a whole. Since Rousseau chose to publish *Emile* alone, with its happy ending and with no reference to Emile's subsequent experiences, *Emile* can and should be considered a whole unto itself. At the same time, it is *not* a complete whole, as there is more to the story.

Emile and Sophie can be understood as simultaneously continuous with and separate from *Emile*. In this respect its structure is the mirror image of book V, which has its own subtitle ("Sophie, or The Woman") and thus stands somewhat apart from the other books of *Emile*, even as it is part of the larger whole. In its very structure, then, *Emile* is an incomplete whole, which I believe reflects Rousseau's understanding of the human soul as neither simply whole nor simply incomplete but as characterized by a wholeness that is both threatened and enriched by our capacity for self-reflection.

Emile and Sophie invites us to reflect on and judge *Emile* in three different respects. First, and most directly, the letters concern Emile's judgment of Sophie after her infidelity. The epistolary form of his account allows the reader to survey all that transpires without accompanying commentary by Jean-Jacques, whose narration governed *Emile*. The narrator is absent to the reader as well as to Emile and Sophie. In other words, the reader, too, becomes "solitary," and this creates the second level of judgment, as the reader is put in a position to judge the choices and reactions of the two characters without the intervention of Rousseau's commentary. Finally, the striking contrast between the two works with regard to the fate of the supposedly ideal couple—happiness versus misery—calls for critical reflection on Rousseau's claims about the character of their relationship and their respective educations. Just as Emile must compare Sophie's fallen reality with the image he has loved for so long, the reader must compare the dissolved relationship with the image of perfect harmony that was cultivated in *Emile*. In other words, three judgments take place: Emile must judge Sophie, we must judge Emile and Sophie, and we must judge *Emile*. We reflect on the most fundamental controlling image (Sophie) in Emile's education, as he does, but also on Emile, and on the happy couple—that is, on the controlling images in the reader's education. In this way *Emile and Sophie* can be understood not simply as the "test" of the education that was fully completed in *Emile* but as its final lesson—one that can only be learned in complete freedom from the guiding hand of an authority figure. We should keep in mind Rousseau's insistence that an educator must omit furnishing the pupil with the moral of a fable, so that the student may discern it independently.

What is the lesson of *Emile and Sophie*? Some scholars interpret the work as evidence of the success of Emile's natural education insofar as he reverts to his natural independence, while others argue that it represents the failure of his social education insofar as the goal is the achievement of a positive form of interdependence. Taking the first approach, for example, Patrick Deneen argues that *Emile and Sophie* illustrates Rousseau's principle that solitude is preferable to the happiness of love because it protects us from the misery that inevitably results from entanglements with others. Reading *Emile* as a work designed explicitly to create a human being who approximates as closely as possible the asocial man of the original state of nature, Deneen argues that Emile is successful in freeing himself from his relationship to Sophie "in accordance with the principles of his education," which was designed to "allow him to retain the ability to unencumber himself of all needs and affections beyond those that will allow him to leave, again and again."[1] Similarly, Thomas Kavanagh judges Emile's education a resounding success in that Emile has freed himself from human passions. According to Kavanagh, Emile's passionlessness allows him to become, finally, his own master, led only by reason.[2]

Such interpretations discount the significance of the second half of Emile's education, beginning in book IV: the education in pity, sociability, and love. They present Emile's final state of mind as a return to himself. But this implies that the new needs and desires that grew out of the experience of loving Sophie form no part of Emile's actual self, and that they have not indelibly altered his original form. In fact, however, owing to human perfectibility, Emile is no more able to return to an earlier version of himself, living in the simplicity and independence of the state of nature, than anyone else is. Emile's soul may not be as deformed as that of most human beings, who resemble the statue of Glaucus, rendered virtually unrecognizable by the elements (the image with which Rousseau opens his *Second Discourse*), but he has tasted "the sweetest sentiments known to man—conjugal love and paternal love" (*SD*, 146–47; 3:168) and is thus irreversibly altered. To deny the significance of the second half of Emile's education is to ignore the fundamental role of perfectibility in Rousseau's understanding of human nature, and thus to beg the deepest question Rousseau raises. Given human perfectibility, what is finally "natural" for such a being? In terms of the overall project of *Emile*, this question becomes, what would it mean for Emile to be himself, once he has changed? We have tracked the tension between integrity and change throughout Emile's education; this tension reaches its peak in *Emile and Sophie*.

Other scholars, such as Judith Shklar and Marie-Hélène Huet, read the work as a tragic portrayal of inevitable decline that reflects Rousseau's pessimism about the long-term prospects of any legitimate social order.[3] In this view, the sequel signifies not a triumphant return to individual autonomy but a failure of interdependence in which the fragmentation of domestic order prefigures the fragmentation of a political order that cannot be preserved without the guiding hand of a wise and manipulative authority figure.[4]

Thus the question whether *Emile and Sophie* signals the success or failure of Rousseau's project turns on how we understand the ideal of human freedom that governs that project. If we assume that Rousseau aims to reproduce the self-sufficiency of natural man, then one picture emerges. If we assume (taking what is generally understood as the Kantian view of Rousseau) that the ideal is willing submission to the whole of the family (which, in its wholeness, independence, and virtue, stands in for the virtuous republic), then a less triumphant picture emerges. My reading moves past this either/or interpretive framework. If we consider the possibility that Rousseau may be aiming at neither of these two wholes (radical autonomy or complete cohesion) but rather at a middle state, another sort of reading is possible, one in which self-consciousness becomes the central issue. This failure of Emile's marriage opens up and is connected to the possibility of achievement on another scale, insofar as Emile is finally thrust into a position of self-consciousness (which is excluded from the unselfconscious wholeness of natural man and the seamless cohesion of the domestic/political republic) and confronts the challenges of genuine self-rule. Having judged the physical and social worlds under the guidance of his tutor, only now, in the absence of any compass to guide him, is Emile finally positioned to exercise truly independent judgment. This requires that he become the judge of his judges—that he reflect critically on his education, on his beloved Sophie, and on himself.

The "test" of *Emile and Sophie* is thus a test of the human capacity for reflection and judgment. The tutor's absence is of critical importance insofar as it creates an opportunity for self-consciousness and self-rule. Just as the *Second Discourse* considers what humanity would become if left to itself (i.e., in the absence of God, the Author), the sequel to *Emile* considers what Rousseau's new and improved natural man, equipped with the "philosophy and experience" that original man lacked, might become under the same conditions—in the absence of the tutor, the "author" of his being. Moreover, the epistolary form of the sequel puts the reader in the same abandoned position as the human race (and as a newly conceived Adam and Eve: Emile and Sophie), as the reader is deprived of Rousseau's running commentary, or the hand of the author. The solitude of the sequel's subtitle—*Les Solitaires*—resonates in all three registers.

Sophie's Fall and Emile's Response

Emile's first letter to his tutor opens with a lamentation over the loss of his freedom and happiness. Emile and Sophie are no longer a couple. Emile claims that he has lost everything and wonders whether he will be able to bear living much longer. He wonders whether the tutor is dead or alive; either way, he says, the tutor is dead for him. But of course the tutor is *not* dead for Emile, since Emile chooses to address his letters to him. It is true that he does not expect an answer, so one might argue that he is self-sufficient in his writing, writing for himself rather than for another. But he does not simply keep a diary; he writes to another who is both present and absent to him.

The letter goes on to recount the events that led Emile into his present state of mind. Emile explains that Sophie's parents and beloved daughter died in rapid succession. Sophie became inconsolable. To distract Sophie from her grief, Emile persuaded her to accompany him to Paris. There, the lovers grew apart as they began to participate in its corrupt society. Emile's attention wandered from Sophie, and while Sophie was indeed distracted from her grief, she was also distracted from Emile. They befriended another couple with what we would call an open marriage, and then began to drift apart. They started to treat each other differently in private and in public. Their relationship became a superficial shell, their hearts invested not in each other but in worldly affairs.

Finally, Sophie became upset and withdrawn. She refused to see her new friends, to tell Emile what was wrong, or to let him touch her. Her stubbornness reignited Emile's passion for her, and he became determined to win her back. He did not, however, perceive the cause of Sophie's withdrawal. Whereas her initial seclusion followed the death of her daughter, the cause of the second remained mysterious—a repetition of the pattern we have seen numerous times in Rousseau: the narrative returns to a subject or situation that arose earlier but with something decisive omitted or concealed, which occasions the exercise of judgment. In this case, Emile is challenged to understand the change in Sophie's behavior. He tells himself that she persists in her refusals out of pride, and he decides to help her out by providing her with the cover of a little coercion on his part. This plan backfires; at the last minute, she pulls away from him and announces that she is pregnant by another man, adding, "I am no longer anything to you. . . . You will not touch me again in my life" (*ES*, 692–93; 4:890). The rest of the letter is about Emile's reaction to this revelation.

We might expect Emile to absorb this shocking blow without flinching, given that during his courtship with Sophie, when he was madly infatuated with her, the tutor tested him by asking, "What would you do if you were informed that Sophie is dead?" (*E*, 442; 4:814). Emile had reacted badly to the question, and the tutor used the occasion to teach a lesson about the need to remain in control of one's passions and attachments. Now, years later, Sophie is not literally dead, but she has betrayed Emile and her virtue. Her fall from virtue might be a fate worse than death, as far as Emile is concerned; it is the death of the illusion that was the true object of his love. Had Sophie died, she might have lived on in his memory with her lovely virtue intact and continued to serve as a regulating ideal in Emile's life. The death of the illusion presents a greater challenge, but also a more significant opportunity for Emile to become self-ruling. Instead of being unconsciously governed by an idealized image furnished by his tutor, he might become critically self-aware of what truly moves him.

The role of illusions is as important in the sequel as it was in *Emile*. As the young couple approached Paris, Emile explains in his letter, he was struck by a sense of foreboding and began to fear that he was leading them into a "pit of prejudices and vices to which innocence and happiness proceed from every direction in order to be ruined" (*ES*, 688; 4:885). He dismissed this premonition at the time, treating it as "a chimera." Here we see the true nature and significance of Emile's lapse of judgment. He did not forget about the dangers of Paris or his tutor's warnings about the corruption of big cities. He made a more fundamental mistake: he confused image and reality with regard to himself and his relationship. What he took to be a chimera in this case was actually real. The disintegration of his relationship with Sophie (which began long before she committed adultery) was not a simple matter of ardor cooling and attention beginning to wander. Both of these things happened, but the fundamental problem is not that his scope of vision has broadened but that it is not broad *enough*, insofar as it does not encompass critical reflection on his own judgments.

Emile agonizes over his marital crisis for three days, and the letter offers a very detailed account of his thought process, which unfolds in three stages. Put simply, on the first day, Emile is too undone to judge at all; on the second day, he judges with his heart; and on the third day, he judges strictly rationally. On the first day, when Emile learns of Sophie's infidelity, he wanders through the city in the throes of despair, disorientation, and disillusionment. He realizes that the object of his affection for so many years was nothing but a chimera. In this agitated state, he cannot form any judgments. "I was in no condition to see anything, to compare anything, to deliberate, to resolve, to judge about anything" (694; 4:892). The next morning, he sets out for a long walk. He leaves the city limits and heads out into the countryside, where he continues to walk all day. He becomes, we might say, a solitary walker. As he walks, he reflects, and his reflections are guided solely by his sentiments. He continually refers to what his heart is inclining him to feel and to believe about Sophie and their situation, and he strives mightily to hold on to the image of Sophie as pure and virtuous. The alternative is too painful to bear. Vacillating wildly between loving Sophie and hating her, Emile has little control over his emotions during this second stage. Although unable to bear the "horrible idea" of Sophie "debased and despicable," he finds himself "going back over that fatal object in spite of [him]self," and feels "forced to despise her" (697; 4:895). Finally, unable to bridge the chasm between what Sophie was and what she has become, Emile concludes that Sophie is "the most odious of all monsters" (697; 4:896).

But not all complexity is necessarily monstrosity. Emile does not consider this possibility; he needs, or thinks he needs, a perfectly seamless whole. Seeking to preserve Sophie's wholeness in his imagination, he decides that the entire episode was his fault, for it was he who drew Sophie to Paris, he who neglected her and left her vulnerable. In order to hold Sophie blameless, he resorts to a kind of mind/body dualism, convincing himself that only her body committed adultery, while her heart remained pure (698; 4:897). He decides that he should hate himself rather than her. Finally, he goes so far as to express admiration for Sophie, noting that nothing forced her to reveal her infidelity but her own sense of honor and pride and respect for the institution of fatherhood. Indeed, he tells himself, her virtue was not sullied but actually enhanced by her confession. The virtue of the confession canceled out the sin confessed. Drawn to this "more bearable" judgment by his "heart's inclination," Emile experiences joy and relief in "imagining [Sophie] to be less disfigured" than he had thought at first (699; 4:898–99).

Having managed to explain away Sophie's adultery with a view to restoring her pristine image, Emile eats his dinner and sleeps peacefully until morning, his world intact. His heart has taken him full circle. Whereas he had been blinded by pain and anger, he now sees Sophie as she used to be, a beautiful image of virtue with her flaw buffed away. He is no longer blinded by anger, but he is still blind. He has attached himself to the imperishable beauty of her unsullied image, but this image is nothing but a noble lie. As we observe Emile's anguish and confusion as he tries to come to terms with Sophie's betrayal, we cannot help but notice that he fails to do one obvious thing: he does not ask Sophie for an explanation. Although his tutor has taught him (in book IV of *Emile*, in the context of another revelation) to demand reasons before submitting to authority, Emile accepts Sophie's declaration that he will never touch her again without asking a single question. He is tossed to and fro by passion, without engaging reason.

On the morning of the third day, Emile resolves to begin anew, deciding that he must face reality with no illusions. He now strives to disengage his heart and judge by reason alone. But before he closes himself off completely to the urgings of his heart, he rests for a moment in an interesting equilibrium between passion and reason. This, to my mind, is the most significant moment in the letter. Until this point, he has been driven by passion, which has consistently blinded him—first to anything but Sophie's flaw, then to the flaw itself. He will soon become completely detached from her, and rather cold and sanctimonious in his supposedly rational arguments. But, for a moment, he manages to incorporate Sophie's lapse into a more complex understanding of virtue—not by restoring her to perfection but by appreciating the value of her imperfection. "Sophie," he states, "having remained estimable even in crime, will be respectable in her repentance; she will be all the more faithful because her heart made for virtue has felt what it costs it to offend against it" (701; 4:900). The self-consciousness that Emile sees as a potential outgrowth of Sophie's situation implies a divided self, as opposed to a seamless, unmediated whole. Moreover, this divided self is presented in a positive light, as something that might contribute to greater virtue over the long term in someone who understands the cost of losing it. Emile's reflections intimate the possibility that he could love Sophie—a flawed but still lovable Sophie—on new terms, neither seduced by her illusory perfection nor utterly disenchanted. This middle perspective is captured in Emile's own assessment of his thought process. Whereas he initially vacillated between complete attachment and complete detachment, he now moves toward a middle ground. He observes that in order to think through his situation properly, his heart, which was accustomed to feeling "indissolubly united" with his family, would have to be detached from them, "*at least in part, and that was even more painful than to detach it completely*" (705; 4:905, emphasis added).

Like the flawed but still lovable image of Sophie, Emile's own experience of partial detachment makes only a brief appearance in the letter. Emile does not remain in this fragile state but detaches himself emotionally in favor of proceeding on the basis of reason alone. He decides that what he had loved was nothing but a chimera, and he categorically turns his back on that illusion, and with it, on Sophie. She is nothing to him now. This categorical rejection looks and feels quite similar to the blind fury he experienced on the first day. Before Emile leaves Sophie for good, however, he must decide what to do about his son. Again, Rousseau does not simply announce Emile's conclusion; he details the evolution of his thinking. At first, Emile decides that he must take his son away from Sophie as punishment for her infidelity. His anger returns, and he states that he would rather see his son dead than raised by another man (704; 4:904). But before he can act on this decision, he is prompted to reconsider it by an "unforeseen event." Having found work as a carpenter, he learns one day that Sophie has paid a visit to his place of employment and spent some time observing him intently without his awareness. His employers tell him that after much weeping and anguish, Sophie calmly informed her son, "No, he will never want to take your mother away from you; come, we have nothing to do here" (707; 4:907). Hearing this, Emile reconsiders his decision, noticing that the same action that seemed reasonable to him seemed unreasonable to Sophie. "Which was wrong?" he asks (708; 4:908). He tries to look at the matter as he thinks she would, and realizes that in seeking to punish Sophie he would also punish the child. Entering into Sophie's perspective pushes Emile to judge not only whether his decision is reasonable but also whether *he* is being reasonable. He imagines how he must have looked to her as she observed him working intently at his carpentry. "What had she seen?" he wonders. "Emile at peace, Emile at labor. What proof could she draw from this sight?" (708; 4:908). In other words, he asks, how did Sophie interpret this image?

Sophie's overheard remark is an observation about what kind of man Emile is, not a calculation of the relative merit of a course of action. This is in keeping with the "feminine" education that Rousseau prescribed for her, which was grounded in particulars rather than abstractions. But it is also presented here as a corrective to Emile's tendency toward abstract reasoning. Emile is finally looking at himself through her eyes, not in order to impress her but so as to understand his own character. He neither accepts nor rejects her assessment uncritically. And, while she offers a corrective, she does not control or manipulate Emile's own thinking, as she (and the tutor) did so often in the past. Nor does he simply throw off her influence completely. He allows her judgment to inform his own, but not to determine it. This is another moment of partial detachment.

Elizabeth Wingrove characterizes Emile's deliberations quite differently, arguing that the two poles between which he vacillates are not passion and reason but passion and the force of law—that is, the tyranny of love and the tyranny of the state. Emile loves Sophie, but he cannot, as her legal husband, abide her infidelity. Wingrove concludes that although Emile's moral capacity and political identity are secured in his passion for Sophie, that passion relies "in turn on the authorizing, sanctifying, and enforcing power of the husband-as-peerless-father, which is to say, on the ordering and enforcing power of the state."[5] Although Jean-Jacques advised the young couple to go on being lovers after marriage as a way of preserving the freedom of their association, Wingrove's analysis suggests that this apparent freedom rests on an unavoidable paternalism. Thus Rousseau does not ultimately improve substantially upon Hobbes's prescription but simply confirms by an alternate route (erotic passion replaces fear of violent death) that subjection is always and inevitably a feature of political and moral agency.

If the two poles between which Emile oscillates were the only possibilities indicated in his letter, then Wingrove's conclusion would perhaps be warranted. However, Emile considers a third possibility, that of partial detachment, and this, along with his reaction to Sophie's visit, suggests that our choices are not necessarily limited to the tyranny of love or the tyranny of the state. Rousseau's depiction, in book V of *Emile*, of Sophie's rule as neither tyrannical nor submissive points beyond these two poles as well.

Detachment and Freedom

After Emile cuts all ties with Sophie and his son, he sets sail and eventually falls into slavery, an experience that he describes in his second (unfinished) letter. Despite being enslaved, Emile insists that this is the time of his greatest freedom, that he is freer than he has ever been in his life (715; 4:916). One wonders what to make of this claim. Perhaps Emile's situation is meant to be a twist on Rousseau's famous dictum that there is no slavery so complete as that which has the appearance of freedom; Emile's example might suggest that complete freedom has the external appearance of slavery. It is just as plausible, however, that Emile ran to meet his chains thinking that he was embracing freedom, as Rousseau puts it in the *Second Discourse*. Once again, the reader must judge, although at this point, unlike in previous instances throughout *Emile*, we do not have Rousseau's express invitation. Here, Emile expresses his judgment of his situation, and the reader is implicitly asked to make an independent judgment about the soundness of Emile's judgment.

Rationalizing his status as a slave, Emile remarks, "In order not to fall into nothingness I needed to be animated by someone else's will for lack of my own." He is not so much a whole unto himself as an empty vessel. It is only for this reason that he has no problem with being driven by the will of another. He thrives because of his enslavement, not in spite of it. After all, he muses, "if I had my freedom, what would I do with it? In the condition I am in, what can I want?" (714; 4:917). Deprived of all attachments and desires, he is free of the pain that human longing can cause, but this does not make him self-ruling. He consents to being a slave, which Rousseau in other contexts insists is illegitimate. He avoids doing injustice to others or causing himself unhappiness, but he is neither virtuous nor happy. And he cannot be said to be free in light of Rousseau's contention that human freedom consists, above all, in not being subject to the will of another human being.[6] Emile's own will is not opposed by anyone only because he has no will of his own.[7] He justifies this submission by appealing to his tutor's lessons about submitting to necessity. "Was I not born the slave of necessity? What new yoke can men impose on me?" (715; 4:916–17).

Has Emile learned his tutor's lessons extraordinarily well, or has he misunderstood them? Although Emile sees no difference between his present yoke of conventional slavery and the yoke of necessity imposed by nature, we cannot lose sight of Rousseau's primary concern for protecting individuals from subjection to the will of others. That Emile thinks there is no difference suggests a failure of judgment on his part. He simply fails to distinguish at all, just as he failed to distinguish between chimera and reality when heading to Paris. Moreover, earlier in his education, when Emile declared to his tutor that he had learned that in order to be free one must "do nothing," the tutor had criticized him for his "extravagant disinterestedness" and reminded him that he had duties no matter where he lived, and no matter how corrupt the laws of that land. Now Emile reverts to his indifference, stating that it does not matter to him where he is (714; 4:915). To be sure, the social contract is not observed in most places, so Emile is supposed to carry it with him in his heart wherever he goes. But these are not simply abstract principles that allow him to turn away from the particulars of any regime. The lesson of book V was that he must honor these principles, and the laws of his country, simultaneously. The goal is to see the real in the ideal, and the ideal in the real, and to be inside and outside a particular political order. This is a complex, challenging, and potentially transformative perspective reminiscent of Sophie's inside/outside perspective in her relationship with Emile.

Emile's lack of passion recalls Rousseau's well-known critique of the Enlightenment project of attempting to govern the human soul by reason alone: often, when it appears that reason is moving us, the opposite is in fact the case; vanity is driving reason. Emile demonstrates this beautifully in spite of himself when he flees the pain of remembering Sophie. He attempts to rid himself of his passion in order to purify his reason but ends up allowing his passion to determine his course. In deciding what to do with the rest of his life, Emile explains, "I followed the direction contrary to the object that I had to flee" (711; 4:912). Sophie had been a positive pole attracting him but now becomes a negative pole repelling him; in neither case is Emile indifferent. We see a similar entanglement in Emile's celebration of the fact that he is driven by a will other than his own, insofar as his purported detachment depends so completely upon that from which he is supposedly detached. In short, divesting himself of all desire does not make Emile the good, reasonable judge that he aspires to be. It leaves him enslaved by his passions—exactly the problem suggested by Rousseau's general critique of Enlightenment rationalism. Rousseau observes that anyone truly moved by reason is moved because he or she *loves* reason, and this love is not simply the result of rational calculation. Of course, this suggests that only sentiment and the illusions that inspire it can move us, and that we are thus inescapably governed by something outside ourselves. We seem to be left with the impossibility of self-rule, and the inevitability of some form of (possibly concealed) subjection, *unless* there is a way of relating to those illusions that both allows them to move us and mitigates their hold on us. It is this possibility that Rousseau explores throughout Emile's education, and that Emile exemplifies when he experiences partial detachment from the controlling image of his beloved Sophie.

Partial Detachment and Partial Freedom

Emile's struggle to navigate his relationship to both the image of his idealized Sophie and the reality of his fallen Sophie reflects the broader question of the proper stance of human beings toward poetic images and chimeras. Rousseau believes that, at best, such images can reorient our sensibilities, enabling us to see and to judge what is truly good, but at the same time they may cause us to suspend critical judgment and thus circumvent reflection on the question of what is truly good. Emile himself is one such image, one of Rousseau's "ideals" intended to move us to see differently, to judge soundly. *Emile and Sophie* helps us think about how we should look at Emile—not simply by providing a vantage point from which to reflect retrospectively on his education but also by suggesting what it would mean to do it well. In this latter sense, it is about how to look not only at Emile in particular but at images in general. I have argued that the first letter in *Emile and Sophie* explores several ways of addressing the tension between the perfect ideal and the flawed reality. I have emphasized the importance of Emile's momentary hovering in the middle ground of "partial detachment," which allows him to draw on both reason and sentiment in order to judge well. The possibility of partial detachment is introduced and then abandoned. We cannot determine definitively Rousseau's final word on Emile and the possibilities he represents, because the work was left unfinished.[8] But just as the flawed but still lovable Sophie makes a brief appearance in Emile's new life, his own observation about partial detachment offers a brief glimpse of a middle ground between complete attachment (or being "one" with someone or something) and complete detachment (being "one" alone).

Rousseau reinforces this understanding of partial detachment in the way that he conveys his own ideals. By drawing attention to the imperfections of his imaginary ideals, Rousseau invites precisely this partially detached perspective. "I present my dreams as dreams, which others are not careful to do," he writes in *Emile*, "leaving it to the reader to find out whether they contain something useful for people who are awake" (112; 4:351). Rousseau's depiction of the failure of this supposedly perfect marriage, and the corruption of the perfect man and woman, is for the reader what Sophie's fall from grace is for Emile: a destabilization that opens up the possibility of another perspective, one that neither loves blindly nor is utterly detached. If the project of *Emile* is to educate judgment, it has to strike this balance, even if Emile himself ultimately cannot do it, or can do it only fleetingly. It is in part because of his failure, and the failure of his marriage, not despite them, that the reader learns to judge. Rousseau's beautiful images have to move us in order to seduce us away from our own corrupt standards of judgment, but they cannot be so seductive that we become incapable of judging for ourselves. Rousseau reminds his readers of this at every turn, each time he asks us to judge in the middle of a story that is supposed to teach us to judge.

Throughout *Emile*, Rousseau associates wisdom with knowing how to stay in one's place, a notion that is neither as simple nor as static as it first appears. I have returned to this phrase numerous times throughout this book, to explore its meaning as the idea is developed throughout Emile's education and to reflect on the implications for Rousseau's understanding of the possibility of self-rule. We can trace the downfall of Emile and Sophie's marriage to Emile's oversimplification of what it means to stay in place. He assumes that even when he and Sophie move to Paris, staying in place—that is, remaining the couple that they are—will take care of itself, since this has always been taken care of for him. The challenge they face, however, is not strictly the physical change in location or even the new culture to which they are exposed; Emile has withstood such pressures before. The fundamental problem is that Emile assumes he can withstand the temptations of a decadent culture simply because he withstood them the last time he was there. He assumes that staying in place simply means remaining the same, and that it requires no new tools. But it does *not* simply mean staying the same, because change is part of the human condition, as Rousseau makes clear again and again. After he abandons Sophie, Emile does not claim to have returned unscathed to his original or true self but to have made a complete break, in effect becoming a new being. To be sure, this new being bears some resemblance to the self-contained physical being that he was prior to book IV, and much of Emile's self-presentation in his second letter echoes Rousseau's own rhetoric in the early books of *Emile*. But just as we should not assume when reading the *Second Discourse* that Rousseau sees the ideal as a return to the original state of nature, we should not assume that Emile's ideal response to Sophie's betrayal is to return to an earlier version of himself.

Thus the fundamental question is not whether Emile can continue on "autopilot" once his tutor departs, but whether he can preserve the spirit of the tutor's work by adapting his perspective to unforeseen circumstances that challenge the simplicity of that perspective. Again, the issue is the possibility of combining growth/change and integrity/remaining oneself. This combination requires more than rigidly resisting all change. Rousseau suggests the limitations of a perspective that resists change in his account of Emile's sense of foreboding as the couple approached Paris. In the background is his earlier trip to Paris, when the tutor forced him to take a break from Sophie and learn about the world. However, circumstances have changed. The first time Emile went to Paris, he was immune to the temptation of the superficial pleasures of city life because his conditioning protected him against their appeal. This result depended completely on the tutor's machinations, however. By showing that Emile's conditioning fails him the second time around, Rousseau presents not a pessimistic view that all, even the most carefully inculcated conditioning, must decay, but an understanding that conditioning *cannot* confer invulnerability in the absence of reflection that directs, mobilizes, and adapts it in order to preserve its effects.

This is clearly one of the lessons of Rousseau's discourse on taste in book V of *Emile*, where he argues that the key to good taste (and to happiness generally) is to seek true rather than chimerical pleasures. One must be able to see the difference between them—which means both to *taste* and to *understand* the difference between them. Rousseau signals the need for both tasting and understanding as early as book II, as we saw in chapter 2. In book IV, Jean-Jacques offered himself as a model because Emile's tastes were too pure to serve as an example. I argued in chapter 5 that the implication of this substitution was that Emile made the "right" choices too automatically, without reflection. In other words, he had been *too* well conditioned, only "tasting" without knowing the *why*. This conditioning served him well the first time in Paris, because his tutor controlled his environment and his interaction with it. But it does not suffice when circumstances change, which Rousseau depicts vividly in *Emile and Sophie*.

It takes good judgment to know when to modify and when to resist; we are reminded of the description, in *Emile*, of Sophie's knowing when to submit and when to lead (383; 4:731). For all his conditioning, Emile initially falters when faced with such decisions in the absence of external guidance. The root of his difficulty is that he tends to confuse the real with the chimerical. His conflation of the two in his presentiment of doom as the couple approached Paris had tragic consequences. Also contributing to Emile's faulty judgment is the fact that he lacks any sense of fragility or contingency regarding his relationship with Sophie, as we see in *Emile and Sophie* when Emile states that he is "certain" (*sûr*) of her and of himself (688; 4:885). His unshakable certainty and sense of security are what lead him to dismiss his presentiment of the threats that await them in Paris. His confidence is in part a testament to the strength and depth of the bond he shares with Sophie, but he fails to consider the degree to which this bond is an illusion based on erotic attachment. The drawback of existing wholly inside this bond is ignorance of the larger context that supports it. An education *about* love (which Sophie receives to some degree but the reader receives even more comprehensively) and its contingency is a necessary complement to being *in* love. On the one hand, it might threaten the magic of being in love; on the other, it alone creates the possibility that our prospects are not limited to falling in love and falling radically out of love.[9]

Emile understands only in retrospect why he was immune to the temptations of Paris the first time around. To the degree that he initially lacks this understanding—that is, *self*-understanding—Emile does not rule himself and is not truly free, no matter how free he may subjectively feel. Over time, his education shows that proper conditioning is one form of preparation for self-rule, but the cultivation of self-awareness is another—which is why the "enlightenment" scene in book IV, in which the "cords and pulleys" of Emile's education are revealed, is so important. The goal is not simply the cementing of Emile's attachment to the tutor. This is certainly one effect, insofar as Emile now consents to the tutor's rule (which had theretofore remained invisible to him), but the tutor then criticizes Emile's eagerness to submit. This critique points beyond the moment of Emile's consent to be ruled toward the possibility of a more substantive form of self-rule. The longer-term goal is not momentary (and arguably illusory) self-rule that creates the opportunity to consent to giving that capacity away, but rather ongoing self-government. This is made possible not by further, deeper conditioning but by awareness of the movements of one's own soul. Rousseau understands the source of the soul's motion as simultaneously intrinsic and extrinsic to it, just as the source of the general will is both internal and external to the people, as we see in the tension between the independence of the general will and the formative role of the legislator who shapes that will. This underlies his understanding of human freedom, which is not identical to the chimerical ideals of freedom that he parades before his readers' eyes. It is, finally, neither a romantic nor a pessimistic view of freedom: insofar as we can be partially detached from the illusions that inevitably influence our judgments, we can be partially free.

Throughout this book, I have argued that Rousseau continually introduces new requirements that alter the meaning of "staying in place," and thus of human wisdom, as *Emile* unfolds. I submit that *Emile*'s ultimate lesson is that human happiness and freedom are achieved not by remaining immobile and static but by combining integrity and change.[10] Only then might one grow old forever learning, as Rousseau phrases it (quoting Solon) in the third walk of the *Reveries*.[11] Only then might one reconcile the idea of human nature with the idea of human perfectibility. Only then might one *be* a self (authentically, unselfconsciously, and without division) even as one *rules* oneself (which requires self-reflection for the purpose of self-direction). Rousseau grappled with these tensions, in one form or another, throughout his works. His point was not to identify one side or the other as definitive but to clarify the nature of the tension itself, in order to recognize and distinguish between its healthy and unhealthy forms. *Emile* is an exploration of what it means to *live* the tension as something dynamic and invigorating and conducive to human freedom, rather than as something that renders the human soul incoherent. Living this tension, however, does not mean resolving it. It means achieving an understanding of it that elevates us above being merely a victim to it, even as we remain within it. Insofar as freedom is made possible by self-knowledge, Rousseau suggests, it does not result in a godlike overcoming of nature but allows us to occupy our place in nature in a manner that is compatible with the requirements of human dignity and self-rule.

8

JUDGMENT AND CITIZENSHIP

The limits of the possible in moral matters are less narrow than we think. (*SC*, 189; 3:425)

The success of the first foundation will make change necessary afterwards. (*CC*, 128; 3:906–7)

I have argued that the ultimate purpose of Rousseau's educational project as it unfolds in *Emile* is the cultivation of good judgment, the cornerstone of which he sees as the ability to discern the illusions that cloud our view of human relationships without becoming either thoroughly seduced or thoroughly disillusioned. As we have seen, *Emile* advocates a large dose of manipulation and deception in early childhood, but as his pupil reaches adolescence Rousseau introduces a shift, such that Emile is ultimately educated away from such contrivances and toward independent judgment and self-knowledge. This is reflected in Rousseau's depiction of a form of love that does not rely on illusion and, more directly, in his education of the reader with regard to the illusory ideals that he presents in the book. Rousseau's engagement of the reader consistently operates on two levels: first, he turns us away from the deceptions that surround us by seducing us with new ideals of happiness and freedom; and second, he weans us away from dependence even on these ideals by drawing attention to their limitations and showing why they are nevertheless necessary. Thus the same illusions that make self-rule possible, in Rousseau's view, also make it necessary: they motivate us but cannot substitute for the judgment that is necessary to political life over the long term.

My reading of *Emile* suggests that it is difficult, but not impossible, to achieve this partially detached perspective; Emile, Sophie, and Rousseau himself succeed in this to varying degrees—and it is possible also for the reader, whom Rousseau invites to judge both his fictional characters and himself. But is it conceivable that such a perspective could come into play in political communities, which Rousseau insists must be rooted in love of country? On the surface, there seems to be very little continuity between the education of judgment that we see in *Emile* and the civic education that Rousseau describes in such political works as the *Discourse on Political Economy* and *Considerations on the Government of Poland*. Whereas Emile is challenged to think his own thoughts, the citizens in these works are conditioned to be fervently patriotic. In the *Political Economy*, for example, Rousseau remarks, "Do we want people to be virtuous? Let us begin by making them love their fatherland" (*PE*, 152; 3:255), and then in the service of fostering this love recommends a program of civic education that relies heavily on manipulation and illusions. Similarly, in the *Government of Poland*, Rousseau prescribes a rigorous life-long program of civic education designed to produce citizens who are "patriotic by inclination, passionately, of necessity" (*GP*, 19; 3:966). Both works suggest the need for an educational authority resembling the godlike legislator of the *Social Contract*, that "supreme illusionist"[1] who mythologizes the community's origins and encourages citizens' reverence for an idealized political identity. We might see Rousseau himself as taking on this role when, in his "Dedication to Geneva" in the *Second Discourse*, he attempts to deepen the emotional attachment of the citizens of Geneva to their regime. That is, he presents such a highly embellished image of Geneva that we may wonder if he is trying to manipulate the people into feeling uncritical reverence for their fatherland. In each of these cases, passionate attachment seems to trump judgment as Rousseau's foremost concern.

There is nevertheless evidence that Rousseau is concerned with increasing the human capacity for judgment on the political level. In the *Discourse on Political Economy*, after extolling the virtues of a deeply nationalistic education, Rousseau remarks that citizens should one day become "the fathers of the country whose children they have been for so long" (*PE*, 156; 3:261). Of course, this raises a vexing question: how can children subjected to a rigorous, parochial civic education, trained to be utterly obedient to the "mother" state, suddenly stop behaving like obedient children and become like "fathers"? If they are to succeed in this transformation, they cannot simply be the products of such an education. They must come to understand its principles and purposes in order to adapt them to changing circumstances over time. As a result, they must become conscious of its artful quality—just as Emile would have to read *Emile* in order to replicate his own education for his children.

Citizens who are manipulated and seduced into loving virtue and country would seem to be in a state of perpetual dependence upon the authority figures who do the seducing and manipulating, even if they are blind to that dependence. Even if they fully internalize the myths they are spoon-fed, the passions stimulated by these myths are likely to wane over time, as all passions do, replaced by the kind of moral and social decay that, Rousseau maintains, spells the death of freedom. Thus illusions and the passions they generate serve a necessary but problematic function in Rousseau's understanding of citizenship, which requires deep conditioning but at the same time must be more than a deeply conditioned, unconscious reflex if it is to be sustained. To what degree does Rousseau's account of civic education address this paradoxical notion of citizenship?

Rousseau merely hints at this challenge in the *Discourse on Political Economy*; he devotes most of what he says about civic education to the education of children, who must be taught to love their country from an early age. If they are, then the rest—or most of it—will follow. "Anywhere the populace loves its country, respects its laws and lives simply, little else remains to do to make it happy" (*PE*, 157; 3:262). "Little else" is not *nothing* else, of course. The question remains: what exactly is required if a person is not only to be "made" happy but to remain happy over the long term—after the legislator (or the tutor) departs?

It can perhaps be said that expecting long-term happiness is unrealistic, for Rousseau was notoriously pessimistic about the prospects of maintaining the health of any social arrangement over the long term. Nothing is exempt from the law of decay. But planning for the long term is not the same as hoping for immortality. Health and vigor can be maximized and prolonged, even if nothing lasts forever. "It is not within the power of men to prolong their life; it is within their power to prolong that of the State as far as possible" (*SC*, 188; 3:424). What is required is the preservation of a strong sense of identity and reverence toward long-standing laws; "the prejudice favoring antiquity renders [the laws] more venerable each day. In contrast, wherever the laws weaken as they grow older . . . the State is no longer alive" (*SC*, 189; 3:425). But prejudice favoring antiquity is not Rousseau's only concern. It is not enough to preserve the law as a venerated but antiquated artifact; Rousseau's concern is not mere preservation but ongoing vitality. To be sure, this vitality requires the citizens' passionate patriotic devotion, and the festivals and other public activities that nurture that devotion, but it also requires the exercise of judgment. When, in the *Discourse on Political Economy*, Rousseau speaks of teaching the citizens to love "one object more than another," he is not simply suggesting they be led to love some dazzling illusion, for he adds that they must learn to love "what is truly beautiful [*ce qui est véritablement beau*] more than what is deformed" (*PE*, 155; 3:259).

Past and Future in Geneva

Rousseau's advice to the Genevans in the dedication to the *Second Discourse* follows the pattern I have identified in *Emile*: Rousseau presents an idealized image and then provokes a critical response to it. After pointing out that the Genevans have been fortunate insofar as their ancestors bequeathed to them a well-ordered republic, he identifies *their* task: "Henceforth it is for you alone, not to create your happiness, since your ancestors have saved you the trouble, but to make it lasting by the wisdom of using it well" (*SD*, 84–85; 3:116). What kind of "wisdom" is required for preserving the effects of this good fortune? Two features of Rousseau's letter suggest that he sees patriotic devotion as essential but insufficient.

To be sure, the overall tone of the dedication stresses the importance of loyalty and passionate patriotism, suggesting that deeply felt attachment to the political community is all that is necessary to preserve Geneva as a free and virtuous republic. "It is upon your perpetual unity, your obedience to the laws, and respect for their ministers that your preservation depends." Some commentaries on the letter focus exclusively on this dimension.[2] However, Rousseau immediately follows this statement by imploring the people to "consult the secret voice of your conscience" (*SD*, 85; 3:116). This implies that even the fundamental requirements of obedience to the law and respect for the magistrates are subject to the dictates of conscience.[3] This hardly seems to encourage the alienation of judgment. Rousseau then lauds the virtue and leadership of the magistrates, but in the form of a series of questions posed to the people. We may be tempted to dismiss his questions as merely rhetorical, but in fact his asking whether the magistrates are virtuous raises the possibility that they may not be.[4] While the *Social Contract* emphasizes the fallibility of the people, here Rousseau indirectly raises the possibility of the magistrates' fallibility.[5] Rousseau thus introduces the slightest degree of contingency into the apparent "perpetual unity" of the regime. This move risks the development of an unhealthy form of detachment, to be sure. Without it, however, the Genevans can never mature as a people, for in order to preserve the regime they have inherited, they must understand its fundamental character. This means judging the actual in light of the ideal, not being blinded by an idealized image. If Rousseau seems to embellish his description of the regime, it may be in order to help the Genevans discern traces of the ideal in it—in other words, to see the ideal as real, if not actualized, just as in the body of his essay he encourages the reader to see the pure state of nature, though not historical or factual, as having a reality that should not be dismissed as merely chimerical.[6]

Rousseau's "last counsel" to the Genevans is that they should avoid "listening to sinister interpretations and venomous discourses, the secret motives of which are often more dangerous than the acts that are their object." Is Rousseau suggesting that all criticism of the regime should be stifled? No, because he immediately distinguishes the "good and faithful guardian [dog] that never barks except at the approach of robbers" from "those noisy animals that continually trouble public repose" (*SD*, 86; 3:120). It turns out, then, that his advice is not designed to prohibit any and all criticism but rather to encourage discernment—knowing when to listen and when to ignore. In other words, the people must *judge*, because sometimes the "public repose" *must* be disrupted, for its own sake. Unanimity is not an end in itself for Rousseau.[7]

Just as the *Discourse on Political Economy* indicates that at some point the childlike citizens must become "the fathers," the dedication to Geneva suggests that the people must enter into the perspective of their founders. While they are certainly reminded of the debt they owe the wisdom of their founders, and encouraged to revere that wisdom, Rousseau also suggests that mere reverence is insufficient. Insofar as the people must take conscious precautions against possible future ills, they must take on an aspect of the founders' forward-looking role. This is what it means for a people to be young and old at the same time. For a people constituted as a people to remain a people and avoid fragmentation after the energy of the initial founding wanes, they cannot simply be passive recipients or products, and their cultivated patriotism is not enough to preserve their founders' handiwork. Zealous affection and rational detachment must be combined in order to preserve from within something that has been externally well ordered.

Thus, while the dedication to Geneva initially expresses Rousseau's wish that a republic "so wisely and so happily constituted" may "endure forever," he links this wish to a series of precautions aimed at maximizing the longevity of the regime (*SD*, 84; 3:116). Somewhere between passive wishing and active constructing—between good luck and good planning—lies a considered view of what is required to exercise good citizenship over the long term. It is one thing to say that Rousseau thought decay inevitable, and quite another to say that he thought there was nothing to be done about it. Some risks are worth taking. Longevity requires some degree of alienation—the very thing, in perverted form, that is potentially the greatest threat to longevity. Alienation is therefore not something to be avoided at all costs.[8] The tension between unity and longevity is not easily resolved, to be sure. But the tension itself is a critical component of Rousseau's political prescription and a reflection of the larger tension in his thought between nature and history.

Imagination and Judgment in Poland's Civic Education

This tension's positive role in maintaining political freedom over the long term comes out most clearly in Rousseau's *Considerations on the Government of Poland*. Rousseau begins by offering his assessment of Poland's circumstances. Poland finds itself in a state of urgency, "depopulated, devastated, and oppressed, wide-open to its aggressors, in the depths of misfortune and anarchy" (*GP*, 2; 3:954). Although its legislative body has never been usurped by a single tyrannical power, its ministers and higher officials are "so many minor despots," and they "set a vicious example, too often imitated," of oppressing the people and abusing the law on a small scale, but frequently and brazenly (33; 3:976). The result is a general contempt for the law that Rousseau defines here as anarchy. Still, Rousseau detects a positive force for change insofar as the crisis has reignited "all the fire of youth. It makes bold, as if it had just sprung to life, to demand government and laws! Poland is in irons but is busy discussing means of remaining free" (2; 3:954). Poland thus finds itself in the ripe circumstances of being young and old at once—a time of opportunity fraught with peril. The challenge, according to Rousseau, is to put this fiery disposition to productive use rather than allow impetuousness to drive the Poles to make hasty and ill-advised changes.

After posing the issue in cautionary terms, Rousseau devotes a chapter to the spirit of ancient institutions, praising the ancients in terms consistent with his other works. The title of his next chapter, "The Foregoing Applied to Poland," leads one to believe that the goal of the book is to revive the spirit of ancient institutions in Poland, although it is a large state populated by modern individuals, not a small republic.[9] In this and the following chapter ("On Education"),

Rousseau strongly emphasizes the need to establish a republic in the hearts of the Poles. "Here we have the important topic: it is education that you must count on to shape the souls of the citizens in a national pattern and so to direct their opinions, their likes, and dislikes that they shall be patriotic by inclination, passionately, of necessity" (19; 3:966). Over time, they should become increasingly indifferent toward their neighbors and concentrate their attention on the great deeds of their own ancestors. By these means they might create a "refuge" for the spirit of ancient republics in their own hearts. This is one basis for critiques of Rousseau that depict him as seeking to alienate the citizens' capacity for judgment.

I propose, however, that we should not let Rousseau's opening chapters on the spirit of ancient republics overcondition our reading of his subsequent arguments. His praise of ancient republics and nationalistic education is followed immediately by an explicit break in the argument. That is, he concludes the last of his four introductory chapters by referring to them as "certain preliminaries that I have deemed indispensable" (24; 3:970), and then opens chapter 5 by signaling a new beginning: "Let us, if possible, not start off by hurling ourselves into unrealistic proposals" (25; 3:970). One must wonder whether this refers to the grand proposals for a system of national education that he presented in chapter 4, the status of which I address below.

Only after these preliminaries does Rousseau explicitly turn to the Polish constitution. After identifying two of Poland's main challenges (its vast territory and the stratification of its hierarchical orders) in chapters 5 and 6, Rousseau devotes his remaining nine chapters to considering the Polish constitution and recommending various changes to the country's constitution, economic system, military organization, political institutions, administrative structures, and electoral processes. Like the system of public education described in chapter 4, these changes are designed to promote public-spiritedness and make honor the most esteemed good. There is a change in Rousseau's tone, however. Whereas the first four chapters depict idealized citizens whose consciousness is wholly absorbed into the body politic and whose obedience to the law stems from the "deepest inward assent," he now portrays the citizen as possessing an independent will, interests, and ambitions that must be harnessed and brought into line with the public good.

The cornerstone of Rousseau's advice is that the Poles' love of money must be replaced with love of public esteem. "Cause money to become an object of contempt, and, if possible, useless besides." The only way to accomplish this is to "discover some more powerful and dependable incentive" (68; 3:1004).

Rather than seeking to abolish the vanity and self-interest that drive the pursuit of wealth, Rousseau's recommendations are designed to redirect vanity and self-interest to nobler ends. In other words, Rousseau works with amour-propre rather than against it. His final and most sweeping recommendation is to devise a comprehensive system of graduated promotions in which public esteem is the only criterion for advancement and thus the only currency of any value:

> It consists in seeing to it that every citizen shall feel the eyes of his fellow-countrymen upon him every moment of the day; that no man shall move upward and win successes except by public approbation; that every post and employment shall be filled in accordance with the nation's wishes; and that everyone—from the least of the nobles, or even the least of the peasants, up to the king himself, if that were possible—shall be so completely dependent upon public esteem as to be unable to do anything, acquire anything, or achieve anything without it. The resulting emulation among all the citizens would produce a ferment that, in its turn, would awaken that patriotic fervor which raises men—as nothing else can raise them—above themselves. (87; 3:1019)

Rousseau's entire argument culminates in this well-known passage. The practical considerations he elaborates in his remaining chapters are explicitly directed at achieving and maintaining this spirit of emulation and transcendence of narrow self-interest. Citizen boards should be created to "draw up accurate and complete lists of persons of all ranks who had so conducted themselves as to merit some distinction or reward" (95; 3:1025–26) and to distribute benefactions, awards, and commendations accordingly. Individuals recognized for their virtue would be promoted along a finely graduated path of honorable posts, reaching from the lowest levels of nobility (to be conferred upon certain burghers who distinguish themselves in virtue and public-spiritedness) all the way to the throne itself. The king should be selected by special lottery from among a group of the most distinguished public servants who "have passed with honor through each of the republic's grades. This testing of a lifetime in all the posts they will have filled, along with the approval of the public, will be all the guarantee you need of their merit and virtue" (103; 3:1031).

At first glance, then, the structure of *Poland* presents a program of reform that consists of a series of progressive measures. In other words, the system of education described in chapter 4 is temporally and logically antecedent to the institutional changes described in later chapters. Individuals raised in such a culture of spirited emulation will grow up to be "patriotic by inclination, passionately, of necessity" (19; 3:966). The games and circuses that Rousseau prescribes for children anticipate and mirror the competition for honor that will occupy grown men in the political sphere, priming the citizens to value public-spiritedness and the common good above all, so that they are perfectly suited to move through the ascending ranks of public office and serve on the citizen review boards that make the system work. At the deepest level of social conditioning, their very inclinations will have been correctly formed, and their souls will have been shaped into a "national pattern." "Upon souls like that," Rousseau observes, "a wisely conceived legislation will take firm hold" (12; 3:961).

All of this should be very familiar to anyone who has read Rousseau's *Considerations on the Government of Poland*. What I would like to emphasize, however, is that this rather neat progression is complicated by Rousseau's insistence that Poland cannot wait for a new generation of citizens to be formed before implementing these reforms. Encouraging reform to begin as soon as possible, he argues that the Poles should not even wait to depose the Russian-installed Poniatowski before beginning (114; 3:1040). Thus Poland's program of reform *cannot* unfold along the lines presented in the text. Rousseau does not assume that citizens' inclinations will have been correctly formed by a fully operational system of civic education *before* they can participate in the institutional arrangements he describes in the later chapters. Instead, he seems to be suggesting that those institutional incentives will themselves *produce* public-spiritedness, and that this public-spiritedness will in turn "rescue" the citizens "from the dissolute way of life to which they are all too prone" (95; 3:1025). But this, of course, raises the possibility that the new incentive structure he proposes could be corrupted at the outset by the very tendencies it is designed to counter. If Rousseau's willingness to work with a citizenry already afflicted by self-interest and a taste for luxury reveals a pragmatic approach, it also suggests that the very reforms he proposes might be futile. One is reminded of Rousseau's remark in the preface to *Emile* that proposing "what can be done" amounts to proposing "what is done," which changes nothing.

Even were the Poles immediately to undertake a system of patriotic education, this risk is very real, for Rousseau makes clear that this reform will require an army of right-thinking teachers motivated only by public-spiritedness (20; 3:966–67). Where might such individuals be found in a populace that Rousseau sees as already afflicted by money lust and self-interest? To implement a truly public education, Rousseau notes, one needs truly public-spirited teachers. To attract men of distinction to the vocation of teaching, it is necessary to make the position of a teacher a stepping-stone to more prestigious positions. But he does not introduce the process of graduated promotions until chapter 13, where he suggests that primary-school inspectors be chosen from among those who have already ascended to the second rank. It appears, then, that the comprehensive system of promotions must be in place before the right sort of educators become available, but at the same time, the right sort of educators must shape a citizenry that is suited to that system.

Given this circular reasoning—which by now should be familiar—it is not surprising that when Rousseau finally introduces his plan for a system of graduated promotions, he acknowledges its potential risks and its openness to abuse by self-interested individuals: "Someone may object at this point: all these certificates of approval, awarded by this or that agency . . . are less likely to be duly awarded to the worthy, the just, and the truthful than to be extorted by the wily and the well-connected. To that I have only one answer: I assumed, in making the proposal, that I was addressing myself to a people that, though not wholly free from vices, still possesses some energy and certain virtues; and the proposal is, on that assumption, a good one" (91–92; 3:1022).

The difficulty, in short, is that the rewards for public-spiritedness have to be awarded in a top-down fashion, by those (at least initially) who have risen to the top through the existing system, in which "contempt for the laws" rather than public-spiritedness is emphasized.[10] Rousseau insists that all officeholders be left in their present positions (115; 3:1040). He takes seriously the possibility of fraud, mentioning it explicitly (105; 3:1033), and while he includes some institutional safeguards against it, the risk nevertheless remains that those who only *seem* to be public-spirited could "game the system" and advance on the basis of feigned patriotism. By acknowledging these limitations, Rousseau suggests that, ultimately, the only check on the advancement of corrupt individuals is the public's correct evaluation of them. This, it would seem, is even more fundamental than patriotism. In other words, the implicit but perhaps most fundamental lesson of *Government of Poland* is that the only *real* means of reviving republican virtue is to cultivate the people's capacity for good judgment. *No institutional mechanism can substitute for this exercise of judgment or operate correctly in its absence*—no matter how well designed the constitution or how patriotic the people.

Thus the "spirit of emulation" is not just a solution to a problem, Poland's problem, but is also itself a problem, or at least is problematic. If the "the public eye" (through the work of tribunals and committees) is expected to pass judgment on civil servants throughout their careers, and on kings posthumously, this "eye" must be highly discerning with regard to genuine versus apparent virtue. People easily dazzled by wealth, for example, are unlikely to judge well, whether they are asked to judge the legacy of a king or one of their fellow citizens. What Poland needs, Rousseau says, is "an entire class of citizens whom it would not be easy to deceive or corrupt" (108; 3:1035). By itself, then, the spirit of emulation does not suffice as a bulwark against deception or corruption. Good judgment is necessary.

Judgment, not unreflective passion, is also the cornerstone of Rousseau's advice to Poland with regard to its foreign relations. In the early chapters of the book, Rousseau encourages the Poles to turn inward, divesting themselves of any concern for the outside world. They must avoid comparing themselves to other European states, which will only lead them to emulate others' vices. It is precisely by avoiding the vices of her more modernized (and wealthy) neighbors, Rousseau argues, that Poland may succeed in deflecting, or at least forestalling, an attack. Whereas the pursuit of wealth brings only "the honor of being dragged into every war fought in Europe" (67–68; 3:1003), eschewing wealth in favor of simple republican virtue may protect Poland from war. Rousseau's defense of this point is telling. He argues not simply that virtue protects against invasion in a direct way, by motivating a vigorous citizen army, but also that it has an indirect effect on judgment—in this case, by influencing the judgment of Poland's neighbors, who may find themselves "duped by their low opinion of republics." If they see that Poland, "instead of trying to fill its coffers, to increase its revenues and to raise large forces of regular troops, is thinking, on the contrary, of disbanding its army and dispensing with money, they will believe that she is striving to weaken herself; and in the belief that, in order to conquer her, they will have only to appear whenever they like, they will let her reform herself at leisure, laughing the meanwhile among themselves at her labors" (113; 3:1039).

Rousseau goes on to contrast Poland's putative good judgment with Russia's supposed lack of it. The "great ministers of state" tend to "judge men in general by themselves and those around them and think they understand them." Such failures of judgment stem from the failure *"to begin to imagine* the strength that love of fatherland and the spirit of virtue are capable of developing in the souls of free men" (112–13; 3:1038–39, emphasis added). Rousseau's education is an education of both imagination and judgment, and he illuminates the connection between the two. To motivate men "to begin to imagine" is to create a beginning point that both addresses existing limitations and transcends them to move toward an ideal, without presupposing the very inclinations that reform is expected to produce.[11] The goal of this imagining, however, is not simply to imagine a different Poland; it is to imagine what is, to Rousseau's mind, the *true* Poland, or to see, in other words, what is *truly* beautiful—Rousseau's phrase in the *Discourse on Political Economy*.

This helps us to make sense of Rousseau's criticism in *Emile* of those who "persist in imagining only what they see," which I discussed in chapter 4. While he anticipates that many readers will relegate his project to the "land of chimeras," he counters that such critics themselves remain in the "land of prejudices." Rousseau seeks to navigate a middle course; his concern with the imagination lies in its power to see beyond prejudice, but without detaching completely from the existing reality of which prejudices form a part. "In separating myself so far from vulgar opinions I do not cease keeping them present in my mind," he says (*E*, 253; 4:549). We can relate this concern for a middle course between chimeras and corrupted reality to other contexts in which Rousseau is explicitly critical of literary works that tempt readers to imagine and yearn for an impossible state of affairs. As Christopher Kelly points out, such works are more likely to lead readers to "futile dissatisfaction" than to any moral or cultural reform.[12] But in *Government of Poland* we detect an attempt to work through the imagination toward what is not a simply fanciful projection but a depiction of an unactualized truth, which, inasmuch as it is unactualized, is both true and illusory at once.

Rousseau's projected image of Poland would therefore function in a revelatory way in the same sense that his image of natural man is designed to reveal the truth of human nature. Just as the *Second Discourse* depicts a state of nature "which perhaps never existed, which probably never will exist, and about which it is nevertheless necessary to have precise notions" (*SD*, 93; 3:123), *Government of Poland* depicts a state of affairs that might never exist, the depiction of which Rousseau nevertheless understands as faithful to the truth and therefore of practical relevance as a source of guidance in regard to Poland's genuine interests. Insofar as part of its rhetorical strategy is to suggest a differently imagined future—one in which different possibilities for what might be "realistically" achieved would exist, because even selfish men would understand their interests not simply differently but more *accurately*—it has the potential to be deeply transformative even as it recommends a certain realism.[13] Recall Rousseau's remark in the *Social Contract* that "the limits of the possible in moral matters are less narrow than we think" (*SC*, 189; 3:425).

Rhetoric alone will not suffice to expand the boundaries of the possible, but without an altered political consciousness, legal or institutional changes are doomed to be ineffective. "Merely prohibiting the things people should not do is a clumsy expedient and a pointless one, unless you see to it first that they are hated and despised; and the law's disapproval is never efficacious except as it reinforces disapproval on the part of the citizen's own judgment" (*GP*, 18; 3:965). By the same reasoning, Rousseau shows, it is pointless to mandate what people ought to do, without first seeing to it that such things are admired. But admiration by itself is not enough. If the strong might someday be expected to restrain themselves from harming the weak, and yet human begins will always act in their own self-interest, then it follows that the best bet for overturning "might makes right" is for the strong to believe that it is not in their interest to harm the weak. Rousseau suggests that this is not accomplished simply by re-arranging superficial incentives (since any such arrangement remains open to abuses) but by educating individuals to distinguish between immediate and more fundamental interests. Salutary illusions play an important role in this education insofar as they reorient one's sensibilities, but they are not the whole story. Judgment is inescapably involved. Perhaps this is why Rousseau concludes with the bold move of recommending that the reformers make their plans public. While in other contexts Rousseau suggests that the ideal legislator operate in secret, here he argues for transparency. This is in keeping, I would argue, with the overall structure of his *Considerations on the Government of Poland*, in which he aims to produce not only passionate attachment but also a degree of reflective detachment.

Reflective Detachment and Social Cohesion in Corsica

Rousseau wrote *Plan for a Constitution for Corsica* in 1764–65, in response to a request from Corsican general Matieu Buttafuco for help with the drafting of a new constitution for the newly independent Corsica, which had been under the control of the Genoese. Rousseau died before he could finish this work, but what he did write allows us to draw some conclusions about the complexity of his understanding of social cohesion.[14] Rousseau's prescriptions for Corsica are carefully designed to arrange institutional and psychological incentives to generate certain salutary opinions and behaviors. However, he also indicates in several ways that it is not only impossible to control such outcomes absolutely or permanently but also undesirable insofar as a static people is also a languorous people.[15] The model of citizenship that emerges in *Constitution for Corsica* is more dynamic and less thoroughly "choreographed" than is often recognized.

What it takes to "make" the people embrace a simple and virtuous way of life and attach them to the collective good turns out to require not only a specific form of socialization but also a people capable of transcending that socialization to some degree. My reading of *Constitution for Corsica* thus lends support to interpretations of the *Social Contract* that emphasize Rousseau's concern for deliberation and active citizenship.[16]

Most of Rousseau's recommendations for the Corsicans are calculated to counter their incipient inclination toward commerce, which he argues produces civic weakness and moral decay. He recommends instead the simplicity and industriousness of rural life, which he sees as the moral foundation of a healthy and independent state. A people's relationship to the land shapes national character. Commerce produces private individuals driven by self-interest, Rousseau argues, whereas the simplicity of rural life, which preserves tradition and keeps a community isolated from the corrupting influences of neighboring states and trading partners, produces a vigorous citizenry. Rousseau praises the "laborious and independent" life of the farming Swiss, the model he recommends for the Corsicans, which he says gives the Swiss "agreement in resolutions and courage in combat." Rousseau extols the "constant union that reigned" among them: "All having the same interests and the same tastes, united without difficulty in order to want and do the same things; the uniformity of their life took the place of law for them" (*CC*, 134–35; 3:915–16).

But if we look closely at Rousseau's praise of the Swiss model, we see that it is qualified in one important respect. The Swiss, Rousseau says, were "good and just without even knowing what justice and virtue were." They developed these qualities, he argues, as a result of their rough climate. Rousseau begins by praising the Swiss for their simplicity, constancy, and independence, but then goes on to explain how they "insensibly" debased themselves by allowing foreign influences to "make them love what they ought to have feared and admire what they ought to have disdained." They developed a "taste for money" and eventually began to feel "disdain for their station," which—again, *insensibly*—"destroyed the virtues that were its work" (134–35; 3:914–15).

In Rousseau's presentation, corruption is introduced almost imperceptibly as one "taste" (*goût*) is replaced by another. The Swiss are not deliberately corrupted by tyrannical rulers but "insensibly" lead themselves into a state of dependence to which they bring the same good qualities that were said to support their prior independence: valor, fidelity, and national pride. "It was surprising to see them bring to the service of princes the same valor that they had put into resisting them, the same fidelity they had kept for the fatherland"

(135; 3:915). The qualities that were foundational to their independence—the qualities that Rousseau seeks to cultivate in the Corsicans—were evidently insufficient to secure it, because they were spontaneous and unselfconscious. Just as human beings in Rousseau's depiction of the state of nature lacked the foresight and imagination to anticipate the pernicious long-term effects of a series of seemingly minor alterations in their environment, citizens who are "good and just without even knowing" it experience a similarly insensible decline. Rousseau may find decline inevitable, but he also indicates that health and vigor can be prolonged. Thus Rousseau advises the Corsicans, "It is less a question of becoming different than you are than of knowing how to preserve yourself that way" (125; 3:903).

This helps us to make sense of what appears to be a contradiction in Rousseau's advice with regard to emulating other states. On the one hand, he tells the Corsicans that they "must not draw conclusions from other nations" (125; 3:903). On the other hand, he devotes considerable time to the example of the Swiss, which he presents to the Corsicans as "the model that you ought to follow to return to your primitive state" (135; 3:915). In fact, it is immediately after this reference to the Swiss model that Rousseau begins to detail the decline of the Swiss. The Swiss are in one sense a model, in another sense not. This is because of their strong national character and good moral "taste" but their inability to preserve these qualities. Presumably, then, part of what Rousseau wishes for the Corsicans is precisely this ability to preserve themselves. But rather than promote a static, unreflective conception of civic virtue, he suggests that something more is required—something between completely unselfconscious simple goodness, on the one hand, and "knowledge" in any theoretical or scientific sense, on the other. As he makes his case for the merits of agriculture, Rousseau distinguishes between "the art of talking about agriculture in a sophisticated way" and "the taste for agriculture" that is characteristic of peasants who "do not know any other life" (126; 3:904). The former is a self-conscious but ultimately empty form of knowledge that one finds in books and academies. While Rousseau is certainly critical of such knowledge, the mere "taste for agriculture" (or any unreflective taste) has also been shown to be insufficient. Rousseau's analysis of the Swiss example suggests that something more than an unconscious inclination is needed, however salutary that inclination may be. We are reminded of his attempt in book 1 of *Emile* to combine the tenderness of the natural mother with the expert detachment of *les sages*.

Rousseau's discussion of the Swiss example also sheds light on his oft-quoted remark in *Constitution for Corsica* that "it is better to use fields badly than men"

(143; 3:925). Rousseau acknowledges that the very same structure designed to promote an agricultural way of life may introduce factors that actually threaten that way of life. Specifically, when individual ambition is limited to the agricultural life, the desire to distinguish oneself and seek glory will prompt competition between farmers over who can reap the largest harvest (144; 3:925). This sort of industriousness is, of course, in keeping with Rousseau's goal of promoting attachment to land and family. Copious yields can support large families, which Rousseau, who insists that a healthy population is a growing population, affirms as a positive development—to a point. But "every people of cultivators multiplies," and finally "multiplies so strongly that the land is no longer sufficient for it" (128; 3:907). For this reason, Rousseau warns against unfettered agricultural production. But he does not advocate systematically producing smaller yields ("using fields badly") as a way of controlling population growth. Instead, "every cultivator can and ought to make this choice in his land and each parish or community in its communal goods" (143; 3:925). Similarly, when discussing the means by which the government will collect public revenue, he notes repeatedly (despite his insistence that the circulation of money should be reduced as drastically as possible) that revenue should be collected partly in produce and partly in money. He presents this neither as a temporary measure nor as a grudging compromise. "The receipts of each jurisdiction are farmed out; they are made in kind or in money *at the choice of the contributors*" (150; 3:933, emphasis added). He reiterates this point about choice a few paragraphs later: "Since private individuals will always be free [*seront toujours libres*] to pay their quota in money or in produce at the levels that will be set every year in each jurisdiction, once the government has calculated the best proportion that ought to be found between these two sorts of quotas, as soon as this proportion is altered it will be in a position to notice this alternation on the spot, to seek its cause and to remedy it" (151; 3:935). The choice whether to pay in money or in produce is not a temporary or transitional measure; Rousseau says that individuals will always be free to make this choice for themselves. He devotes a great deal of energy to steering those choices in the right direction. But he makes clear that there is a difference between steering and determining or guaranteeing. The choice remains.

What it means to use the fields "badly," then, is not simply a matter of consistently undercultivating them. Neither is using the fields "well" strictly a matter of increasing production. There are, Rousseau implies, better and worse ways of using fields badly (and, he says, the Genoese did it poorly). Both models share similarities when it comes to short-term effects. Judgment is required to discern what "badly" and "well" mean relative to a particular population that is necessarily in flux as it interacts with and responds to its own mode of production. Thus the legislator who wishes to attend to time and place in making proposals cannot prescribe a fixed rule or formula, even if such a rule is tailored to a particular population—because population, Rousseau emphasizes, fluctuates over time, even (perhaps especially) when a population is robustly engaged in activities conducive to civic virtue. There is a tension between his principle that a population should remain what it is and his principle that it should grow in size, since the very things that support population growth introduce factors that alter the culture. By drawing attention to the question of how a population both reproduces and maintains its size over time, Rousseau indirectly addresses the challenge of how a population reproduces and maintains its culture, values, and identity over time.

What Rousseau calls for, then, is not a universal rule to be applied unreflectively in all cases but a guiding principle that must "attend to time and place" by taking into account both immediate and long-term effects. Conditioning by means of careful institutional and economic arrangements alone cannot address the long term—not because it can never be as seamless or perfect as his idealized vision requires, but precisely because it is only a first foundation. "The success of the first foundation," says Rousseau, "will make change necessary afterwards" (128; 3:906–7). Insofar as these effects are not entirely predictable, part of what it means to anticipate and attend to them is to make room for the exercise of judgment and deliberate choice on the part of the people. This entails some degree of alienation, which may pose a risk to social cohesion, but Rousseau suggests that this is a risk that any healthy, well-governed community cannot do without, precisely for the sake of maintaining cohesion over the long term. Just as perfectibility is a part of human nature, change is a part of the social body. The success—not the failure—of the first foundation makes change, and thus the exercise of judgment, necessary.

Judgment and Political Identity

Throughout his writings, Rousseau demands that we confront the possibility that our received traditions are deeply flawed and corrupted, and that what we consider a "common-sense" standard of judgment may be insidiously misleading, however widely accepted. Challenging this standard takes imagination, but Rousseau was well aware that imagination could simply disarm judgment.

The complex relationship between imagination and judgment was a major focus of his reflections on political life.

Those who claim that Rousseau reduces education to deceit or manipulation read him as aiming to produce people who are thoroughly embedded in their identities. But Rousseau was acutely aware that complete embeddedness in one's identity—whether individual or civic—is ultimately self-defeating. The correction he proposes in *Emile*, and implies in the more political works, is, ironically, a gap created by self-consciousness, which may pose a risk to cohesive identity in the short term but is necessary for the maintenance of identity over the long term. This irreducible tension implies that neither individuals nor peoples are best served by existing wholly or uncritically inside their identities. Rousseau consistently emphasizes active experience or expression (whether of the general will, patriotic feeling, or passion in general) over mindless repetition. Anything that must be continually and consciously reaffirmed cannot become unselfconsciously "second nature." To the degree that self-consciousness is necessary and serves the cause of self-rule, Rousseau's ideal is *not* the complete absence of opposition or disharmony. Nor is it seamless identification. Not only are threats to wholeness inevitable, we have seen; they are in fact essential. In other words, if Rousseau's recipe for patriotic identification is likely to produce an *almost* seamless identification with the whole, this is not a failure to live up to the ideal but rather a more complex ideal. "Almost" is not second best; it is best. "Almost" is what creates the space for the movement that continual reaffirmation entails. As I argued in chapter 6, this is what elevates the imperfect Sophie over the idealized girl like Sophie who cannot reconcile her perfect ideal with the imperfect reality of average suitors.

Therefore, if Emile and Sophie must be "tested" in the sequel, it is in part to create such a space, not to test whether the seamless whole can be maintained against all forms of complexity and change. Their relationship ends because they fail to fill that space with a renewed, active commitment to each other. To complain that if the tutor had never left that space never would have opened up, and their relationship would have remained secure, is to miss the point. Perfect conditioning creates a seamlessness that does away with that space, which may seem justified on the grounds that any opening can become a fissure that ultimately leads to fragmentation. Although such spaces threaten the immediate experience of wholeness, they provide opportunities for reflection and self-direction that support a more complex wholeness. In my introduction I mentioned several scholars who see evidence of this positive friction in *On the Social Contract*. *Emile* sheds light on the psychology and education that contribute to the positive manifestation of this friction, or tension, and mitigate the potential for its negative manifestations (such as those that characterize the unhappy dividedness of the bourgeois). To that end, Rousseau creates a superficial illusion of absolute control while interweaving various slips, mistakes, and retracings throughout the narrative. These serve two important functions, which we might call poetic and reflective, or aesthetic and philosophical. The poetic or aesthetic function adds vitality and dimension to the dominant image, which might otherwise be static and uninspiring and thus fail to reorient us. The reflective or philosophical function simultaneously draws attention to the chimerical quality of that image. Rousseau both encourages our identification with Emile and actively works against overidentification. The education of the reader is thus an education in partial detachment, a perspective that can discern Emile's superiority to civil man without being blinded or seduced by his example. For Rousseau, it is only through such a double perspective that one can come to see the distorted quality of human beings "as they are" for what it is, and yet to see in those very same human beings something noble, something truly human.

I have attempted to contribute to the growing body of literature on Rousseau as a theorist of middle states (e.g., as a defender of the middle ground between individualism and collectivism, rather than either extreme) by elaborating the character and implications of the equally important (and arguably more fundamental) middle state between seductive enchantment and rational detachment. This addresses what is otherwise a problematic lacuna in Rousseau's political psychology.[17] It is one thing to say that Rousseau makes room for individuality in his theory of political community; it is another to show how his understanding of that fragile balancing act differs from the liberal public/private solution that he criticizes so vehemently. By attending to his concerns about preserving judgment, we see that the point is not divide citizens' passionate attachments—for that is the very problem he seeks to address—or to make citizens *less* attached to the whole (equally problematic), but rather to attach them in a more self-conscious way. Surprisingly enough, this self-conscious attachment, like the wisdom of the human being who knows how to stay in place, is a better foundation for vigorous citizenship than unreflectively conditioned passion.

To be sure, Rousseau indicates this middle state only indirectly and fleetingly when it comes to his imaginary pupil, but there is no prima facie reason to dismiss a possibility that Rousseau explores only briefly; in fact, many of the defining moments in his arguments—such as the euphoria he describes in the fifth walk of the *Reveries*—are marked by brevity. Although Rousseau's description of losing himself in the beauty of nature may seem to suggest that his goal is unmediated assimilation to a larger whole (in this case, nature rather than society), the context suggests that this moment of perfect fusion is not the focal point of the account.[18] In fact, Rousseau identifies emergence from a reverie as the sweetest moment of all, even sweeter than being lost in reverie. In other words, it is precisely at the moment when he is simultaneously seeing both the world before his eyes and the world in his imagination that he is most content. For Rousseau, the optimal moment is the middle state between enchantment and disenchantment. "And finally finding myself brought back by degrees to myself and to what surrounded me, I could not mark out the point separating the fictions from the realities; it was this thorough conjunction of everything which made the absorbed and solitary life I led during this beautiful sojourn so dear to me."[19]

Over the course of the fifth walk, the emphasis shifts from unselfconscious self-forgetting to conscious self-forgetting, as paradoxical as that might seem. At first, Rousseau describes his bliss as a function of becoming lost in the natural beauty that surrounds him. He loses himself, allowing himself to become absorbed into the whole of nature. We see the degree to which he has relinquished power over himself in his desire to be imprisoned there. "I wanted them to make this refuge a perpetual prison for me, to confine me to it for life."[20] At the end of the walk, however, he observes that his memory of the time he spent on the island surpasses the experience of being there. He adds to each intense but "abstract and monotonous" reverie various "charming images which make it more intense." As Michael Davis notes, Rousseau's "editing" of his reveries provides deeper satisfaction than losing himself in them.[21] This requires that he give himself over to the reverie but at the same time direct it, semiconscious that it is a reverie and can be improved by the addition of ingredients that will heighten the experience.

We see the same dynamic at work in the *Confessions*, when Rousseau promises to paint the state of his soul in a double perspective ("je peindrai doublement l'état de mon âme"), at the moment in which an event took place and at the moment in which he described it. This simultaneity requires a double perspective made possible by partial detachment; such a perspective is not possible in a state of either complete absorption or perfect detachment. In his seminal psychological work on Rousseau, Starobinski sees him as vacillating between these two poles: seamless immersion in one's (natural) self and detached observation of that self. Both poles reflect a desire for perfect transparency, Starobinski argues, whether subjective or objective.[22] In other words, Starobinski attributes to Rousseau the oscillation that we see in Emile before he loses Sophie: a tendency to be either wholly inside or completely outside his experience. But, as we have seen, on the whole his education works against this bifurcation. Moreover, Rousseau's rhetorical strategy in *Emile* and elsewhere creates a double inside/outside perspective in the reader as well. This perspective may be fleeting and tenuous for Rousseau's imaginary pupil, but it is a deep and recurring feature of Rousseau's rhetorical strategy.

This double perspective and partial detachment resonate with present-day concerns about the possibility of reconciling strong national identities with universal humanistic claims. If the liberal tradition sees the association of nationalism with unreflective passion as problematic, it is also what makes nationalism interesting to those who defend the positive role of passion in politics. In *Politics and Passion*, for example, Michael Walzer criticizes liberal universalism for ignoring the importance of "passionate intensity," which, much more than cool deliberation, motivates egalitarian politics. Yet even Walzer acknowledges the difficulty of accommodating such passion in a liberal regime: "Accommodation is especially difficult when passion is, as it commonly is, the product of our attachments and belongings."[23] Nevertheless, Walzer insists, accommodation must be made for the sake of liberal democracy itself, which requires passion to sustain a commitment to democratic ideals. In other words, Walzer seeks a middle ground in which passionate intensity and rational choice are mutually correcting. A number of theorists have argued forcefully that liberal democracy requires this middle ground.[24] It is to this middle ground that *Emile* speaks, if we can appreciate its political resonance.

Rousseau recognized that redirecting judgment must have a different character than redirecting passion, inasmuch as judgment cannot be *entirely* directed or it ceases to be judgment. While Rousseau calls for a lawgiver in the *Social Contract* precisely because the people, as a political body, tend to lack judgment, his response is not a matter of working around this deficiency or permanently substituting his judgment for their own. Rather, his response is to correct this tendency, to the degree possible. Immediately after referring to the people as a "blind multitude," he states that the people "must be shown how to assimilate considerations of time and place; taught to weigh the attraction of present, tangible advantages against the danger of remote, hidden ills" (*SC*, 154; 3:380). In claiming that Rousseau takes seriously the need to develop a people's capacity for judgment, I am not claiming that he believes that the multitude can be made philosophical. He concedes that he expects to be understood by a very few highly discerning readers. My more modest aim is to show that his understanding of civic education draws attention to the importance of good judgment on the part of citizens, rather than attempting to circumvent the need for judgment by substituting deep conditioning of the passions. In my reading of Rousseau's advice to the Genevans, Poles, and Corsicans, this is no less true of his understanding of civic education than it is of the individual education proffered in *Emile*.[25] As Christopher Bertram puts it in his illuminating analysis of the *Social Contract*, while the affective unity produced by collective singing and dancing is an important component of Rousseau's conception of political identity, it does not wholly constitute it; "there is a time for dancing and there is a time for individuals to reason together in common as citizens."[26]

Of course, in Rousseau's political works, he does not discuss, on an institutional or procedural level, how or where the deliberations that guide judgment are to take place. This is, from a practical standpoint, a shortcoming. But it may be connected to his view of what an education in judgment requires. This also explains why Rousseau presents his understanding of judgment so indirectly. Perhaps the most important lesson of *Emile*, as I have emphasized throughout this study, is that an education in judgment will necessarily have a tacit dimension. For this reason, such an education resists standardization and cannot be reduced to a set of universally applicable principles or a fixed method. But that is precisely why and how it is an education in judgment.

NOTES

Introduction

1. For a comprehensive overview of the intellectual history of the concept of judgment, see Leslie Paul Thiele, *The Heart of Judgment: Practical Wisdom, Neuroscience, and Narrative* (Cambridge: Cambridge University Press, 2006), chap. 1.

2. Ronald Beiner, *Political Judgment* (Chicago: University of Chicago Press, 1983), 2.

3. Peter J. Steinberger, *The Concept of Political Judgment* (Chicago: University of Chicago Press, 1993), 148.

4. One exception is Ryan Patrick Hanley, who gives sustained attention to Rousseau's understanding of the workings of judgment in "Rousseau's Virtue Epistemology," *Journal of the History of Philosophy* 50 (April 2012): 239–63. Tracy B. Strong also emphasizes the centrality of judgment in the context of Rousseau's critique of the theater in "Music, the Passions, and Political Freedom in Rousseau," in *Rousseau and Freedom*, ed. Christie McDonald and Stanley Hoffmann (Cambridge: Cambridge University Press, 2010), 92–110, esp. 104.

5. The notable exception is Benjamin Barber, who emphasizes Rousseau as an important resource for reinvigorating democratic politics in general and democratic political judgment in particular; see his *Conquest of Politics: Liberal Philosophy in Democratic Times* (Princeton: Princeton University Press, 1988). However, Barber's account of Rousseau's general will as a manifestation of democratic deliberation makes no mention of the problematic figure of the legislator, which many argue undermines his commitment to democratic freedom, as I discuss below.

6. For example, in his incisive defense of rhetoric and judgment, Bryan Garsten presents Rousseau as part of a modern project to disarm judgment in order to eliminate the inherent risk that judgment may be co-opted by the rhetorical wiles of demagogues or other dangerous political actors. Rousseau thus seeks to protect against the dangers of rhetoric by cultivating a nonrational patriotic fervor that internalizes an authoritative perspective in order to circumvent judgment while preserving a purely subjective sense of freedom. Garsten, *Saving Persuasion: A Defense of Rhetoric and Judgment* (Cambridge: Harvard University Press, 2006).

7. Steven Johnston, for example, has argued that because Rousseau seeks to "choreograph" the rhythms and motions of politics in advance, "force of habit . . . is the true foundation of Rousseau's republic." Johnston, *Encountering Tragedy: Rousseau and the Project of Democratic Order* (Ithaca: Cornell University Press, 1999), 118–19.

8. Emile strikes some readers as no more autonomous than a puppet because he is so deeply manipulated by the tutor (and eventually by his beloved Sophie). With regard to Emile's coming of age, Daniel E. Cullen, for example, states, "Emile has been properly 'constituted'; his choice

now is to remain what he ought to be. His act of volition is indistinguishable from one of submission . . . a wholly predictable compliance with authority." *Freedom in Rousseau's Political Philosophy* (DeKalb: Northern Illinois University Press, 1993), 131. Similarly, David Gauthier remarks that "captivity of the will is at the core of Rousseau's account of education," which ultimately produces a freedom that is not genuine but rather "feigned." *Rousseau: The Sentiment of Existence* (Cambridge: Cambridge University Press, 2006), 36, 41. See also Lester Crocker, "Rousseau's *Emile*: Life, Liberty, and the Pursuit of Happiness," in *Rousseau and the Eighteenth Century: Essays in Memory of R. A. Leigh*, ed. Marian Hobson, J. T. A. Leigh, and Robert Wokler (Oxford: Oxford University Press, 1992), 101–15.

9. Jonathan Marks, for example, argues that while Emile does exercise a certain degree of autonomy, he does so only within the confines of a set of necessary prejudices, with which he is equipped to protect himself from corruption. Marks concludes from this that Rousseau is an "antiromantic" who recognizes "that human health depends not upon our liberation from constraints and prejudices but, at least in most cases, on the imposition of new constraints and prejudices." *Perfection and Disharmony in the Thought of Jean-Jacques Rousseau* (Cambridge: Cambridge University Press, 2005), 129.

10. "For it cannot be denied that, as Rousseau presents it, the work of political education (which is the transformation of the self) occurs not in the continuing process of democratic deliberation but in the founding activity of the Legislator, which is later routinized in the permanent influence of *moeurs*. Rousseauian democratic politics is not an exercise in *self*-transformation because it depends upon a prior transformation of the self that occurs outside the legitimate boundaries of the political." Cullen, *Freedom in Rousseau's Political Philosophy*, 132. Similarly, Ruth W. Grant states that "in Rousseau's view self-consciousness is simply not a necessary requirement for freedom. . . . Rather, through manipulation and deception, freedom and virtue together are purchased at the price of a highly developed rational self-consciousness." *Hypocrisy and Integrity: Machiavelli, Rousseau, and the Ethics of Politics* (Chicago: University of Chicago Press, 1997), 138. See also William Connolly, *Political Theory and Modernity* (Oxford: Basil Blackwell, 1988), chap. 3; and Zev Trachtenberg, *Making Citizens: Rousseau's Political Theory of Culture* (London: Routledge, 1993).

11. For a detailed analysis of Rousseau's understanding of the bourgeois, and the influence of his view, see Werner J. Dannhauser, "The Problem of the Bourgeois," in *The Legacy of Rousseau*, ed. Clifford Orwin and Nathan Tarcov (Chicago: University of Chicago Press, 1997), 3–19.

12. The illustration that Rousseau chose as the frontispiece for *Emile* depicts the well-known scene of Thetis dipping her son Achilles into the Styx in an attempt to make him invulnerable.

13. For another analysis of the problem of self-consciousness for Rousseau, see Benjamin Storey, "Rousseau and the Problem of Self-Knowledge," *Review of Politics* 71, no. 2 (2009): 251–74. Storey characterizes Emile's education as an "education in self-knowing sociability" (262). See also the brief discussion in Laurence D. Cooper, *Rousseau, Nature, and the Problem of the Good Life* (University Park: Pennsylvania State University Press, 1999), esp. 171, and the lengthier discussion in Laurence D. Cooper, "Nearer My True Self to Thee: Rousseau's New Spirituality—And Ours," *Review of Politics* 74, no. 3 (2012): 465–88. I return to the issue of self-consciousness in later chapters.

14. Mark Cladis, *Public Vision, Private Lives: Rousseau, Religion, and Twenty-First-Century Democracy* (Oxford: Oxford University Press, 2003), 196.

15. Marks, *Perfection and Disharmony*, 11.

16. This counters Jean Starobinski's reading of Rousseau as conflicted, the paradoxes in his arguments attributable to conflicts in his tortured psyche. See Starobinski, *Jean-Jacques Rousseau: Transparency and Obstruction*, trans. Arthur Goldhammer (Chicago: University of Chicago Press, 1971).

17. See John Charvet, *The Social Problem in the Philosophy of Rousseau* (Cambridge: Cambridge University Press, 1974); and Leo Strauss, *Natural Right and History* (Chicago: University of Chicago Press, 1950), 252–94. John T. Scott takes this line of argument in a new direction, arguing that not the unity of the individual soul but rather the "whole" of the entire order of nature (and our place in it) serves as Rousseau's model. See Scott, "The Theodicy of the *Second Discourse*: The 'Pure State of Nature' and Rousseau's Political Thought," *American Political Science Review* 86, no. 3 (1992): 696–711. Cooper argues that even unnatural states can be consistent with nature as long as they reproduce (and extend the scope of) the "inner wholeness" that characterizes Rousseau's understanding of man's original goodness. This "inner wholeness" is the shared defining feature of Rousseau's three exemplars of the good life: uncivilized natural man, the citizen, and civilized natural man (i.e., Emile and Rousseau himself). See Cooper, *Rousseau, Nature, and the Problem of the Good Life*, esp. 59–66 and 186–88.

18. Marks, *Perfection and Disharmony*, 88. Tracy B. Strong goes even further, stating, "Rousseau is not a theorist of the unified self." *Jean-Jacques Rousseau: The Politics of the Ordinary* (Thousand Oaks, Calif.: Sage Publications, 1994), 84. Strong's argument offers a forceful counterweight to those who see in Rousseau an overriding demand for unity, but he goes to the opposite extreme, which is why he is not among the interpreters I classify as defending the importance of "middle" states in Rousseau. Strong emphasizes multiplicity and fragmentation to such a degree that the idea of integrity drops out altogether, whereas I argue that Rousseau seeks to combine motion and change, on the one hand, and integrity, on the other.

19. Marks, *Perfection and Disharmony*, 85.

20. Parallels between Emile and the people, and the tutor and the political legislator, are frequently drawn. See, for example, Arthur M. Melzer, *The Natural Goodness of Man: On the System of Rousseau's Thought* (Chicago: University of Chicago Press, 1990), 241–52; and Madeleine B. Ellis, *Rousseau's Socratic Aemilian Myths: A Literary Collation of "Emile" and "The Social Contract"* (Columbus: Ohio State University Press, 1977). For an alternative interpretation in which Sophie is understood to symbolize the general will rather than the legislator, see Ann Charney Colmo, "What Sophie Knew: Rousseau's *Emile et Sophie, ou Les Solitaires*," in *Finding a New Feminism: Rethinking the Woman Question for Liberal Democracy*, ed. Pamela Grande Jensen (Lanham, Md.: Rowman & Littlefield, 1996), 67–91.

21. See Hannah Arendt, *The Human Condition* (Chicago: University of Chicago Press, 1989).

22. Linda M. G. Zerilli, "We Feel Our Freedom: Imagination and Judgment in the Thought of Hannah Arendt," *Political Theory* 33, no. 2 (2005): 163.

23. Thiele, *Heart of Judgment*, 13.

24. Charles Larmore, "Moral Judgment," in *Judgment, Imagination, and Politics: Themes from Kant and Arendt*, ed. Ronald Beiner and Jennifer Nedelsky (Lanham, Md.: Rowman & Littlefield, 2001), 63.

25. Beiner, *Political Judgment*, 162.

26. The argument that Rousseau is attempting to seduce his readers toward virtue is found, for example, in Joseph R. Reisert, *Jean-Jacques Rousseau: A Friend of Virtue* (Ithaca: Cornell University Press, 2003).

27. Tracy B. Strong recognizes this in arguing for a distinction between Rousseau and the legislator. Emphasizing the difference between Rousseau and God, as well as between Rousseau and the tutor, Strong states that Rousseau's overall goal is to "empower the reader." The goal is not "to reproduce the situation of Emile with the tutor, but to authorize the understanding of the reader. [Rousseau's works] require of the reader that he or she allow Rousseau to be available. But they do not privilege Rousseau, in the way that the tutor is privileged with Emile. In fact, they show us what is wrong with such privilege." Strong, *Jean-Jacques Rousseau*, 161. In my interpretation I show how taking advantage of such privilege, and its seductive force, is also part (though only part) of the education of the reader's understanding. I also focus more directly and thoroughly on Rousseau's "interaction" with the reader throughout *Emile*.

28. Thus I dispute Robert J. Ellrich's characterization of Rousseau: "Rousseau seems to show little interest in establishing, through contact with his reader-figure, the kind of dialectic that opens up the closed circuit of the mind and facilitates change in perception and comprehension." Ellrich, *Rousseau and His Reader: The Rhetorical Situation of the Major Works* (Chapel Hill: University of North Carolina Press, 1969), 42.

29. Marks, *Perfection and Disharmony*, 115.

30. Arthur M. Melzer argues that Rousseau attempts to resolve the age-old problem of combining wisdom and consent by means of a balance between two types of rule: direct and indirect. Just as the legislator rules the people indirectly, Sophie rules Emile indirectly. See Melzer, *Natural Goodness of Man*, 240–49. However, this leads us back to the challenges raised by Cullen, Johnston, and others, discussed above: if consent follows only from the deepest and most through conditioning, is it rendered indistinguishable from submission? Even Melzer, in a footnote, characterizes the supposedly direct rule of the people as "illusory" and argues finally that in Rousseau we find "a pervasive Platonic strain" that recognizes the necessity of "an absolute rule of wisdom" (232).

31. "Rousseau hopes that his reader is so moved by his encounter with *Emile* that he will come to see himself and his world differently: attracted by the image of Emile's domestic happiness, the (male) reader is to be inspired to imitate Emile." Reisert, *Friend of Virtue*, 169. John T. Scott similarly emphasizes the degree to which Rousseau "consistently uses rhetorical and literary techniques that are meant to change the reader's perspective, to cause the reader to visualize the world differently." Rather than focus on Rousseau's effort to impart virtue, however, Scott argues that Rousseau's primary concern in *Emile* is to get the reader to see and accept the truth of man's natural goodness. Scott, "Do You See What I See? The Education of the Reader in Rousseau's *Emile*," *Review of Politics* 74, no. 3 (2012): 444. While I agree with Reisert and Scott that a major goal of *Emile* is to change how the reader *sees*, my reading of Rousseau's rhetorical strategy differs from theirs in the following respect: whereas Reisert presents Rousseau's goal as

securing the (male) reader's direct identification with Emile, and Scott presents Emile as the embodiment of the truth or principle that Rousseau seeks to impart, I argue that Rousseau educates his reader to achieve a certain critical distance from Emile in order to apprehend a vision that includes but also transcends Emile's example.

32. Melzer, *Natural Goodness of Man*, 249–52.

33. Rousseau refers to Machiavelli's *The Prince* as "a handbook for republicans." He adds in a footnote (in the 1782 edition) the following explanation: Machiavelli was forced to disguise his love of liberty because he lived in a corrupt regime. Rousseau draws our attention to the apparent contradictions between *The Prince* and the *Discourses* and remarks that "this profound political thinker has had only superficial or corrupt Readers until now" (*SC*, 177; 3:1480). If *The Prince* is a handbook for republicans insofar as it makes the prince's mystique intelligible, then we might say the same of the *Social Contract*—despite its apparent defense of a divine legislator.

34. As Tracy B. Strong observes, Rousseau calls attention "to the fact that we will be tempted to find answers in beings that claim superiority." Strong goes on to argue that Rousseau defends the "ordinary" as a way of "forewarning us against the temptations of the inhuman." *Jean-Jacques Rousseau*, 161–62.

35. This is how Joel Schwartz, for example, characterizes the two parts of Emile's education, in *The Sexual Politics of Jean-Jacques Rousseau* (Chicago: University of Chicago Press, 1985).

36. Some have argued that Sophie's education has no integrity of its own but is only geared toward completing Emile's education, thus subordinating Sophie to Emile. I address these readings in chapter 6 and argue that they overlook several important features of Sophie's education.

37. My observation about the significance of the structure of *Emile* resonates with the arguments put forward by Richard Velkley and Michael Davis about the structure of the *Second Discourse*, in which the doubleness of nature is reflected in the disjunction between the body of the text and the notes. See Michael Davis, *The Autobiography of Philosophy: Rousseau's "The Reveries of the Solitary Walker"* (Lanham, Md.: Rowman & Littlefield, 1999), 90–92; Richard L. Velkley, *Being After Rousseau: Philosophy and Culture in Question* (Chicago: University of Chicago Press, 2002), 43–46.

38. Steinberger, *Concept of Political Judgment*, 229.

39. See, for example, Beiner, *Political Judgment*, 162.

40. Thiele, *Heart of Judgment*, 15.

Chapter 1

1. On the significance of Rousseau's understanding of infancy for his political thought, see Jeffrey A. Smith, "Natural Happiness, Sensation, and Infancy in Rousseau's *Emile*," *Polity* 35, no. 1 (2002): 93–120.

2. Laurence D. Cooper has provided an illuminating analysis of the doubleness of Rousseau's idea of nature (as both original condition and telos), arguing that there is a continuity between these two senses of naturalness and thus between the first and second halves of Emile's education, as well as between what is natural for original man and what is natural for historically transformed man. Human beings cannot return to their original nature, but they can achieve a

second-order naturalness by reproducing a similar orderliness of soul. Their "unnatural" qualities (such as amour-propre [vanity], sociability, and advanced mental capacities) can be incorporated to serve the wholeness that Cooper sees as the defining mark of our original nature. Thus natural wholeness can be achieved on a higher level. See Cooper, *Rousseau, Nature, and the Problem of the Good Life* (University Park: Pennsylvania State University Press, 1999). While Cooper's analysis captures one axis of the doubleness of Rousseau's ideal of nature, I argue that in *Emile* a version of this doubleness is built into even the "original" sense of nature as presented in the earliest stages of Rousseau's educational project. Jonathan Marks also observes that the distinction between nature and history in Rousseau's thought is blurred, and that natural man is already "divided." Marks, *Perfection and Disharmony in the Thought of Jean-Jacques Rousseau* (Cambridge: Cambridge University Press, 2005), 25–27.

3. Jennifer Einspahr similarly observes that Rousseau's accounts of human development "present us with layered and complex synchronicities rather than a neat developmental trajectory where sharp lines between 'before' and 'after' can be drawn." Einspahr, "The Beginning That Never Was: Mediation and Freedom in Rousseau's Political Thought," *Review of Politics* 72, no. 3 (2010): 440.

4. For a penetrating discussion of this "getting in the way," see Richard L. Velkley, *Being After Rousseau: Philosophy and Culture in Question* (Chicago: University of Chicago Press, 2002), 31–48.

5. Although her reading of Rousseau diverges sharply from my own, Elizabeth Rose Wingrove also discusses the significance of this ambiguity in the *Second Discourse*. As she puts it, "The putative origins and foundations are already shot through with the political imperatives whose legitimation initially motivated the originary search." *Rousseau's Republican Romance* (Princeton: Princeton University Press, 2000), 60.

6. See Mark Cladis, *Public Vision, Private Lives: Rousseau, Religion, and Twenty-First-Century Democracy* (Oxford: Oxford University Press, 2003), 89–96; Marks, *Perfection and Disharmony*, 15–38; Velkley, *Being After Rousseau*, 31–48; and Wingrove, *Rousseau's Republican Romance*, 60.

7. As I mentioned in my introduction, Jonathan Marks also explores the discrepancy between the idealized account of nature in the *Second Discourse* and the more sober view in *Emile*, but he explains the simultaneous presence of *both* an idealized view and a more sober, considered view within *Emile* itself only in terms of the author's circumspection and political pragmatism. My reading, in contrast, suggests that both dimensions of *Emile* are integral to Rousseau's philosophical project.

8. For a discussion of the educational theorists and intellectual debates that formed the contemporary background to Rousseau's understanding of educational theory, see Natasha Gill, *Educational Philosophy in the French Enlightenment: From Nature to Second Nature* (Surrey, UK: Ashgate, 2010), chap. 9.

9. Jean-Jacques Rousseau, *Rousseau, Judge of Jean-Jacques: Dialogues*, in *The Collected Writings of Rousseau*, ed. Roger D. Masters and Christopher Kelly, 13 vols. (Hanover: University Press of New England, 1990–2009), 1:8–9.

10. Here I disagree with Steven Johnston, who contends (with regard to the legislator specifically) that Rousseau "does not seem to understand quite how serious is his legitimacy problem."

Encountering Tragedy: Rousseau and the Project of Democratic Order (Ithaca: Cornell University Press, 1999), 71.

Chapter 2

1. On the importance of the body in Rousseau's understanding of freedom, see Mathieu Brunet and Bertrand Guillarme, "The Subject and Its Body: Love of Oneself and Freedom in the Thought of Rousseau," in *Rousseau and Freedom*, ed. Christie McDonald and Stanley Hoffmann (Cambridge: Cambridge University Press, 2010), 216–27.

2. For an extended insightful analysis of the importance of authentic language for Rousseau, see Tracy B. Strong, *Jean-Jacques Rousseau: The Politics of the Ordinary* (Thousand Oaks, Calif.: Sage Publications, 1994).

3. There is actually a third: Emile presents himself as reborn yet again in the sequel to *Emile* (*Emile et Sophie, ou Les Solitaires*). I discuss the significance of this third rebirth in chapter 7.

4. In book IV, Rousseau praises the savage as judge, noting that the savage "has a healthier judgment of us than a philosopher does." He goes on to compare his pupil to the savage. Emile is similar to the savage, "with the difference that Emile, having reflected more, compared ideas more, seen our errors from closer up, is more on guard against himself and judges only what he knows" (243–44; 4:535). The ability to "guard against himself," I shall argue, makes all the difference.

5. Joseph R. Reisert observes that "the affair with the Socratic magician reminds [Emile] that possessing power is not a reason to use it: the exercise of theoretical reason must always be subordinate to the dictates of practical reason." *Jean-Jacques Rousseau: A Friend of Virtue* (Ithaca: Cornell University Press, 2003), 157. The question now becomes how Emile is to learn to listen to the dictates of practical reason.

6. "Anything which gives movement to the body without constraining it is always easy to obtain from children. There are countless means of interesting them in measuring, knowing, and estimating distances. Here is a very tall cherry tree. How shall we go about picking the cherries? . . . There are two villages. At which of the two will we arrive sooner for dinner? Et cetera" (140–41; 4:392–93).

7. On the role of sensation in Rousseau's understanding of judgment, see also Ryan Patrick Hanley, "Rousseau's Virtue Epistemology," *Journal of the History of Philosophy* 50 (April 2012): 239–63.

8. On Rousseau's critique of Helvétius, see Natasha Gill, *Educational Philosophy in the French Enlightenment: From Nature to Second Nature* (Surrey, UK: Ashgate, 2010), 163–80; Hanley, "Rousseau's Virtue Epistemology"; Terence Marshall, "Perception politique et théorie de la connaissance dans l'oeuvre de Jean-Jacques Rousseau," *Revue Française de Science Politique* 29, nos. 4–5 (1979): 605–64; and Pierre-Maurice Masson, "Rousseau contre Helvétius," *Revue d'Histoire Littéraire de la France* 18 (1911): 103–24. For an assessment of Helvétius's criticisms of *Emile*, see Jean H. Bloch, "Rousseau and Helvétius on Innate and Acquired Traits: The Final Stages of the Rousseau-Helvétius Controversy," *Journal of the History of Ideas* 40 (January–March 1979): 21–41.

9. Jean-Jacques Rousseau, "Letter to Beaumont," in *The Collected Writings of Jean-Jacques Rousseau*, ed. Roger D. Masters and Christopher Kelly, 13 vols. (Hanover: University Press of New England, 1990–2009), 9:39–40.

10. Here Rousseau seems to follow Glaucon in Plato's *Republic* (358b, 361b), who wishes to see the just soul in itself and by itself, and so to do away with appearances, reputations, rewards, etc. For a discussion of the numerous points of intertextuality between *Emile* and Plato's *Republic*, see Madeleine B. Ellis, *Rousseau's Socratic Aemilian Myths: A Literary Collation of "Emile" and "The Social Contract"* (Columbus: Ohio State University Press, 1977). On metaphysical and ontological affinities between Plato and Rousseau, see David Lay Williams, *Rousseau's Platonic Enlightenment* (University Park: Pennsylvania State University Press, 2007), 168–82.

11. For more on this subject, see Jean Starobinski, *Jean-Jacques Rousseau: Transparency and Obstruction*, trans. Arthur Goldhammer (Chicago: University of Chicago Press, 1971).

Chapter 3

1. Susan Meld Shell, "Eating Crow: Rousseau on Fables," in *Yearbook of the Beast Fable Society* 4 (1992): 76.

2. See, for example, Allan Bloom's introduction to his translation of *Emile*, 8–9; and Jean Starobinski, *Jean-Jacques Rousseau: Transparency and Obstruction*, trans. Arthur Goldhammer (Chicago: University of Chicago Press, 1971), 109, 230. Several commentators have noted the degree to which Crusoe departs from Rousseau's vision of "natural man." See Todd R. Flanders, "Rousseau's Adventure with Robinson Crusoe," *Interpretation* 24, no. 3 (1997): 319–37; Paul Nourrisson, *Jean-Jacques Rousseau et Robinson Crusoé* (Paris: Editions Spes, 1931); and Maximillian E. Novak, *Defoe and the Nature of Man* (New York: Oxford University Press, 1963). While Novak provides the general argument that *Robinson Crusoe* illustrates the misery, rather than the felicity, of human beings in the state of nature, Nourrisson and Flanders devote more focused attention to the question of Rousseau's use of the novel. Nourrisson claims that Rousseau had an "idée fixe" (27), a morbid obsession with solitude, which caused him to misunderstand Defoe's novel. Flanders takes a much more subtle and productive approach, arguing that Rousseau engaged in a wholesale revision of the novel as presented in *Emile*, since Crusoe's religiosity and his Englishness would get in the way of the goals of Emile's "natural" education. Flanders sees in Rousseau's editing an implicit criticism of Crusoe that serves to highlight for the reader the contrast between Crusoe as the quintessential portrait of the problems of civil society (and early modern understandings of society in particular) and Emile as the portrait of the possibilities of original freedom in nature. His reading preserves a dichotomy between Defoe's Crusoe and Rousseau's Crusoe, and between society and nature.

3. Bloom, "Introduction," in *Emile*, 9. In contrast, Christopher Kelly provides a more subtle interpretation of Emile's identification with Crusoe: "Emile does imagine himself to be Robinson Crusoe, but he is aware of differences between himself and the character in the book. Robinson has fears that Emile would never have had and makes mistakes that Emile would never make. Emile identifies with Robinson's situation rather than with the man." Kelly, *Rousseau's Exemplary Life: The "Confessions" as Political Philosophy* (Ithaca: Cornell University Press, 1987),

93. My own reading is more compatible with Kelly's than with Bloom's, although Kelly presents Crusoe's "situation" as characterized by "self-sufficiency" (79), which I shall dispute.

4. For an insightful discussion of Rousseau's understanding of the unnaturalness of the human desire for knowledge, particularly as the issue is presented in the *Lettres Morales*, see Kelly, *Rousseau's Exemplary Life*, 40–45. Kelly goes on to argue that the *Confessions* is Rousseau's attempt to overcome this problem, and therefore serves as a foundation for Rousseau's system as a whole.

5. For a stimulating interpretation of the various ways in which the "compass" functions as an allegory in book III, see Madeleine B. Ellis, *Rousseau's Socratic Aemilian Myths: A Literary Collation of "Emile" and "The Social Contract"* (Columbus: Ohio State University Press, 1977), 155–67.

6. Hilail Gildin, *Rousseau's Social Contract: The Design of the Argument* (Chicago: University of Chicago Press, 1983), 66.

7. Many commentators have identified the parallels between *Emile* and *On the Social Contract*, and in particular between Emile and the people. See, for example, Stephen Ellenberg, *Rousseau's Political Philosophy: An Interpretation from Within* (Ithaca: Cornell University Press, 1973), 271–318; Ruth W. Grant, *Hypocrisy and Integrity: Machiavelli, Rousseau, and the Ethics of Politics* (Chicago: University of Chicago Press, 1997), 125–34; Arthur M. Melzer, *The Natural Goodness of Man: On the System of Rousseau's Thought* (Chicago: University of Chicago Press, 1990), 245–49; and Judith N. Shklar, *Men and Citizens: A Study of Rousseau's Social Theory* (Cambridge: Cambridge University Press, 1969), 165.

8. Gildin, *Rousseau's Social Contract*, 87–88.

9. Plutarch, *Lives of the Noble Greeks*, trans. Ian Scott-Kilvert (London: Penguin Books, 1973), 44.

10. Tracy B. Strong offers an alternative explanation for Rousseau's opposition to books: "From the beginning, the reason for the opposition to books is Rousseau's resistance to permanent definition. . . . What is wrong with precision is that it eliminates the human from the world." Strong, *Jean-Jacques Rousseau: The Politics of the Ordinary* (Thousand Oaks, Calif.: Sage Publications, 1994), 38.

11. Rousseau makes one final suggestion before turning to *Robinson Crusoe*. Almost as an aside, he suggests that a tutor comment on a child's development with reference to the child's own past rather than by comparison with other children. "I see no problem in his being his own competitor," he says (184; 4:454). Another way to translate this sentence would be, "I see no problem in his emulating himself." A younger Emile would function as "another self" to an older Emile. But Rousseau does not elaborate on this point, nor is the reader given any example of how it might work. The problem, of course, is that this purported solution requires a stable identity over time, and therefore assumes in advance that which it is meant to bring into existence: a sense of oneself as an "I." This is the problem that remains to be resolved in book III.

12. Note that in the *Letters from the Mountain* and the letters to Beaumont and Franquieres, Rousseau has much more to say about how *not* to interpret his work than he does about how one ought to. He is, of course, defending the works against critics who have (in his view) completely missed the point. However, his explication of their mistakes does not always include positive

guidance toward a "correct" view. This circumspection is not surprising from one who admonishes his reader that "if you need to be told, you do not understand me."

13. It is of course important that absent from these needs is the one that would be the most threatening to Emile's education at this point—sexual desire. Just as Emile has not yet felt "the most violent, the most terrible" need of sexual desire, Crusoe lacks "the lust of the flesh." Only in this very limited sense can it be said that the two men have more strength than they do needs, or that they are independent beings.

14. Clearly, the seeds of morality have been planted in Emile, and indeed cultivated to some degree, long before their fruits become apparent; for example, he learns a basic lesson about property in book II. Rousseau highlights the preparatory significance of that incident in discussing the lessons about the division of labor that Emile will be prompted to consider upon reading *Robinson Crusoe*: "The society of the arts consists in exchange of skills, that of commerce in exchange of things, that of banks in exchange of signs and money. All these ideas are connected, and the elementary notions are already grasped. We laid the foundation for all this at an early age with the help of Robert, the gardener" (189; 4:461).

15. Flanders, "Rousseau's Adventure with Robinson Crusoe," 321, 325. Flanders argues that Rousseau in effect creates a new Crusoe out of whole cloth.

16. Daniel Defoe, *Robinson Crusoe*, ed. Michael Shinagel (New York: W. W. Norton, 1994), 36.

17. Novak, *Defoe and the Nature of Man*, 25.

18. Nourrisson argues that Rousseau's fixation on Crusoe's parasol arises from the illustration of Crusoe that graced the edition of the novel that Rousseau most probably encountered. Nourrisson, *Jean-Jacques Rousseau et Robinson Crusoé*, 28.

19. It is unlikely that Rousseau overlooked this important detail. In his *Confessions*, book VII, Rousseau refers to himself as "another Robinson Crusoe" as he prepares to spend twenty-one days in a spare lazaretto after the passengers of a ship he was traveling on are quarantined. His Crusoe-like preparations entail choosing carefully the provisions he will bring from the ship, including not only clothing and linens but also paper, ink, and a dozen books. Ironically, he has two trunks of supplies at his disposal as he bravely endures his "bare" solitude.

20. Defoe, *Robinson Crusoe*, 47.

21. Ibid.

22. Ibid., 43.

23. Ibid., 95.

24. "Similarly, in the *Second Discourse*, natural man makes sense only as that for which civil man longs. That natural man has no real existence apart from this looking back seems clear from the difficulty Rousseau has in finding appropriate examples, all of which prove to be either animals or already in some measure civil." Michael Davis, *The Autobiography of Philosophy: Rousseau's "The Reveries of the Solitary Walker"* (Lanham, Md.: Rowman & Littlefield, 1999), 111n22.

25. Rousseau may be attempting to resolve a similar problem in the *Second Discourse* when he describes how natural man first compared himself to animals, and sensed his superiority to them, before comparing himself to other human beings (*SD*, 144; 3:165–66).

Notes to Pages 78–87 ❧ 207

26. See discussion of this issue in Davis, *Autobiography of Philosophy*, esp. 265–67; Sarah Herbold, "Rousseau's Dance of Veils: The *Confessions* and the Imagined Woman Reader," *Eighteenth-Century Studies* 32, no. 3 (1999): 333–53; and Strong, *Jean-Jacques Rousseau*, 17.

27. For a discussion of how Rousseau's rejection of humankind in the first part of the *Reveries* can be read as an obsession with others, see Davis, *Autobiography of Philosophy*, 89–103, 126–29, 232–40.

28. Morgenstern provides a detailed analysis of the way in which the tutor monitors the development of pity in Emile in order to teach him that he has *semblables*. While she considers the role that the imagination plays in this development, she focuses on the role that the study of history plays. My analysis is intended to show that Emile must be self-aware before he can see that he has *semblables*. See Mira Morgenstern, *Rousseau and the Politics of Ambiguity: Self, Culture, and Society* (University Park: Pennsylvania State University Press, 1996), 63–71.

29. The significance of this apparent contradiction in the *Reveries* is thoroughly explored and illuminated in Davis, *Autobiography of Philosophy*. I am deeply indebted to Davis on this point.

30. See, for example, the *Confessions*, book XII.

31. A parallel can be drawn to amour-propre, which is employed as a necessary but dangerous tool throughout *Emile* despite Rousseau's criticisms of it. For the most thorough treatment of the positive qualities of amour-propre, see Laurence D. Cooper, *Rousseau, Nature, and the Problem of the Good Life* (University Park: Pennsylvania State University Press, 1999), chap. 4. See also Frederick Neuhouser, *Rousseau's Theodicy of Self-Love: Evil, Rationality, and the Drive for Recognition* (Oxford: Oxford University Press, 2010).

32. Jean-Jacques Rousseau, *The Reveries of the Solitary Walker*, trans. Charles E. Butterworth (Indianapolis: Hackett, 1992), 141.

33. He makes this task explicit for himself (and reflects on its ultimate impossibility) in *Reveries*, book III. On the general theme of the differences between Emile and Rousseau (as he presents himself in the *Confessions*), see Kelly, *Rousseau's Exemplary Life*, chap. 3.

34. In a similar vein, Rousseau goes on to indicate in book IV of *Emile* that even when a more mature man sees himself reflected in his beloved's eyes, he needs to reflect on that reflection. "From the need for a mistress is soon born the need for a friend" (215; 4:494).

Chapter 4

1. "Soul" (*l'âme*) occurs a second time in book III, but only in reference to the tutor's soul, which is moved by a beautiful vista. Rousseau immediately makes clear the impossibility of sharing this experience with a young pupil (168–69; 4:431).

2. According to Allan Bloom, the "primary function" of Emile's education in pity is "to make Emile social while remaining whole." See Bloom's introduction to his edition of *Emile*, 20.

3. For an argument that Rousseau's understanding of pity nevertheless fosters relationships of power and inequality, see Richard Boyd, "Pity's Pathologies Portrayed: Rousseau and the Limits of Democratic Compassion," *Political Theory* 32, no. 4 (2004): 519–46.

4. "The Stoic wise man is a man of feeling, but his feelings do not control, or even influence, his decisions and his actions . . . he is passionless (*apathés*), but not without rational feelings." John M. Rist, *Stoic Philosophy* (Cambridge: Cambridge University Press, 1977), 260. For an alternative analysis of the relationship between Rousseau and Stoicism, but one that agrees that "Rousseau's working through his Stoic inheritance eventually undermines its assurance of the harmony and unity of the mind," see Amélie Oksenberg Rorty, "The Two Faces of Stoicism: Rousseau and Freud," *Journal of the History of Philosophy* 34, no. 3 (1996): 352.

5. For a detailed discussion of the role of the imagination in Rousseau's understanding of compassion, see David Marshall, *The Surprising Effects of Sympathy: Marivaux, Diderot, Rousseau, and Mary Shelley* (Chicago: University of Chicago Press, 1988), 148–52.

6. For a critique of Rousseau's view of pity on the grounds that he treats suffering as mere spectacle, see Boyd, "Pity's Pathologies Portrayed." Boyd argues that the perspective Rousseau attributes to the one who feels pity is "voyeuristic," in that one may feel repugnance at the sight of human suffering but not be moved to act to alleviate it. Clifford Orwin similarly emphasizes the limitations of pity: "As we needed a compassionate morality to supplement the coldness of reason, we need a rational one to restrain the impulsive warmth of compassion." Orwin, "Rousseau and the Discovery of Political Compassion," in *The Legacy of Rousseau*, ed. Clifford Orwin and Nathan Tarcov (Chicago: University of Chicago Press, 1997), 308. On the relationship between pity, sympathy, and self-love, see Charles L. Griswold, "Smith and Rousseau in Dialogue: Sympathy, *Pitié*, Spectatorship, and Narrative," in *The Philosophy of Adam Smith*, ed. Vivienne Brown and Samuel Fleischacker (London: Routledge, 2010), 59–84.

7. Morgenstern and Velkley argue that even in the state of nature as depicted in the *Second Discourse*, pity has a reflective dimension. See Mira Morgenstern, *Rousseau and the Politics of Ambiguity: Self, Culture, and Society* (University Park: Pennsylvania State University Press, 1996), 65–72; and Richard L. Velkley, *Being After Rousseau: Philosophy and Culture in Question* (Chicago: University of Chicago Press, 2002). For a general overview of the status of pity in Rousseau's state of nature, see Marc F. Plattner, *Rousseau's State of Nature: An Interpretation of the Discourse on Inequality* (DeKalb: Northern Illinois University Press, 1979), 84–87.

8. Jonathan Marks argues similarly that in *Emile* pity and reason are intertwined, and that therefore pity is not simply opposed to judgment. Marks, "Rousseau's Discriminating Defense of Compassion," *American Political Science Review* 101 (November 2007): 727–39.

9. Those who emphasize the degree to which Emile's education in pity underscores human differences as much as (or even more than) human commonality (with different implications than my reading suggests) include Boyd, "Pity's Pathologies Portrayed," and William Connolly, *Identity/Difference: Democratic Negotiations of Political Paradox* (Minneapolis: University of Minnesota Press, 2002), 158–60, 172–73.

10. There is an explicit reference to this particular exchange in the *Republic* (including a footnote to the precise location in the text) later in book IV of *Emile*, in the context of the "Profession of Faith of the Savoyard Vicar" (*E*, 307; 4:626).

11. See Plato *Republic* 9.571a–580b.

12. See Jean Starobinski, *Jean-Jacques Rousseau: Transparency and Obstruction*, trans. Arthur Goldhammer (Chicago: University of Chicago Press, 1971).

13. The entry on "physionomie" in the *Encyclopédie* warned against the oversimplification of associating goodness and fairness. On the status of physiognomy in the eighteenth-century French novel (including Rousseau's *La nouvelle Heloise*), see Angelica Goodden, *The Complete Lover: Eros, Nature, and Artifice in the Eighteenth-Century French Novel* (Oxford: Clarendon Press, 1989), 153–87.

14. See, for example, Joseph R. Reisert, *Jean-Jacques Rousseau: A Friend of Virtue* (Ithaca: Cornell University Press, 2003).

Chapter 5

1. Peter Emberley, "Rousseau Versus the Savoyard Vicar: The Profession of Faith Considered," *Interpretation* 14, no. 3 (1986): 324.

2. Allan Bloom, *Love and Friendship* (New York: Simon & Schuster, 1993), 78.

3. See, for example, Roger D. Masters, *The Political Philosophy of Rousseau* (Princeton: Princeton University Press, 1976), 72.

4. Bloom, *Love and Friendship*, 73.

5. Bloom points out that in the earliest draft of *Emile*, Rousseau wrote and then crossed out the following statement: "If I am asked how it is possible for the morality of human life to emerge from a purely physical revolution, I will answer that I do not know." See his translation of *Emile*, 488n2.

6. Following the profession of faith, we are told merely that "this" is what Rousseau will limit himself to with regard to his pupil (313–14; 4:636), but there is no scene depicting Emile receiving "this" (or any) religious education.

7. For a careful analysis of the will in Descartes, including an overview of the scholarly controversy about the role of the will in Descartes's theory of judgment, see David M. Rosenthal, "Will and the Theory of Judgment," in *Descartes' Meditations: Critical Essays*, ed. Vere Chappell (Lanham, Md.: Rowman & Littlefield, 1997). See also David M. Rosenthal, "Descartes and the Theory of Judgment," in *Essays on Descartes' Meditations*, ed. Amélie Oksenberg Rorty (Berkeley: University of California Press, 1986), 405–34.

8. Bernard Williams, *Descartes: The Project of Pure Enquiry* (New York: Penguin Books, 1978), 183.

9. René Descartes, *Discourse on Method and Meditations on First Philosophy*, trans. Donald A. Cress (Indianapolis: Hackett, 1998), 52.

10. Ibid., 6.

11. There is much more complexity in Descartes's argument than I am addressing for the purposes of this comparison. I am working with the most accessible and influential understanding of his project, precisely because it was so influential. It might make more sense to say that Rousseau's target is "Cartesianism."

12. Descartes, *Discourse on Method*, 52.

13. Ibid., 3.

14. Plato *Phaedrus* 241e. Parenthetical references to the *Phaedrus* are to the translation by Stephen Scully (Newburyport, Mass.: Focus, 2003).

15. Masters, *Political Philosophy of Rousseau*, 72.

16. Arthur M. Melzer, "The Origin of the Counter-Enlightenment: Rousseau and the New Religion of Sincerity," *American Political Science Review* 90, no. 2 (1996): 359. See also Joshua Mitchell, *Not By Reason Alone: Religion, History, and Identity in Early Modern Political Thought* (Chicago: University of Chicago Press, 1993), chap. 4, in which Mitchell concludes that Rousseau "silences" reason in favor of listening to the heart, but adds the nuance that Rousseau, like Luther, does so in order to disrupt "any world that listens to reason alone" (124).

17. Melzer, "Origin of the Counter-Enlightenment," 355. See also Jennifer Einspahr, "The Beginning That Never Was: Mediation and Freedom in Rousseau's Political Thought," *Review of Politics* 72, no. 3 (2010): 437–61, esp. 452–54.

18. For an excellent discussion of the positive qualities of amour-propre, see Laurence D. Cooper, *Rousseau, Nature, and the Problem of the Good Life* (University Park: Pennsylvania State University Press, 1999), chap. 4.

19. We cannot, of course, assume that the Vicar's position is Rousseau's position, even if Rousseau claims some affinity between the two. Emberley, for example, has argued that the two differ in quite fundamental ways; see "Rousseau Versus the Savoyard Vicar," esp. 300–323. Joseph Cropsey contends that "Rousseau's own understanding of man and his natural matrix is closer to that of Descartes than to that of the Vicar." Cropsey, *Political Philosophy and the Issues of Politics* (Chicago: University of Chicago Press, 1977), 326. See also Marc F. Plattner, *Rousseau's State of Nature: An Interpretation of the Discourse on Inequality* (DeKalb: Northern Illinois University Press, 1979). Even when he leaves the Vicar's voice behind, however, Rousseau confirms the point I have been making about how conscience and reason must operate in tandem. For example, the tutor tells Emile that "the eternal laws of nature and order," which, for the wise man, "take the place of positive law," are "written in the depth of his heart by conscience and reason" (473; 4:857). I am not identifying the Vicar's religious teaching in general with Rousseau's own view, but I do maintain that on this particular point there is an affinity. The profession of faith illustrates the interconnection between reason and sentiment in its presentation of conscience, confirming a pattern that persists throughout *Emile*. For a broad discussion of Rousseau's religious views, see Victor Gourevitch, "The Religious Thought," in *The Cambridge Companion to Rousseau*, ed. Patrick Riley (Cambridge: Cambridge University Press, 2001), 193–246.

20. Ronald Grimsley, *Rousseau and the Religious Quest* (Oxford: Clarendon Press, 1968), 63. Although he arrives at his conclusion quite differently than I do, Grimsley similarly argues that "to establish an absolute antithesis between feeling and reason [in Rousseau's thought] is to misunderstand an outlook which seeks to do justice to both" (71).

21. Bloom, *Love and Friendship*, 73.

22. Ibid., 79, emphasis added.

23. Ibid., 82.

24. Melzer makes an important point that parallels this one. He argues that Rousseau attacks both Christianity and modern philosophy on similar grounds; philosophy "is politically dangerous in ways resembling Christianity. Through the combination of abstract universalism and restless skepticism, it tends to subvert all particular worldly attachments and thus to destroy the wholeness of political life, just like Christian revelation." "Origin of the Counter-Enlightenment," 351.

25. For an overview of Rousseau's own remarks to this effect, in various contexts, see Grimsley, *Rousseau and the Religious Quest*, 36–40.

26. Emberley, "Rousseau Versus the Savoyard Vicar," 299–329. Emberley implies that the figure of the Vicar functions as a noble lie meant to "inspire virtue by portraying a simulacrum of virtue, dazzling in its charm and beauty and capable of alluring men away from vice" (324). I argue, however, that Rousseau makes clear the flaws in the figure of the Vicar (even as I defend some aspects of the Vicar's teaching, which he does not always live up to), thus inviting the reader to judge, just as the Vicar invites the young man to form his own independent views.

27. Bloom, *Love and Friendship*, 78.

28. Mary P. Nichols similarly draws the parallel for Emile between the tutor and God. See her "Rousseau's Novel Education in the *Emile*," *Political Theory* 13, no. 4 (1985): 535–58.

29. Ruth W. Grant, *Hypocrisy and Integrity: Machiavelli, Rousseau, and the Ethics of Politics* (Chicago: University of Chicago Press, 1997), 138.

Chapter 6

1. Rousseau draws attention to Sophie's great "maturity of judgment" (*E*, 399; 4:754).

2. For an excellent and detailed discussion of the common thread guiding the education of both Emile and Sophie, see Penny A. Weiss, *Gendered Community: Rousseau, Sex, and Politics* (New York: New York University Press, 1993), 10–35.

3. Specific examples of this argument can be found in M. E. Brint, "Echoes of Narcisse," *Political Theory* 16, no. 4 (1988): 617–35; and Lynda Lange, "Rousseau and Modern Feminism," in *Feminist Interpretations and Political Theory*, ed. Mary Lyndon Shanley and Carole Pateman (University Park: Pennsylvania State University Press, 1991), 100–101.

4. Weiss, *Gendered Community*, 26.

5. See Joel Schwartz, *The Sexual Politics of Jean-Jacques Rousseau* (Chicago: University of Chicago Press, 1985), chap. 4. See also Arthur M. Melzer, *The Natural Goodness of Man: On the System of Rousseau's Thought* (Chicago: University of Chicago Press, 1990), 244–49.

6. And perhaps more swiftly than the reader expects, given that Rousseau has just made the general claim that women are not made to run (437; 4:807). This is yet another instance in which Sophie's example challenges Rousseau's generalizations about women.

7. See Laurence D. Cooper, *Rousseau, Nature, and the Problem of the Good Life* (University Park: Pennsylvania State University Press, 1999), chap. 4. See also Frederick Neuhouser, *Rousseau's Theodicy of Self-Love: Evil, Rationality, and the Drive for Recognition* (Oxford: Oxford University Press, 2010).

8. Melissa A. Mathes, *The Rape of Lucretia and the Founding of Republics: Readings in Livy, Machiavelli, and Rousseau* (University Park: Pennsylvania State University Press, 2000), 146.

9. Tracy B. Strong, *Jean-Jacques Rousseau: The Politics of the Ordinary* (Thousand Oaks, Calif.: Sage Publications, 1994), 135.

10. Bonnie Honig, *Democracy and the Foreigner* (Princeton: Princeton University Press, 2001), 30–32.

11. For an alternative interpretation of Sophie's symbolic role, see Ann Charney Colmo, "What Sophie Knew: Rousseau's *Emile et Sophie, ou Les Solitaires*," in *Finding a New Feminism: Rethinking the Woman Question for Liberal Democracy*, ed. Pamela Grande Jensen (Lanham, Md.: Rowman & Littlefield, 1996), 67–91. Colmo argues that Sophie represents the general will and not the legislator because she does not in fact govern, as the failure of the marriage in *Emile et Sophie* attests. Even if we understand Sophie to represent the general will, however, my point about her inside/outside position remains applicable, since Sophie, as an individual, would presumably be a particular will as well.

12. For an interesting discussion of Rousseau's views on arranged versus freely chosen marriages, see Judith N. Shklar, *Men and Citizens: A Study of Rousseau's Social Theory* (Cambridge: Cambridge University Press, 1969), 85–88.

13. On this point I disagree with Susan Meld Shell, who argues that the story of the girl like Sophie is designed to highlight an important difference between male and female desire, which is that men are "for good or ill, the 'sublimer'—hence the more poetic—sex." In other words, they are more likely to translate their eros into love of abstract ideals. Shell, "*Emile*: Nature and the Education of Sophie," in *The Cambridge Companion to Rousseau*, ed. Patrick Riley (Cambridge: Cambridge University Press, 2001), 291–92. Rousseau himself, by contrast, claims that the story reveals a similarity between the sexes. It shows, he says, that "in spite of the prejudices born of the morals of our age, enthusiasm for the decent and the fine is no more foreign to women than to men, and that there is nothing that cannot be obtained under nature's direction from women as well as from men" (*E*, 405; 4:763).

14. For an alternative interpretation of the girl like Sophie, see Allan Bloom, *Love and Friendship* (New York: Simon & Schuster, 1993), 121–22.

15. It must be acknowledged that Sophie's experience of dependence will obviously be different from Emile's insofar as she is economically dependent on the relationship in a way that he is not. Rousseau accepts the prevailing lack of economic opportunity for women in the eighteenth century and hardly addresses the issue. His greater concern is with the moral, emotional, and intellectual dependence that can exist among individuals, and therefore I have focused on these aspects of dependence.

16. Of course, it remains difficult to translate Sophie into an explicitly *political* model of rule, since women are absent from political participation in the regime governed by the general will. But if her most important characteristic is her exercise of judgment, then the absence of women in the *Social Contract* provides us with a symbolic clue as to why it is so difficult to distinguish between radical democracy and authoritarianism in the "ideal" regime. The legislator becomes necessary to the degree that judgment is lacking in the people.

17. This argument can be found in Allan Bloom's introduction to his edition of *Emile*, 22. See also Laurence D. Cooper, *Eros in Plato, Rousseau, and Nietzsche: The Politics of Infinity* (University Park: Pennsylvania State University Press, 2007), 192.

18. Bloom, *Love and Friendship*, 108.

19. For an illuminating discussion of the mathematical analogies in the *Social Contract*, 3.1–2, see Christopher Bertram, *Routledge Philosophy Guidebook to Rousseau and the Social Contract* (London: Routledge, 2004), 151–56.

20. Ibid., 153.

21. In the *Social Contract*, by contrast, the need for a legislator is introduced following the observation that the general will is always right but tends to lack judgment (*SC*, 154; 3:380).

Chapter 7

1. Patrick J. Deneen, *The Odyssey of Political Theory* (Lanham, Md.: Rowman & Littlefield, 2003), 158–59. In supporting his argument, Deneen points to a passage in book IV that refers to Emile's independence from all bonds to humanity and his recognition only of the bonds of necessity (472; 4:856). However, this thought is expressed by Emile himself, not by the tutor or Rousseau, and the tutor immediately corrects Emile's perspective and reminds him of his bonds to humanity and his duties to whatever country he lives in, however imperfect (473; 4:858).

2. Thomas M. Kavanagh, *Writing the Truth: Authority and Desire in Rousseau* (Berkeley: University of California Press, 1987), 78–101.

3. See, for example, Marie-Hélène Huet, "Social Entropy," in *Exploring the Conversible World: Text and Sociability from the Classical Age to the Enlightenment*, ed. Elena Russo, *Yale French Studies* 92 (New Haven: Yale University Press, 1997), and Judith N. Shklar, *Men and Citizens: A Study of Rousseau's Social Theory* (Cambridge: Cambridge University Press, 1969).

4. On this point, see Diane Berrett Brown, "The Constraints of Liberty at the Scene of Instruction," in *Rousseau and Freedom*, ed. Christie McDonald and Stanley Hoffman (Cambridge: Cambridge University Press, 2010), 159–73; Ann Charney Colmo, "What Sophie Knew: Rousseau's *Emile et Sophie, ou Les Solitaires*," in *Finding a New Feminism: Rethinking the Woman Question for Liberal Democracy*, ed. Pamela Grande Jensen (Lanham, Md.: Rowman & Littlefield, 1996); and Nancy Senior, "Les solitaires as a Test for Emile and Sophie," *French Review* 49, no. 4 (1976): 528–35.

5. Elizabeth Rose Wingrove, *Rousseau's Republican Romance* (Princeton: Princeton University Press, 2000), 91.

6. In *Letters from the Mountain*, for example, Rousseau states, "Liberty consists less in doing one's will than in not being subject to that of another." *Oeuvres complètes de Jean-Jacques Rousseau*, ed. Bernard Gagnebin and Marcel Raymond, 5 vols. (Paris: Gallimard, 1959–95), 3:841.

7. On the centrality of free will to Rousseau's understanding of freedom, see Roger D. Masters, *The Political Philosophy of Rousseau* (Princeton: Princeton University Press, 1976), 69.

8. For a discussion of the various possible endings, see Michel Launay, *Une grève d'esclaves à Alger au XVIIIeme siècle* (Paris: Jean-Paul Rocher, 1998), 84–89.

9. Cf. Steven Johnston, *Encountering Tragedy: Rousseau and the Project of Democratic Order* (Ithaca: Cornell University Press, 1999), 71.

10. My argument here is consistent with Jonathan Marks's observation that Rousseauian freedom requires a middle ground between passivity and activity. Emile must "negotiate a middle position between acting in the world and restraining himself or staying in place." Marks, *Perfection and Disharmony in the Thought of Jean-Jacques Rousseau* (Cambridge: Cambridge University Press, 2005), 86.

11. For an analysis of Rousseau's treatment of the problem of learning in time in the *Reveries*, see Michael Davis, *The Autobiography of Philosophy: Rousseau's "The Reveries of the Solitary Walker"* (Lanham, Md.: Rowman & Littlefield, 1999), chap. 7.

Chapter 8

1. Judith N. Shklar, "Rousseau's Images of Authority," in *The Cambridge Companion to Rousseau*, ed. Patrick Riley (Cambridge: Cambridge University Press, 2001), 183.

2. See, for example, James Miller's reading in *Rousseau: Dreamer of Democracy* (New Haven: Yale University Press, 1984). See also Michael Palmer, *Masters and Slaves: Revisioned Essays in Political Philosophy* (Lanham, Md.: Lexington Books, 2001). "The only precaution left for [the Genevans] to take," Palmer writes, "is to remain united, obey the laws, and respect their magistrates" (131).

3. Compare, in book V of *Emile*, Rousseau's admonition that women bow to the dictates of convention only when they do not conflict with the dictates of conscience. I discuss the implications of this in chapter 6.

4. Christopher Kelly discusses an instance in which Rousseau explicitly addresses the implications of putting issues in the form of questions. See his *Rousseau as Author: Consecrating One's Life to the Truth* (Chicago: University of Chicago Press, 2003), 47.

5. Whereas he presents the sovereign people with a series of questions about the merit of the magistrates, he confronts the magistrates with a series of stern assertions, reminding them that the people are their equals by education, nature, and birth, unequal only in "their will and by the preference they owe your merit" (*SD*, 87; 3:118).

6. Christopher Kelly's discussion of how Rousseau uses classical heroes (especially heroic republican citizens such as Brutus, Cato, and Lucrezia) to inspire good citizenship supplies yet another example of this balance. According to Kelly, "Rousseau's analysis shows us the dangers of heroes even as it magnifies their allure." *Rousseau as Author*, 115. This is just one example of how Rousseau mitigates his readers' unreflective attachment to the ideals he promotes.

7. Several other readings draw attention to this dimension in the *Social Contract*. Focusing on the underlying conditions that make the proper expression of the general will possible, Christopher Kelly emphasizes the need for active (if limited) public deliberation. Although Rousseau at times associates debate with corruption (as dissension may indicate the dominance of private interests), at other points he notes that unanimity can also coexist with corruption; it can mask the practice of selling votes. Unanimity can be either healthy or unhealthy, and the unanimity of Sparta, according to Kelly, represents the "frictionless extreme." Rousseau may praise Sparta for its "excellent regulations," but he also refers to those regulations as "monstrously perfect." According to Kelly, Rousseau's true model is Rome. "The case for Rome, the turbulent domestic history of which makes it an unlikely example of total social cohesion, is a case for a sort of patriotism that is intimately linked with freedom." Ibid., 122–25. In a similar vein, Katrin Froese argues that the articulation of the general will requires an *active* transcendence of the self and therefore feeds on a necessary *tension* between the general and the particular will. "Commonality requires difference because there would be no need to assemble if our interests were naturally

compatible." Froese, *Rousseau and Nietzsche: Toward an Aesthetic Morality* (Lanham, Md.: Lexington Books, 2001), 57. Tracy B. Strong argues that the general will, "far from being the expression of a single, unitary overarching collective consciousness," is in fact "the expression of the multiplicity and mutability of my being." Strong, *Jean-Jacques Rousseau: The Politics of the Ordinary* (Thousand Oaks, Calif.: Sage Publications, 1994), 83. Finally, see Joshua Cohen, *Rousseau: A Free Community of Equals* (Oxford: Oxford University Press, 2010), 68–73.

8. Similarly, there are healthy and unhealthy forms of amour-propre, in Rousseau's view. For the most detailed discussion of this point, see Laurence D. Cooper, *Rousseau, Nature, and the Problem of the Good Life* (University Park: Pennsylvania State University Press, 1999), chap. 4.

9. For a detailed discussion of this theme, see Jeffrey A. Smith, "Nationalism, Virtue, and the Spirit of Liberty in Rousseau's *Government of Poland*," *Review of Politics* 65, no. 3 (2003): 409–37.

10. Claiming that Rousseau seriously underestimates this difficulty, Steven Johnston points out that such heavy demands of public service "may well backfire" as service comes to be viewed as a "resented extraction" rather than as a valued contribution. Moreover, Johnston argues, this represents a fundamental contradiction in Rousseau's thought—one that ultimately subverts the very freedom that the system of rigorous public service is purported to promote. *Encountering Tragedy: Rousseau and the Project of Democratic Order* (Ithaca: Cornell University Press, 1999), 98–99.

11. Joshua Cohen draws a useful distinction between "motivational possibility" and "institutional possibility" in considering the question of Rousseau's realism. Cohen, *Rousseau: A Free Community of Equals*, 16–20.

12. Kelly, *Rousseau as Author*, 109.

13. For a detailed account of the contemporary reception and impact of Rousseau's work in Poland, see Jerzy Lukowski, "Recasting Utopia: Montesquieu, Rousseau, and the Polish Constitution of 3 May 1791," *Historical Journal* 37 (March 1994): 65–87. Lukowski focuses on the debates in the Four-Year Sejm (parliament) of 1788–92 and discusses in detail the degree to which Rousseau's prescriptions were taken seriously in the debates, as various participants "appealed . . . to the authority of Montesquieu and Rousseau" (69). While the new constitution ultimately disregarded two major pieces of Rousseau's advice, abolishing both the elective monarchy and the *liberum veto*, it did incorporate others, such as the enforcement of a national curriculum through a new Commission for National Education. With regard to the status of the serfs, the changes were modest in terms of concrete material effects but fairly significant in terms of rhetoric. "Article IV put the peasantry under the protection of the law; it was little enough, but it was the only starting point from which 'freedom,' as the Enlightenment understood it, was possible" (83). Just as important—perhaps even more so—there was a discernible shift in the imagery and terminology surrounding the peasantry. "There was no reference to the demeaning *poddani*—that is, subjects or serfs. Instead the constitution spoke of 'the rural peasantry,' 'the agrarian population,' and sought to give them their own dignity" (83). Moreover, they were characterized (in language, I would add, that closely echoes Rousseau's own words) as a chief source of the country's riches. Only a generation earlier, Lukowski notes, such language would have been unthinkable. See also Lukowski, *Disorderly Liberty: The Political Culture of the Polish-Lithuanian Commonwealth in the Eighteenth Century* (London: Continuum, 2010), 137–38.

14. For a longer and more developed version of the argument that follows, see my "Attending to Time and Place in Rousseau's Legislative Art," *Review of Politics* 74, no. 3 (2012): 421–41.

15. This view is consistent with Jeffrey A. Smith's argument, in "Nationalism, Virtue, and the Spirit of Liberty," that *Considerations on the Government of Poland* shows that a people, in order to remain free, should retain some sense that their freedom is in peril.

16. Christopher Bertram, for example, notes that although affective identification among citizens (strengthened by public festivals and spectacles) is an important foundation for Rousseau's model of citizenship, it does not exhaust "all that Rousseau values. . . . There is a time for dancing and a time for individuals to reason together in common as citizens." Bertram, *Routledge Philosophy Guidebook to Rousseau and the Social Contract* (London: Routledge, 2004), 146. Christopher Kelly similarly emphasizes the need for active (if limited) public deliberation in Rousseau's ideal regime, arguing that unanimity for Rousseau "is not simply desirable at any cost." *Rousseau as Author*, 122. See also Ethan Putterman, who argues that citizenship, for Rousseau, is more "active and robust" than is commonly recognized. Putterman, *Rousseau, Law, and the Sovereignty of the People* (Cambridge: Cambridge University Press, 2010), 173.

17. See Cheryl Hall, *The Trouble with Passion: Political Theory Beyond the Reign of Reason* (New York: Routledge, 2005), 87.

18. For a more complete analysis of the fifth walk, see Michael Davis, *The Autobiography of Philosophy: Rousseau's "The Reveries of the Solitary Walker"* (Lanham, Md.: Rowman & Littlefield, 1998), chap. 9.

19. Jean-Jacques Rousseau, *The Reveries of the Solitary Walker*, trans. Charles E. Butterworth (Indianapolis: Hackett, 1992), 70.

20. Ibid., 63.

21. See Davis, *Autobiography of Philosophy*, 92–93.

22. See Jean Starobinski, *Jean-Jacques Rousseau: Transparency and Obstruction*, trans. Arthur Goldhammer (Chicago: University of Chicago Press, 1971).

23. Michael Walzer, *Politics and Passion: Toward a More Egalitarian Liberalism* (New Haven: Yale University Press, 2006), xii.

24. In addition to Walzer, see also Hall, *Trouble with Passion*, and Sharon R. Krause, *Civil Passions: Moral Sentiment and Democratic Deliberation* (Princeton: Princeton University Press, 2008).

25. For a helpful discussion of the status of "public reason" in Rousseau, see Frederick Neuhouser, *Rousseau's Theodicy of Self-Love: Evil, Rationality, and the Drive for Recognition* (Oxford: Oxford University Press, 2010), 201–17.

26. Bertram, *Routledge Philosophy Guidebook*, 146.

INDEX

abstraction, 104–6

Adventures of Telemachus (Fénelon), 139–40, 144, 146–47, 148, 149

agriculture, 187–90

Alexander, 59, 69–70

amour-propre

children and, 90

desires and, 44–46, 66, 89–90, 115, 142

freedom and, 89, 168–69

humiliation and, 45–46, 96–100

identity and, 78–79

judgment and, 89, 96–100

love and, 141–43

as necessary, 207n. 31, 215n.8

pity and, 86–87, 88–90, 96–100

politics and, 180–86

reason and, 119, 168–69

religion and, 119

running and, 142

self-consciousness and, 96–100, 141–43

society and, 86–87, 88–90

soul and, 168–69

wholeness and, 141–43

appearances. *See* seeing

Arendt, Hannah, 7–8

Aristophanes, 152

Aristotle, 15, 48–49, 59, 60

attachment. *See* detachment

authority

amour-propre and, 141–43

freedom and, 124–29, 160–61

gender and, 140–44

illusions and, 141, 142, 144

imagination and, 125, 126–28

judgment and, 108–9, 127–29, 138, 143–44, 161

love and, 135, 140–44

movement and, 119–20, 126–27, 142

politics and, 143–44, 175–76, 177

reason and, 108–9, 114, 119–23, 126, 128–29

reflection and, 127–29, 143–44, 161

religion and, 108–9, 119–23, 129

self-consciousness and, 140–44, 161

self-rule and, 128, 143–44, 161

senses and, 120, 125–26

sentiment and, 114, 119–23, 126

truth and, 114, 120

tutors and, 124–29, 138, 143

wholeness and, 127, 140–44

autonomy. *See* self-rule

Barber, Benjamin, 197n. 5

beauty, 110–11, 114, 116–17, 149, 151, 193

Beiner, Ronald, 1, 8–9

Bertram, Christopher, 154, 195, 216n. 16

biographies, 94–95. *See also* books

Bloom, Allan

on pity, 207n. 2

on reason, 107, 111, 120, 121

on revision, 209n. 5

on wholeness, 152

body

books and, 69, 73, 75–76

children and, 24–25, 37–47, 69

desires and, 43–45, 46–47

freedom and, 20, 43–44

gender and, 137, 140

happiness and, 40–42

independence and, 45, 47, 65, 87, 140

judgment and, 36, 87–88, 140

movement and, 38, 39, 42–45, 46–47, 85, 115–16

nature and, 20, 24–25, 110–11

pity and, 87–88, 93

body *(continued)*
  property and, 54
  reason and, 46–47, 109–11, 115–16
  reflection and, 81
  religion and, 109–11
  running and, 37–38, 42–45
  society and, 25, 87–88
  virtue and, 164
  wholeness and, 87–88
books
  Adventures of Telemachus (Fénelon), 139–
    40, 144, 146–47, 148, 149
  biographies, 94–95
  body and, 69, 73, 75–76
  children and, 63–66, 68–72
  death and, 72, 74–75
  desires and, 65–66
  experience and, 63–65, 81, 82–83
  fables, 51, 63–64, 68–69, 71–72, 75, 104, 116
  freedom and, 65, 68
  history, 69–70, 71, 80, 94
  identity and, 73–74, 78–80
  illusions and, 73–74, 76, 81–82
  independence and, 76–77, 78–80, 82–83,
    139–40
  judgment and, 64, 69–72, 77, 104, 135, 139–
    40, 146–47
  knowledge and, 64, 65–66
  learning and, 65–66, 77
  love and, 139–40, 144, 146–47, 148, 149
  movement and, 68
  nature and, 64–65, 68, 73–74, 77–78, 81
  pity and, 94–95
  prejudices and, 78
  reason and, 63–64, 116
  rebirths and, 73–74
  reflection and, 77–78, 80–83
  Robinson Crusoe (Defoe), 53–54, 64–65,
    72–83
  self-consciousness and, 65–66, 73–74,
    77–80, 82–83
  society and, 65, 72–78
  utility and, 66–68, 72, 74, 75–77, 78,
    80–83, 135
  virtue and, 65, 69, 76
Boyd, Richard, 208n. 6, 208n. 9
Buttafuco, Matieu, 186

change. *See* movement
character
  of children, 37, 44, 51–52, 60
  illusions and, 151–53
  judgment and, 100–106
  love and, 151–53, 166
  society and, 103
children
  amour-propre and, 90
  body and, 24–25, 37–47, 69
  books and, 63–66, 68–72
  character of, 37, 44, 51–52, 60
  desires and, 25–29, 43–47
  education of, generally, 21–23, 30–31, 36–38
  foresight and, 61, 66
  freedom and, 43–44
  habit and, 51–54
  happiness and, 40–42, 46
  identity and, 44, 46
  illusions and, 61–62
  imitation and, 51–54
  judgment and, 37–38, 50, 56–60, 69–72
  language and, 26, 28, 38–39
  man compared with, 22, 29, 30, 157
  maturity and, 37–38, 42–43, 50–51
  movement by, 38, 39, 42–45, 46–47
  nature and, 21–31, 36, 40–42, 52
  prejudices and, 22
  reason and, 38, 39, 46–47, 50, 63–64, 109
  rebirths of, 12, 39–40
  religion and, 109
  running and, 37–38, 42–45, 46–47
  seeing and, 37–38, 47–50, 58–60
  self-consciousness and, 46
  senses and, 37–38, 46–50, 58–60
  society and, 22, 25, 26
  virtue and, 36, 51–54
  wholeness and, 58–59, 60–62
  will and, 25–26, 28–29
  wisdom and, 63
chimeras. *See* illusions
citizenship. *See* politics
Cladis, Mark, 4
Cohen, Joshua, 215n.11
collectivism, 2–5, 192. *See also* society
Colmo, Ann Charney, 212n. 11
common sense, 49–50

conditioning. *See also* illusions; prejudices
  freedom and, 2–3, 135–36
  identity and, 2–3, 191–92
  illusions and, 2–3, 134
  judgment and, 1–3, 6, 172, 191–92
  love and, 134, 135–36
  movement and, 171, 191
  politics and, 1–2, 2–3, 190, 191–92
  self-consciousness and, 172–73, 191–92
  self-rule and, 2–3, 6, 172–73
  taste and, 130, 132, 171–72
  wholeness and, 191–92
Confessions (Rousseau), 55, 80, 193, 206n. 18
Connolly, William, 208n. 9
conscience, 113–14, 120, 138, 177, 210n. 19,
  214n. 3. *See also* sentiment
Considerations on the Government of Poland
  (Rousseau), 2, 3, 175, 179–86
Cooper, Laurence D., 199n. 17, 201n. 2
Corsica, 186–90
courage, 69–70
Cropsey, Joseph, 210n. 19
Cullen, Daniel E., 197n. 8, 198n. 10

Davis, Michael, 193, 201n. 37
death, 60, 61–62, 72, 74–75, 162–63
Deenan, Patrick J., 159–60, 213n. 1
Defoe, Daniel, 53–54, 64–65, 72–83, 135
democracy. *See* politics
Deneen, Patrick J., 213n. 1
Descartes, René, 112–13, 114–16, 117, 119
desires
  amour-propre and, 44–46, 66, 89–90, 115,
    142
  body and, 43–45, 46–47
  books and, 65–66
  children and, 25–29, 43–47
  detachment and, 169
  equilibrium and, 66, 145
  faculties and, 40–42, 66, 142, 145
  freedom and, 43–44, 65, 66
  gender and, 212n. 13
  happiness and, 40–42, 66, 101–2, 145
  knowledge and, 45–46, 65–66, 115
  mothers and, 25–29
  movement and, 43–45, 46–47, 115, 133
  nature and, 25–29

reason and, 111, 115
religion and, 111
running and, 43–45, 65
self-rule and, 65–66
sexuality and, 206n. 13
society and, 25, 26, 29, 89–90
soul and, 133
suffering and, 101–2
utility and, 66–67
virtue and, 66
will and, 25–26, 28–29
detachment. *See also* perspective
  freedom and, 167–73, 179
  illusions and, 5, 11, 156–57, 165–66, 168,
    169–70, 174–75
  judgment and, 3–9, 14, 87, 100, 143–44,
    147–49, 162–63, 165–66, 167–69,
    169–70, 174–75, 177–79, 192
  love and, 89, 143–44, 147–49, 151–52,
    162–63, 165–66
  partial, 144, 157, 165–66, 167, 169–73, 192,
    193–94
  politics and, 156–57, 175, 177–79, 186–90,
    192
  reason and, 165–66
  self-consciousness and, 192
  self-rule and, 6–7
  wholeness and, 5
Discourse on Political Economy (Rousseau)
  beauty in, 185
  education in, 3, 6, 11
  love in, 175, 176, 177
  self-rule in, 6, 175
domination, 25–26, 28

education
  authority and, 160–61
  of children, generally, 21–23, 30–31, 36–38
  freedom and, 2, 4–8, 158, 159–61
  gender and, 12–13, 137–38, 141, 143–45,
    149, 152, 166
  identity and, 3–5, 11–13, 205n. 11
  independence and, 159–61
  of judgment, 2, 5–7, 9–11, 13–15, 37–38,
    135–36, 195
  judgment of, 13, 21–23, 57–60, 100–106,
    129, 135–36, 139, 158–61, 169–73

education *(continued)*
    meaning of, 3–7
    nature and, 16–18, 30–31, 32, 35, 36, 159–61
    negative v. positive, 17–18, 30, 36–38,
        53–54, 116, 157
    origins of, 31–35, 53
    overviews of, 2, 3–7, 9–15, 30–31, 36–38
    politics and, 10–11, 175–77, 179–86, 194–95
    reflection and, 2–3, 15, 161
    in religion, 112
    self-consciousness and, 3–4, 161
    self-rule and, 2, 5–7, 10–11, 161
    wholeness and, 53, 143–44
Einspahr, Jennifer, 202n. 3
Ellrich, Robert J., 200n. 28
Emberley, Peter, 107, 121, 210n. 19, 211n. 26
Emile, or On Education (Rousseau)
    education in, reader's judgment of, 13,
        21–23, 57–60, 100–106, 129, 135–36, 139,
        158–61, 169–73
    education in, negative v. positive, 17–18,
        30, 36–38, 53–54, 116, 157
    education in, origins of, 31–35, 53
    education in, overviews of, 2, 3–7, 9–15,
        30–31, 36–38
    education of judgment in, generally, 2,
        5–7, 9–11, 13–15, 37–38, 135–36, 195
    structure of, 158–59
Emile and Sophie, or The Solitaries
    (Rousseau)
    education and, 13, 136, 169–70
    freedom in, 167–73
    identity and, 13
    judgment and, 136, 148, 158–61
    love in, 158, 159, 161–67
equilibrium
    desires and, 66, 145
    foresight and, 4, 40, 41
    gender and, 142, 145, 147–48
    happiness and, 40–42, 142, 145
    love and, 142, 145, 147–48, 165
    nature and, 20, 28
    self-consciousness and, 142, 145
    self-rule and, 147–48
experience
    books and, 63–65, 81, 82–83
    humiliation and, 45–46, 96–100

judgment and, 96–100, 191
    tutors and, 34, 126

fables. *See also* books
    desires and, 68–69
    judgment and, 63–64, 71–72, 75, 104
    reason and, 116
    virtue and, 51
faculties, 40–42, 66, 142, 145
faith. *See* religion
family
    politics and, 189
    society and, 141, 143–44, 161
    tutors and, 30–31, 32
    wholeness and, 138–39, 141–44, 161
fathers, 31
feeling. *See* sentiment
Fénelon, François, 139–40, 144, 146–47, 148,
    149
First Discourse (Rousseau), 64
Flanders, Todd R., 204n. 2, 206n. 15
foresight
    children and, 61, 66
    death and, 75
    equilibrium and, 4, 40, 41
    harm and, 55
    knowledge and, 56–57
    mothers and, 23–24, 30–31, 35, 71
freedom. *See also* independence; self-rule
    amour-propre and, 89, 168–69
    authority and, 124–29, 160–61
    body and, 20, 43–44
    books and, 65, 68
    children and, 43–44
    conditioning and, 2–3, 135–36
    desires and, 43–44, 65, 66
    detachment and, 167–73, 179
    education and, generally, 2, 4–8, 158,
        159–61
    family and, 161
    gender and, 135–36, 145
    happiness and, 40, 41, 145, 161–62, 168, 173
    identity and, 2–3, 4–5, 44
    illusions and, 2–3, 5–6, 152, 168, 169, 173,
        174–75, 176
    judgment and, 2–3, 5–8, 35, 109, 112, 135–
        36, 145, 156, 167–69, 173

knowledge and, 152
language and, 124–27
love and, 135–36, 145, 152, 156, 158, 159–61, 161–62, 166–67, 168–69
movement and, 43–44, 86, 124, 126–27, 170–73
nature and, 20, 159–61, 173
partial, 169–73
pity and, 109
politics and, 2, 7–8, 84, 107, 156, 166–67, 168, 176, 179, 189
prejudices and, 5–6, 35, 145
reason and, 109, 112, 115, 124, 167–69
reflection and, 124, 161
religion and, 109, 112, 124
self-consciousness and, 5, 126–27, 128, 161, 173
self-rule and, 161, 168, 173
sentiment and, 120, 124, 169
sexuality and, 89
sincerity and, 124
slavery and, 167–69
soul and, 86, 168–69, 173
truth and, 152
tutors and, 124–29
virtue and, 168, 173, 176
wholeness and, 145, 167
will and, 44, 115, 167–69
wisdom and, 170–73
Froese, Katrin, 214n. 7

Garsten, Bryan, 197n. 6
Gauthier, David, 198n. 8
gender
amour-propre and, 141–43
authority and, 140–44
body and, 137, 140
conscience and, 138, 214n. 3
desires and, 212n. 13
education and, 12–13, 137–38, 141, 143–45, 149, 152, 166
equilibrium and, 142, 145, 147–48
freedom and, 135–36, 145
ideal, feminine, 134–44
illusions and, 134–53
independence and, 137–40, 147–48
judgment and, 136, 137–40, 143–50

love and, 138–53
perspective and, 138, 148
politics and, 212n. 16
prejudices and, 137–39, 145, 146–47, 148
reason and, 137–38, 140, 147
reflection, 143–44
running and, 142
self-consciousness and, 139, 140–44, 148
self-rule and, 137, 143–44, 147–48
sentiment and, 147
sexuality and, 136–37
virtue and, 137, 140, 146–47, 148
wholeness and, 136–37, 152
Geneva, 33, 84, 122, 175, 177–79, 214n. 2
good. See virtue
governor. See tutors
Grant, Ruth W., 128, 198n. 10
Grimsley, Ronald, 120, 210n. 20

habit, 26–27, 51–54. See also conditioning; prejudices
Hanley, Ryan Patrick, 197n. 4
happiness
amour-propre and, 96–100
books and, 68
character and, 100–106
children and, 40–42, 46
desires and, 40–42, 66, 101–2, 145
equilibrium and, 40–42, 142, 145
faculties and, 40–42, 145
foresight and, 30–31
freedom and, 40, 41, 145, 161–62, 168, 173
illusions and, 97, 136, 151–52, 174
judgment and, 95–96, 96–100, 100–106, 136, 145
knowledge and, 60, 83
love and, 86, 136, 145, 151–52, 159–60, 161–62
pity and, 87, 90, 91, 95–96, 96–100
politics and, 153, 176, 177
reflection and, 40–42, 96–100, 145
seeing and, 100–106
self-consciousness and, 41, 46, 96–100, 145
soul and, 101, 102
suffering and, 95–96, 100–106
taste and, 130–32
virtue and, 103–4, 173

happiness *(continued)*
    wholeness and, 60, 97, 127, 141, 145
    wisdom and, 41–42, 177
harm, 54–56, 91
Helvétius, 48, 50
history, 69–70, 71, 80, 94. *See also* books
Hobbes, Thomas, 18, 114, 156
Honig, Bonnie, 143
Huet, Marie-Hélène, 160
humanity. *See* man
humiliation, 45–46, 96–100. *See also* suffering

ideas, 20, 105, 148–49
identity
    books and, 73–74, 78–80
    children and, 44, 46
    conditioning and, 2–3, 191–92
    education and, 3–5, 11–13, 205n. 11
    freedom and, 2–3, 4–5, 44
    illusions and, 2–3, 5, 83, 191
    judgment and, 2–3, 190–95
    love and, 158, 160, 167–69, 171, 191–92,
        194–95
    movement and, 79–80, 171, 191
    pity and, 91
    politics and, 2–3, 176–77, 190–95
    self-consciousness and, 3–4, 46, 67, 73–74,
        191–94
    society and, 73–74, 78–80
    wholeness and, 3–5, 11–13, 83, 191–92
ignorance, 56–57, 150
illness, 39
illusions. *See also* conditioning; prejudices
    authority and, 141, 142, 144
    books and, 73–74, 76, 81–82
    character and, 151–53
    children and, 61–62
    conditioning and, 2–3, 134
    death and, 61–62
    detachment and, 5, 11, 156–57, 165–66, 168,
        169–70, 174–75
    education and, generally, 5–6, 9, 10–12,
        14
    family and, 142
    freedom and, 2–3, 5–6, 152, 168, 169, 173,
        174–75, 176
    gender and, 134–53

happiness and, 97, 136, 151–52, 174
identity and, 2–3, 5, 83, 191
judgment and, 2–3, 5–6, 9, 10–12, 14,
    61–62, 105–6, 107, 134–36, 143–50,
    153–57, 163–66, 169–70, 172, 173,
    174–75, 185, 191
knowledge and, 151–53
love and, 134–36, 142, 144–53, 163–66,
    169–70, 172, 174
nature and, 73–74, 156–57, 178
pity and, 95
politics and, 1–2, 2–3, 10–11, 68, 144, 151,
    153–57, 175–78, 185, 191
prejudices and, 5–6, 10–12, 163
reason and, 147, 164–66
reflection and, 5, 14, 162–66
religion and, 107
self-consciousness and, 5, 62, 142, 165
self-rule and, 2–3, 5–6, 10–11, 163, 169,
    174–75
sentiment and, 147, 163–64
society and, 156–57
taste and, 171–72
truth and, 5–6, 62, 150–53
utility and, 134–35
virtue and, 107, 146–47, 163–66, 169
wholeness and, 61–62, 83, 97, 141, 147, 164,
    165
wisdom and, 149–50
imagination
    authority and, 125, 126–28
    happiness and, 41
    judgment and, 8, 105–6, 184–86, 190–91
    movement and, 127–28
    nature and, 20–21, 111
    pity and, 90–91, 111
    politics and, 184–86, 190–91
    reason and, 111
    reflection and, 20–21
    religion and, 111
    sexuality and, 125
imitation, 51–54, 57
independence. *See also* freedom; self-rule
    body and, 45, 47, 65, 87, 140
    books and, 76–77, 78–80, 82–83, 139–40
    education and, generally, 159–61
    equilibrium and, 147–48

foresight and, 30–31
gender and, 137–40, 147–48
habit and, 27
judgment and, 11–12, 18–19, 87, 137–40, 147–48
love and, 135, 138–40, 147–48
nature and, 3–4, 18–19, 28
self-consciousness and, 161
self-rule and, 147–48, 161
senses and, 87
society and, 18–19, 73, 76–77, 78–80, 82–83, 159, 160–61
soul and, 86
utility and, 76–77
individualism, 2–5, 192
integrity. *See* nature; virtue

Johnston, Steven, 197n. 7, 202n. 10, 215n.10
judgment. *See also* reflection
abstraction and, 104–6
amour-propre and, 89, 96–100
authority and, 108–9, 127–29, 138, 143–44, 161
body and, 36, 87–88, 140
books and, 64, 69–72, 77, 104, 135, 139–40, 146–47
character and, 100–106
children and, 37–38, 50, 56–60, 69–72
conditioning and, 1–3, 6, 172, 191–92
death and, 61–62
detachment and, 8–9, 14, 87, 100, 143–44, 147–49, 162–63, 165–66, 167–69, 169–70, 174–75, 177–79, 192
determinate v. reflective, 7–8
of education, 13, 21–23, 57–60, 100–106, 129, 135–36, 139, 158–61, 169–73
education of, 2, 5–7, 9–11, 13–15, 37–38, 135–36, 195
experience and, 96–100, 191
freedom and, 2–3, 5–8, 35, 109, 112, 135–36, 145, 156, 167–69, 173
gender and, 136, 137–40, 143–50
happiness and, 95–96, 96–100, 100–106, 136, 145
humiliation and, 96–100
identity and, 2–3, 190–95
ignorance and, 56–57

illusions and, 2–3, 5–6, 9, 10–12, 14, 61–62, 105–6, 107, 134–36, 143–50, 153–57, 163–66, 169–70, 172, 173, 174–75, 185, 191
imagination and, 8, 105–6, 184–86, 190–91
imitation and, 57
independence and, 11–12, 18–19, 87, 137–40, 147–48
knowledge and, 56–57
learning and, 47, 57–60
love and, 134–36, 138–40, 143–50, 156, 159, 161–67, 169–70, 172, 174–79, 180, 192, 194–95
maturity and, 37–38
meaning of, 1, 7–8, 15
mothers and, 23, 24, 29–31, 35, 71, 100, 188
movement and, 114, 123–24, 191
nature and, 16–17, 21–23, 24, 100
perspective and, 58–60, 91–93, 99–100, 138, 192, 193–94
philosophy and, 16, 100, 203n. 4
pity and, 87–88, 91–100, 138
politics and, 1–3, 7–8, 10–11, 153–57, 174–79, 180, 183–86, 189–95
prejudices and, 2, 9–12, 14, 16, 21, 35, 135, 145, 146–47, 148, 185
reason and, 1, 7–8, 107–12, 114–15, 121, 123–24, 128–29, 139, 164–66
reflection and, 2–3, 8–9, 14, 15, 161–67, 191–92
religion and, 107–12, 114, 121, 123–24, 129
seeing and, 47–50, 56–57, 58–60, 100–106, 138
self-consciousness and, 96–100, 139, 140–44, 148, 165, 191–94
self-rule and, 2–3, 5–7, 10–11, 161
senses and, 1, 47–50, 56–57, 58–60, 87, 110–11, 114
sentiment and, 109, 114, 121, 123–24, 163–64
sincerity and, 123–24
society and, 92, 103, 138
spectatorship and, 9
suffering and, 100–106
taste and, 129–33
transparency and, 62
utility and, 77, 134–35
virtue and, 103–4, 161–66, 169

judgment. *See also* reflection *(continued)*
  wholeness and, 58–59, 60–62, 87–88,
    143–44, 164, 165, 191–92
  will and, 1–2, 114–15
justice, 101–2, 113, 118, 204n. 10

Kant, Immanuel, 7, 161
Kavanagh, Thomas, 160
Kelly, Christopher
  on books, 185, 204n. 3
  on desires, 205n. 4
  on politics, 214n. 6, 214n. 7, 216n. 16
  on questions, 214n. 4
knowledge
  books and, 64, 65–66
  desires and, 45–46, 65–66, 115
  experience and, 98–99
  happiness and, 60, 83
  humiliation and, 45–46, 98–99
  illusions and, 151–53
  imitation and, 51–54
  judgment and, 56–57
  learning and, 72–73
  love and, 151–53
  perspective and, 99–100
  pity and, 98–99
  reason and, 113
  self-rule and, 65–66
  sentiment and, 113, 132
  of soul, 110
  truth and, 113, 132, 151–53
  wholeness and, 60
  wisdom and, 132

labor, 54
La Fontaine, Jean de, 63, 68–69
language, 26, 28, 38–39, 124–27, 137
Larmore, Charles, 8
learning. *See also* education
  books and, 65–66, 77
  desires and, 45–46, 65–66
  equilibrium and, 42
  gender and, 13
  identity and, 79
  imitation and, 51–54
  judgment and, 47, 57–60
  knowledge and, 72–73

  to learn, 50–56
  movement and, 37–38, 42–47, 63
  seeing and, 37–38, 48–50, 60
  self-rule and, 65–66
  utility and, 77
legislator, 1–2, 67–68, 143, 144, 173. *See also*
  politics
Letters from the Mountain (Rousseau), 205n.
  12, 213n. 6
Locke, John, 18, 38, 39, 70, 109–10
love. *See also* amour-propre; family
  amour-propre and, 141–43
  authority and, 135, 140–44
  beauty and, 116–17, 149, 151
  books and, 139–40, 144, 146–47, 148, 149
  character and, 151–53, 166
  conditioning and, 134, 135–36
  death and, 162–63
  desires and, 89
  detachment and, 89, 143–44, 147–49, 151–
    52, 162–63, 165–66
  equilibrium and, 142, 145, 147–48, 165
  freedom and, 135–36, 145, 152, 156, 158,
    159–61, 161–62, 166–67, 168–69
  gender and, 138–53
  happiness and, 86, 136, 145, 151–52, 159–60,
    161–62
  identity and, 158, 160, 167–69, 171, 191–92,
    194–95
  illusions and, 134–36, 142, 144–53, 163–66,
    169–70, 172, 174
  independence and, 135, 138–40, 147–48
  judgment and, 134–36, 138–40, 143–50,
    156, 159, 161–67, 169–70, 172, 174–79,
    180, 192, 194–95
  knowledge and, 151–53
  movement and, 116–17, 133, 149, 152–53,
    170–71, 191
  nature and, 111, 146–47
  perspective and, 145, 148, 150–53, 168
  pity and, 111, 160
  politics and, 143, 151, 156, 166–67, 175–90,
    192, 194–95, 197n. 6
  prejudices and, 145, 146–47, 148, 163,
    170–71
  reason and, 111, 116–17, 139, 147, 163,
    164–66, 168–69

rebirths and, 85–86
reflection and, 143–44, 161–67, 207n. 34
religion and, 111
seeing and, 134
self-consciousness and, 140–44, 148, 161, 165, 191–92
self-rule and, 135, 143–44, 147–48, 163, 170–71
sentiment and, 147, 163–64
soul and, 116–17, 160, 168–69
truth and, 132, 146–47, 150–53
tutors and, 135, 136, 139
utility and, 134–35
virtue and, 134, 146–47, 148, 152, 161–66, 170–71, 175, 176, 177–78, 179–90
wholeness and, 145, 147, 152, 164, 165, 191–92
will and, 212n. 11
wisdom and, 117, 133, 149–50
Lukowski, Jerzy, 215n.13
Lycurgus, 67–68

Machiavelli, Niccolò, 201n. 33
man. *See also* gender
children compared with, 22, 29, 30, 157
desires and, 89–90
movement and, 83–84
nature of, 17–21, 35, 40–42, 83–84, 114, 156–57, 159–61, 173, 185, 206n. 24, 206n. 25
sexuality and, 136–37
suffering of, 90–96
wholeness and, 136–37, 143–44
Marks, Jonathan
on freedom, 213n. 10
on nature, 202n. 2, 202n. 7
on pity, 208n. 8
on self-rule, 198n. 9
on virtue, 4, 5
marriage. *See* family; love
Masters, Roger, 118–19
maturity, 37–38, 42–43, 50–51
Melzer, Arthur M., 10–11, 119, 120, 200n. 30, 210n. 24
Montesquieu, 155
morality. *See* virtue
Morgenstern, Mira, 207n. 28, 208n. 7

mothers, 22–31, 35, 71, 100, 188
movement. *See also* running
authority and, 119–20, 126–27, 142
body and, 38, 39, 42–45, 46–47, 85, 115–16
books and, 68
by children, 38, 39, 42–45, 46–47
conditioning and, 171, 191
desires and, 43–45, 46–47, 115, 133
freedom and, 43–44, 86, 124, 126–27, 170–73
identity and, 79–80, 171, 191
imagination and, 127–28
judgment and, 114, 123–24, 191
learning and, 37–38, 42–47, 63
love and, 116–17, 133, 149, 152–53, 170–71, 191
pity and, 91, 93–94
reason and, 46–47, 111, 113, 114–18, 119–20, 123–24
reflection and, 123–24
religion and, 114, 119–20, 123–24
self-consciousness and, 191, 192–93
self-rule and, 170–73
senses and, 111, 114
sentiment and, 113, 114, 119–20, 123–24
sincerity and, 119–20, 123–24
soul and, 84, 85–86, 93–94, 115, 116–17, 133, 173
taste and, 132–33
truth and, 114–16
will and, 113, 115–16
wisdom and, 83–84, 117, 132–33, 170–73

nature
authority and, 160–61
beauty of, 110–11, 114, 193
body and, 20, 24–25, 110–11
books and, 64–65, 68, 73–74, 77–78, 81
children and, 21–31, 36, 40–42, 52
desires and, 25–29
education and, 16–18, 30–31, 32, 35, 36, 159–61
equilibrium and, 20, 28
freedom and, 20, 159–61, 173
illusions and, 73–74, 156–57, 178
imagination and, 20–21, 111
independence and, 3–4, 18–19, 28

nature *(continued)*
  judgment and, 16–17, 21–23, 24, 100
  language and, 26, 28
  learning and, 63
  love and, 111, 146–47
  of man, 17–21, 35, 40–42, 83–84, 114, 156–57, 159–61, 173, 185, 206n. 24, 206n. 25
  meaning of, 17, 35
  mothers and, 22–31
  perspective and, 100
  prejudices and, 10
  reason and, 108, 110–11, 112
  reflection and, 20–21, 77–78, 80–81, 161
  religion and, 108, 110–11, 112, 114
  self-consciousness and, 62, 77–78, 161, 193
  self-rule and, 161
  senses and, 110–11
  society and, 16–17, 18–19, 25, 77–78, 80–81, 114, 156–57, 204n. 2
  soul and, 201n. 2
  truth and, 108, 156–57
  utility and, 81
  virtue and, 157
  wholeness and, 16, 36, 201n. 2
  will and, 25–26, 28–29
  wisdom and, 41–42, 83–84
Nietzsche, Friedrich, 116
Nourrisson, Paul, 204n. 2, 206n. 18
Novak, Maximillian E., 204n. 2

obedience. *See* authority
On the Social Contract (Rousseau)
  conditioning in, 1–2, 191–92
  education in, 10–11
  Emile, or On Education (Rousseau) compared with, 7
  freedom in, 84
  identity in, 195
  illusions in, 10–11, 153–57
  judgment in, 1–2, 10–11, 187, 194, 213n. 21
  politics in, 10–11, 32–33, 67, 143, 175
  The Prince (Machiavelli) compared with, 201n. 33
  society in, 32–33
  virtue in, 174, 177, 185
opinions. *See* prejudices
Orwin, Clifford, 208n. 6

Palmer, Michael, 214n. 2
passion. *See* desires; love
perspective. *See also* detachment
  gender and, 138, 148
  identity and, 192, 193–94
  judgment and, 58–60, 91–93, 99–100, 138, 192, 193–94
  love and, 145, 148, 150–53, 168
  movement and, 171
  pity and, 91–93, 99–100, 156–57
  politics and, 156–57, 168, 192, 193–94
  reflection and, 91–93, 99–100
  self-consciousness and, 99–100, 148
  soul and, 193–94
philosophy
  judgment and, 16, 100, 203n. 4
  politics and, 194–95
  prejudices and, 16, 123
  religion and, 109, 122, 123, 210n. 24
  truth and, 112–13, 122
  virtue and, 123
physicality. *See* body
pity
  amour-propre and, 86–87, 88–90, 96–100
  body and, 87–88, 93
  books and, 94–95
  freedom and, 109
  happiness and, 87, 90, 91, 95–96, 96–100
  harm and, 54–55, 91
  imagination and, 90–91, 111
  judgment and, 87–88, 91–100, 138
  knowledge and, 98–99
  love and, 111, 160
  maxims of, 91, 92–93
  movement and, 91, 93–94
  perspective and, 91–93, 99–100, 156–57
  reason and, 88, 119
  reflection and, 87–88, 92–100
  self-consciousness and, 96–100
  senses and, 92
  sentiment and, 120
  sexuality and, 88–90, 111
  society and, 86–87, 88, 92, 96
  soul and, 86–87
  suffering and, 54–55, 90–96, 101, 109
  truth and, 120
  wholeness and, 87–88, 91–92

Plan for a Constitution for Corsica (Rousseau), 174, 186–90

Plato
 on authority, 123
 on education, 33, 72–73
 on ideas, 20, 105, 148–49
 on illusions, 10
 on justice, 101–2, 118, 204n. 10
 on love, 152
 on soul, 84, 116–17, 204n. 10

pleasure. *See* happiness; taste

Plutarch, 67–68

poetry, 67–68

Poland, 179–86

politics. *See also* society
 amour-propre and, 180–86
 authority and, 143–44, 175–76, 177
 conditioning and, 1–2, 2–3, 190, 191–92
 detachment and, 156–57, 175, 177–79, 186–90, 192
 education and, 10–11, 175–77, 179–86, 194–95
 freedom and, 2, 7–8, 84, 107, 156, 166–67, 168, 176, 179, 189
 gender and, 212n. 16
 happiness and, 153, 176, 177
 identity and, 2–3, 176–77, 190–95
 illusions and, 1–2, 2–3, 10–11, 68, 144, 151, 153–57, 175–78, 185, 191
 imagination and, 184–86, 190–91
 judgment and, 1–3, 7–8, 10–11, 153–57, 174–79, 180, 183–86, 189–95
 love and, 143, 151, 156, 166–67, 175–90, 192, 194–95, 197n. 6
 origins of, 32–33
 perspective and, 156–57, 168, 192, 193–94
 prejudices and, 10–11, 176–77, 185
 reflection and, 11, 191–92
 self-consciousness and, 191–94, 198n. 10
 self-rule and, 2–3, 10–11
 truth and, 151, 153–57
 tutors and, 182–83
 virtue and, 143, 175, 176, 177–78, 179–90
 wealth and, 180–81
 wholeness and, 67–68, 143–44, 191–92
 will and, 1–2, 173

prejudices. *See also* conditioning; illusions
 books and, 78
 children and, 22
 education and, generally, 2, 9–12, 14
 freedom and, 5–6, 35, 145
 gender and, 137–39, 145, 146–47, 148
 illusions and, 5–6, 10–12, 163
 judgment and, 2, 9–12, 14, 16, 21, 35, 135, 145, 146–47, 148, 185
 love and, 145, 146–47, 148, 163, 170–71
 philosophy and, 16, 123
 politics and, 10–11, 176–77, 185
 reason and, 110, 116, 122–23, 139
 reflection and, 2–3, 5, 10, 163
 religion and, 110, 122–23
 self-consciousness and, 139
 self-rule and, 2, 10–11
 utility and, 135
 wholeness and, 137–39

property, 19, 54, 206n. 14. *See also* wealth

Putterman, Ethan, 216n. 16

reading. *See* books

reason
 amour-propre and, 119, 168–69
 authority and, 108–9, 114, 119–23, 126, 128–29
 body and, 46–47, 109–11, 115–16
 books and, 63–64, 116
 children and, 38, 39, 46–47, 50, 63–64, 109
 conscience and, 210n. 19
 desires and, 111, 115
 freedom and, 109, 112, 115, 124, 167–69
 gender and, 137–38, 140, 147
 illusions and, 147, 164–66
 judgment and, 1, 7–8, 107–12, 114–15, 121, 123–24, 128–29, 139, 164–66
 love and, 111, 116–17, 139, 147, 163, 164–66, 168–69
 movement and, 46–47, 111, 113, 114–18, 119–20, 123–24
 nature and, 108, 110–11, 112
 origins of, 114–15
 pity and, 88, 119
 practical v. theoretical, 203n. 5
 prejudices and, 110, 116, 122–23, 139
 reflection and, 122–24, 128–29

reason (continued)
   religion and, 107–14, 118–24, 128, 129
   senses and, 48, 50, 110–11, 113, 114, 120, 122
   sentiment and, 108, 109, 112–14, 116, 117–24, 147
   sexuality and, 111, 125
   sincerity and, 113, 118–24
   soul and, 113, 115, 116–17, 168–69
   taste and, 130
   truth and, 108, 112–16, 120, 122
   tutors and, 98–99
   virtue and, 107, 108–9, 117–18, 121–22, 123
   will and, 113, 114–15, 115–16, 167–69
rebirths, 12, 39–40, 73–74, 85–86, 98, 158
reflection. See also judgment
   authority and, 127–29, 143–44, 161
   books and, 77–78, 80–83
   conditioning and, 171
   education and, 2–3, 15, 161
   equilibrium and, 145
   freedom and, 124, 161
   happiness and, 40–42, 96–100, 145
   illusions and, 5, 14, 162–66
   judgment and, 2–3, 8–9, 14, 15, 161–67, 191–92
   love and, 143–44, 161–67, 163, 207n. 34
   nature and, 20–21, 77–78, 80–81, 161
   perspective and, 91–93, 99–100
   pity and, 87–88, 92–100
   politics and, 11, 191–92
   prejudices and, 2–3, 5, 10, 163
   reason and, 122–24, 128–29
   religion and, 122–24
   self-consciousness and, 96–100, 161, 191–92
   self-rule and, 84, 161
   sentiment and, 122–24
   society and, 77–78, 80–83, 161
   taste and, 129–33
   wholeness and, 84, 143–44, 191–92
Reisert, Joseph R., 200n. 31, 203n. 5
religion
   authority and, 108–9, 119–23, 129
   education in, 112
   freedom and, 109, 112, 124–29

   judgment and, 107–12, 114, 121, 123–24, 129
   movement and, 114, 119–20, 123–24
   nature and, 108, 110–11, 112, 114
   philosophy and, 109, 122, 123, 210n. 24
   prejudices and, 110, 122–23
   reason and, 107–14, 118–24, 128, 129
   reflection and, 122–24
   senses and, 110–11, 113, 114, 120, 122
   sentiment and, 108, 109, 112–14, 118–24
   sincerity and, 118–24
   truth and, 108, 112–14, 120, 122
   virtue and, 107, 108–9, 121–22, 123
The Reveries of the Solitary Walker (Rousseau), 80, 82–83, 173, 192–93
Rist, John M., 208n. 4
Robinson Crusoe (Defoe), 53–54, 64–65, 72–83, 135
Rousseau, Jean-Jacques
   Confessions, 55, 80, 193, 206n. 18
   Considerations on the Government of Poland, 2, 3, 175, 179–86
   Discourse on Political Economy, 3, 6, 11, 175, 176, 177, 185
   Emile, or On Education (see *Emile, or On Education*)
   Emile and Sophie, or The Solitaries, 13, 72, 136, 148, 158–73
   First Discourse, 64
   Letters from the Mountain, 205n. 12, 213n. 6
   The Reveries of the Solitary Walker, 80, 82–83, 173, 192–93
   Rousseau, Judge of Jean-Jacques, 33
   Second Discourse (see *Second Discourse*)
Rousseau, Judge of Jean-Jacques (Rousseau), 33
running, 37–38, 42–47, 65, 142. See also movement

Schwartz, Joel, 140, 141
Scott, John T., 199n. 17, 200n. 31
Second Discourse (Rousseau)
   children in, 25, 26–29
   freedom in, 167
   habit in, 26–27
   harm in, 54, 55
   imagination in, 21

judgment in, 122

language in, 26, 28

love in, 27, 175, 177–79

man in, 17–21, 22, 40, 114, 161, 206n. 24, 206n. 25

mothers in, 25, 26–29

nature in, 10, 16–21, 28–29, 185, 201n. 37, 206n. 24, 206n. 25

pity in, 93

reflection in, 21

self-consciousness in, 4

soul in, 160

seeing. *See also* perspective; senses

children and, 37–38, 47–50, 58–60

education and, 200n. 31

judgment and, 47–50, 56–57, 58–60, 100–106, 138

love and, 134

religion and, 122

self-consciousness

amour-propre and, 96–100, 141–43

authority and, 140–44, 161

books and, 65–66, 73–74, 77–80, 82–83

conditioning and, 172–73, 191–92

education and, generally, 3–4, 161

equilibrium and, 142, 145

experience and, 96–100, 191

freedom and, 5, 126–27, 128, 161, 173

gender and, 139, 140–44, 148

happiness and, 41, 46, 96–100, 145

identity and, 3–4, 46, 67, 73–74, 191–94

illusions and, 5, 62, 142, 165

judgment and, 96–100, 139, 140–44, 148, 165, 191–94

love and, 140–44, 148, 161, 165, 191–92

movement and, 191, 192–93

nature and, 62, 77–78, 161, 193

perspective and, 99–100, 148

politics and, 191–94, 198n. 10

reflection and, 96–100, 161, 191–92

self-rule and, 161, 172–73

society and, 62, 73–74, 77–80, 82–83, 161

wholeness and, 62, 140–44, 165, 191–92

wisdom and, 79, 83–84

self-rule. *See also* freedom; independence

authority and, 128, 143–44, 161

books and, 65–66

conditioning and, 2–3, 6, 172–73

detachment and, 6–7

education and, generally, 2, 5–7, 10–11, 161

freedom and, 161, 168, 173

gender and, 137, 143–44, 147–48

identity and, 2–3

illusions and, 2–3, 5–6, 10–11, 163, 169, 174–75

independence and, 147–48, 161

judgment and, 2–3, 5–7, 10–11, 161

love and, 135, 143–44, 147–48, 163, 170–71

movement and, 170–73

politics and, 2–3, 10–11

prejudices and, 2, 10–11

reflection and, 84, 161

self-consciousness and, 161, 172–73

society and, 161

wholeness and, 84

senses. *See also* seeing

authority and, 120, 125–26

children and, 37–38, 46–50, 58–60

common, 49–50

judgment and, 1, 47–50, 56–57, 58–60, 87, 110–11, 114

movement and, 111, 114

pity and, 92

reason and, 48, 50, 110–11, 113, 114, 120, 122

religion and, 110–11, 113, 114, 120, 122

sentiment and, 113, 114, 120

sentiment

authority and, 114, 119–23, 126

freedom and, 120, 124, 169

illusions and, 147, 163–64

judgment and, 109, 114, 121, 123–24, 163–64

knowledge and, 113, 132

love and, 147, 163–64

movement and, 113, 114, 119–20, 123–24

reason and, 108, 109, 112–14, 116, 117–24, 147

reflection and, 122–24

religion and, 108, 109, 112–14, 118–24

senses and, 113, 114, 120

truth and, 112–14, 120, 122

virtue and, 117–18, 121–22

wisdom and, 132, 208n. 4

sexuality
authority and, 124–26
desires and, 206n. 13
movement and, 85–86
pity and, 88–90, 111
reason and, 111, 125
wholeness and, 136–37
Shell, Susan Meld, 63, 212n. 13
Shklar, Judith, 160
sight. *See* seeing
sincerity, 113, 118–24
slavery, 167–69
Smith, Jeffrey A., 216n. 15
society. *See also* politics
amour-propre and, 86–87, 88–90
body and, 25, 87–88
books and, 65, 72–78
children and, 22, 25, 26
desires and, 25, 26, 29, 89–90
education and, generally, 30, 31
family and, 141, 143–44, 161
harm and, 56
identity and, 73–74, 78–80
illusions and, 156–57
independence and, 18–19, 73, 76–77,
78–80, 82–83, 159, 160–61
judgment and, 92, 103, 138
mothers and, 25, 26
nature and, 16–17, 18–19, 25, 77–78,
80–81, 114, 156–57, 204n. 2
origins of, 32–33
pity and, 86–87, 88, 92, 96
politics and, 32–33
property and, 19
rebirths and, 73–74
reflection and, 77–78, 80–83, 161
self-consciousness and, 62, 73–74, 77–80,
82–83, 161
utility and, 75–77, 80–83
virtue and, 103–4, 157
wholeness and, 141, 143–44
will and, 26, 29
Socrates, 101–2, 116–17, 118, 123, 149–50
soul
freedom and, 86, 168–69, 173
happiness and, 101, 102

immortality of, 113
justice and, 113, 204n. 10
knowledge of, 110
love and, 116–17, 160, 168–69
movement and, 84, 85–86, 93–94, 115,
116–17, 133, 173
nature and, 201n. 2
pity and, 86–87
reason and, 113, 115, 116–17, 168–69
self-consciousness and, 193–94
social contract and, 84, 86
suffering and, 101, 102
wholeness and, 87–88, 143–44, 159, 201n. 2
spectatorship, 9, 94–95, 99, 147
Starobinski, Jean, 193–94, 199n. 16
Steinberger, Peter J., 1
Storey, Benjamin, 198n. 13
Strong, Tracy B.
on books, 205n. 10
on judgment, 197n. 4
on tutors, 200n. 27, 201n. 34
on wholeness, 199n. 18
on will, 215n.7
on women, 142
suffering, 54–55, 90–96, 100–106, 109. *See
also* humiliation

taste, 129–33, 137, 171–72
teachers. *See* tutors
Thales, 67–68
Thiele, Leslie Paul, 8
Thucydides, 71
transparency, 62
truth. *See also* illusions; wisdom
authority and, 114, 120
gender and, 137
illusions and, 5–6, 62, 150–53
knowledge and, 113, 132, 151–53
love and, 132, 146–47, 150–53
nature and, 108, 156–57
philosophy and, 112, 122
politics and, 151, 153–57
prejudices and, 10
religion and, 108, 112–14, 120, 122
sentiment and, 112–14, 120, 122
vice and, 36

Index ❧ 231

tutors
    authority and, 124–29, 138, 143
    death and, 162
    education and, generally, 31, 33–35
    experience and, 34, 126
    family and, 30–31, 32
    love and, 135, 136, 139
    politics and, 182–83
    reason and, 98–99
    seeing and, 66
    virtue and, 52–53
    wisdom and, 34, 97–99, 126

utility
    books and, 66–68, 72, 74, 75–77, 78,
        80–83, 135
    gender and, 137
    of ink, 66–68, 80
    judgment and, 77, 134–35
    love and, 134–35
    question of, 66
    society and, 75–77, 80–83
    virtue and, 66, 76

vanity. See amour-propre
Velkley, Richard L., 201n. 37, 208n. 7
vice, 36, 69. See also virtue
virtue
    books and, 65, 69, 76
    children and, 36, 51–54
    freedom and, 168, 173, 176
    gender and, 137, 140, 146–47, 148
    happiness and, 103–4, 173
    harm and, 54–56
    illusions and, 107, 146–47, 163–66, 169
    judgment and, 103–4, 161–66, 169
    love and, 134, 146–47, 148, 152, 161–66,
        170–71, 175, 176, 177–78, 179–90
    nature and, 157
    politics and, 143, 175, 176, 177–78, 179–90
    property and, 206n. 14
    reason and, 107, 108–9, 117–18, 121–22,
        123
    religion and, 107, 108–9, 121–22, 123
    sentiment and, 117–18, 121–22
    society and, 103–4, 157

soul and, 113
tutors and, 52–53
utility and, 66, 76
wholeness and, 164, 165

Walzer, Michael, 194
wealth, 130–32, 180–81. See also property
Weiss, Penny, 138, 141
wholeness
    authority and, 127, 140–44
    children and, 58–59, 60–62
    death and, 60, 61–62
    education and, generally, 53, 143–44
    of Emile, or On Education, 158–59
    family and, 138–39, 141–44, 161
    freedom and, 145, 167
    gender and, 136–44, 152
    happiness and, 60, 97, 127, 141, 145
    identity and, 3–5, 11–13, 83, 191–92
    illusions and, 61–62, 83, 97, 141, 147, 164,
        165
    judgment and, 58–59, 60–62, 87–88,
        143–44, 164, 165, 191–92
    love and, 145, 147, 152, 164, 165, 191–92
    man and, 136–37, 143–44
    nature and, 16, 36, 201n. 2
    perspective and, 99
    pity and, 87–88, 91–92
    politics and, 67–68, 143–44, 191–92
    prejudices and, 137–39
    reflection and, 84, 143–44, 191–92
    self-consciousness and, 62, 140–44, 165,
        191–92
    self-rule and, 84
    society and, 141, 143–44
    soul and, 87–88, 143–44, 159, 201n. 2
    virtue and, 164, 165
    will and, 28
will
    children and, 25–26, 28–29
    freedom and, 44, 115, 167–69
    judgment and, 1–2, 114–15
    love and, 212n. 11
    movement and, 113, 115–16
    politics and, 1–2, 173
    reason and, 113, 114–15, 115–16, 167–69

will *(continued)*
  society and, 26, 29
  wholeness and, 28
Williams, Bernard, 115
Wingrove, Elizabeth Rose, 166–67, 202n. 5
wisdom. *See also* truth
  children and, 63
  freedom and, 170–73
  happiness and, 41–42, 177
  illusions and, 149–50
  love and, 117, 133, 149–50

movement and, 83–84, 117, 132–33, 170–73
nature and, 41–42, 83–84
politics and, 177
prejudices and, 10
self-consciousness and, 79, 83–84
senses and, 48–49
sentiment and, 132, 208n. 4
soul and, 117
tutors and, 34, 97–99, 126

Zerilli, Linda, 7–8